Learn Qt 5

Build modern, responsive cross-platform desktop applications
with Qt, C++, and QML

Nicholas Sherriff

BIRMINGHAM - MUMBAI

Learn Qt 5

Commissioning Editor: Kunal Chaudhari
Acquisition Editor: Siddharth Mandal
Content Development Editor: Flavian Vaz
Technical Editor: Akhil Nair
Copy Editor: Shaila Kusanale
Project Coordinator: Devanshi Doshi
Proofreader: Safis Editing
Indexer: Tejal Daruwale Soni
Graphics: Jason Monteiro
Production Coordinator: Arvindkumar Gupta

First published: Febraury 2018

Production reference: 1060218

Published by Packt Publishing Ltd.
Livery Place
35 Livery Street
Birmingham
B3 2PB, UK.

ISBN 978-1-78847-885-4

www.packtpub.com

`mapt.io`

Mapt is an online digital library that gives you full access to over 5,000 books and videos, as well as industry leading tools to help you plan your personal development and advance your career. For more information, please visit our website.

Why subscribe?

- Spend less time learning and more time coding with practical eBooks and Videos from over 4,000 industry professionals

- Improve your learning with Skill Plans built especially for you

- Get a free eBook or video every month

- Mapt is fully searchable

- Copy and paste, print, and bookmark content

PacktPub.com

Did you know that Packt offers eBook versions of every book published, with PDF and ePub files available? You can upgrade to the eBook version at `www.PacktPub.com` and as a print book customer, you are entitled to a discount on the eBook copy. Get in touch with us at `service@packtpub.com` for more details.

At `www.PacktPub.com`, you can also read a collection of free technical articles, sign up for a range of free newsletters, and receive exclusive discounts and offers on Packt books and eBooks.

Contributors

About the author

Nicholas Sherriff (Nick) spent the majority of his career at a major utility company in the UK, working predominantly on the Microsoft Windows platform with C#, ASP.NET, and SQL Server. While leading the native application development function there, he experimented with C++ before eventually discovering Qt, utilizing it on a major greenfield project serving several thousand users. He currently works for a communications recording software house. At home, Nick enjoys music, video games, and half-hearted calisthenics.

About the reviewer

Marthala Vishnu Vardhan Reddy is an enthusiastic software engineer. He is a Qt software developer and has been working in the automation industry since 2013. He completed his master's in information technology from the University of Stuttgart, Germany. He is currently working on the digitization of metal cutting tool data in the manufacturing industry in the direction of Industry 4.0.

He has done his bachelor's thesis from Institut supérieur d'électronique de Paris, France, where he published an IEEE publication on 5G networks as well.

Packt is searching for authors like you

If you're interested in becoming an author for Packt, please visit authors.packtpub.com and apply today. We have worked with thousands of developers and tech professionals, just like you, to help them share their insight with the global tech community. You can make a general application, apply for a specific hot topic that we are recruiting an author for, or submit your own idea.

Table of Contents

Preface

Qt is a mature and powerful framework for delivering sophisticated applications across a multitude of platforms. It is widely used in embedded devices, including TVs, satellite set-top boxes, medical equipment, car dashboards, and much more. It also has a rich history in the Linux world, with KDE and Sailfish OS using it extensively and many apps in the stores being developed using Qt. It has also made great strides in the mobile arena over the past few years. However, in the Microsoft Windows and Apple macOS X worlds, the dominance of C#/.NET and Objective-C/Cocoa means that Qt is often overlooked.

This book aims to demonstrate the power and flexibility of the Qt framework and show how you can write your application once and deploy it to multiple operating system desktops. The reader will build a complete real-world **Line of Business** (**LOB**) solution from scratch, with distinct library, user interface, and unit test projects.

We will cover building a modern and responsive user interface with QML and wiring it up to rich C++ classes. We will control every aspect of our project configuration and output with QMake, including platform detection and conditional expressions. We will build "self-aware" data entities that can serialize themselves to and from JSON. We will persist those data entities in a database and learn how to find and update them. We will reach out to the internet and consume an RSS feed. Finally, we will produce an installation package so that we can deploy our application onto other machines.

This is a suite of essential techniques that cover the core requirements for most LOB applications and will empower the reader to progress from blank page to shipped application.

Who this book is for

This book targets application developers looking for a powerful and flexible framework for creating modern and responsive applications on Microsoft Windows, Apple Mac OS X, and Linux desktop platforms. Although focused on desktop application development, the techniques discussed are largely applicable to mobile development also.

What this book covers

Chapter 1, *Hello Qt*, covers how to install and configure the Qt Framework and associated IDE, Qt Creator.

Chapter 2, *Project Structure*, showcases how to create a new multi-project solution that will be the foundation of our example application.

Chapter 3, *User Interface*, explores the user interface markup language QML and sketches out our UI's layout.

Chapter 4, *Style*, explains how to give our UI a modern look and feel with shared resources and reusable components.

Chapter 5, *Data*, discusses managing the most critical part of any LOB application—the data.

Chapter 6, *Unit Testing*, gets you started with integrating unit testing into our solution using Qt's testing framework—QtTest.

Chapter 7, *Persistence*, focuses on persisting our data to disk in a SQLite database.

Chapter 8, *Web Requests*, assists in using HTTP requests to pull data from a live RSS feed.

Chapter 9, *Wrapping Up*, dives into packaging and deploying our application.

To get the most out of this book

The reader should be comfortable with C++, but no prior knowledge of Qt or QML is required. On Mac OS X, you will need to install XCode and have launched it at least once. On Windows, you may optionally install Visual Studio in order to have the MSVC compiler available.

Download the example code files

You can download the example code files for this book from your account at www.packtpub.com. If you purchased this book elsewhere, you can visit www.packtpub.com/support and register to have the files emailed directly to you.

You can download the code files by following these steps:

1. Log in or register at www.packtpub.com.
2. Select the **SUPPORT** tab.
3. Click on **Code Downloads & Errata**.
4. Enter the name of the book in the **Search** box and follow the onscreen instructions.

Once the file is downloaded, please make sure that you unzip or extract the folder using the latest version of:

- WinRAR/7-Zip for Windows
- Zipeg/iZip/UnRarX for Mac
- 7-Zip/PeaZip for Linux

The code bundle for the book is also hosted on GitHub at https://github.com/PacktPublishing/Learn-Qt-5. We also have other code bundles from our rich catalog of books and videos available at https://github.com/PacktPublishing/. Check them out!

Conventions used

There are a number of text conventions used throughout this book.

CodeInText: Indicates code words in text, database table names, folder names, filenames, file extensions, pathnames, dummy URLs, user input, and Twitter handles. Here is an example: "Create the SplashView.qml file in cm-ui/ui/views".

A block of code is set as follows:

```
<RCC>
    <qresource prefix="/views">
        <file alias="MasterView">views/MasterView.qml</file>
    </qresource>
    <qresource prefix="/">
        <file>views/SplashView.qml</file>
        <file>views/DashboardView.qml</file>
        <file>views/CreateClientView.qml</file>
        <file>views/EditClientView.qml</file>
        <file>views/FindClientView.qml</file>
    </qresource>
</RCC>
```

When we wish to draw your attention to a particular part of a code block, the relevant lines or items are set in bold:

```
QT += sql network
```

Any command-line input or output is written as follows:

```
$ <Qt Installation Path> \Tools \QtInstallerFramework \3.0\ bin\
binarycreator.exe -c config\config.xml -p packages
ClientManagementInstaller.exe
```

Bold: Indicates a new term, an important word, or words that you see onscreen. For example, words in menus or dialog boxes appear in the text like this. Here is an example: "Replace the **Hello World** title with **Client Management** and insert a **Text** component inside the body of the **Window**".

 Warnings or important notes appear like this.

 Tips and tricks appear like this.

Get in touch

Feedback from our readers is always welcome.

General feedback: Email feedback@packtpub.com and mention the book title in the subject of your message. If you have questions about any aspect of this book, please email us at questions@packtpub.com.

Errata: Although we have taken every care to ensure the accuracy of our content, mistakes do happen. If you have found a mistake in this book, we would be grateful if you would report this to us. Please visit www.packtpub.com/submit-errata, selecting your book, clicking on the Errata Submission Form link, and entering the details.

Piracy: If you come across any illegal copies of our works in any form on the Internet, we would be grateful if you would provide us with the location address or website name. Please contact us at copyright@packtpub.com with a link to the material.

If you are interested in becoming an author: If there is a topic that you have expertise in and you are interested in either writing or contributing to a book, please visit authors.packtpub.com.

Reviews

Please leave a review. Once you have read and used this book, why not leave a review on the site that you purchased it from? Potential readers can then see and use your unbiased opinion to make purchase decisions, we at Packt can understand what you think about our products, and our authors can see your feedback on their book. Thank you!

For more information about Packt, please visit packtpub.com.

1
Hello Qt

Qt is a mature and powerful framework for delivering sophisticated applications across a multitude of platforms. It is widely used in embedded devices including TVs, satellite set-top boxes, medical equipment, car dashboards, and much more. It also has a rich history in the Linux world, with KDE and Sailfish OS using it extensively and many apps in the stores being developed using Qt. It has also made great strides in the Mobile arena over the past several years. However, in the Microsoft Windows and Apple Mac OS X worlds, the dominance of C#/.NET and Objective-C/Cocoa mean that Qt is often overlooked.

This book aims to demonstrate the power and flexibility of the Qt framework and show how you can write your application once and deploy it to multiple operating system desktops. We will build a complete real-world **line of business (LOB)** solution from scratch, with distinct library, user interface, and unit test projects.

We will cover building a modern, responsive user interface with QML and wiring it up to rich C++ classes. We will control every aspect of our project configuration and output with QMake, including platform detection and conditional expressions. We will build "self-aware" data entities that can serialize themselves to and from JSON. We will persist those data entities in a database and learn how to find and update them. We will reach out to the internet and consume an RSS feed. Finally, we will produce an installation package so that we can deploy our application onto other machines.

In this chapter, we will install and configure the Qt framework and associated **Integrated Development Environment (IDE)** Qt Creator. We will create a simple scratchpad application that we will use throughout the remainder of the book to demonstrate various techniques. We will cover the following topics:

- Installing Qt
- Maintaining your installation

- Qt Creator
- Scratchpad project
- qmake

Installing Qt

Let's start things off by visiting the Qt website at `https://www.qt.io`:

The site layout changes fairly frequently, but what you are looking for is to download Qt Open Source for **Desktop & Mobile**:

1. From the top-level menu, select **Products** and then **IDE & Tools**
2. Click on **Start for Free**
3. Select **Desktop & Mobile Applications**
4. Click on **Get your open source package**

If you continue to use Qt beyond these personal projects, ensure that you read the licensing information available on the Qt website (`https://www.qt.io/licensing/`). Upgrade to the commercial Qt license if the scope of your projects requires it or if you want access to the official Qt support and the benefits of a close strategic relationship with the Qt company.

The site will detect your operating system and suggest a recommended download:

On Windows, you will be recommended the online installer *.exe file, while on Linux you will be offered a *.run file, and a .dmg file if you are running Mac OS X. In all cases, download and launch the installer:

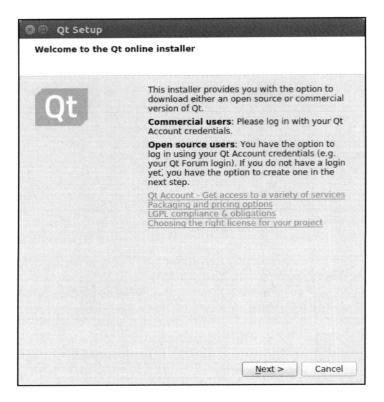

 On Linux, once downloaded, you may need to first navigate to the *.run file and mark it as executable in order to be able to launch it. To do this, right-click on the file in the file manager and click on **Properties**. Click on the **Permissions** tab and tick the box that says **Allow executing file as program**.

After the initial welcome dialog, the first thing you are presented with is the option to sign up for or log in with a Qt account. Feel free to create one if you wish, but for now we'll go ahead and **Skip**:

You are then asked to select which components you wish to install.

Your first decision is which version(s) of the Qt framework you want. You can have multiple versions installed side by side. Let's select the latest and greatest (Qt 5.10 at the time of writing) and leave all the older versions unchecked.

Next, expand the selected version and you will see a secondary list of options. All the options where the description reads "Qt 5.9.x Prebuilt Components for ..." are what is known as a **Kit**. A Kit is essentially a toolset enabling you to build your application with a specific compiler/linker and run it on a particular target architecture. Each kit comes with Qt framework binaries compiled specifically for that particular toolset as well as necessary supporting files. Note that kits do not come with the referenced compiler; you will need to install those ahead of time. One exception to this on Windows is MinGW (which includes GCC for Windows), which you can optionally install via the Tools component list at the bottom.

On Windows, that is exactly what we'll do, so we select the **MinGW 5.3.0 32 bit** kit and also the **MinGW 5.3.0** development environment from the Tools section. On my (64-bit) machine, I already have Microsoft Visual Studio 2017 installed, so we will also select the MSVC 2017 64-bit kit to help demonstrate some techniques later in the book. On Linux, we select GCC 64-bit, while on Mac OS, we select macOS 64-bit (which uses the Clang compiler). Note that on Mac OS, you must have XCode installed, and it's a good idea to launch XCode at least once to give it an opportunity to complete its initialization and configuration.

Feel free to press pause, go and install whatever other IDEs or compilers you want to use, and then come back and pick the kits to match. It doesn't matter too much which you go for—the techniques explained throughout the book are applicable regardless of the kit, you may just get slightly different results. Note that the available kits you are presented with will differ depending on your operating system and chipset; for example, if you are on a 32 bit machine, you won't be offered any 64 bit kits.

 Below the kits are some optional Qt APIs (such as Qt Charts), which we won't need for the topics covered in this book, but feel free to add them in if you want to explore their functionality. Note that they may have different licensing agreements from the core Qt framework.

Regardless of kits and APIs, you will note in the **Tools** section that Qt Creator is installed by default and that is the IDE we will be using throughout this book:

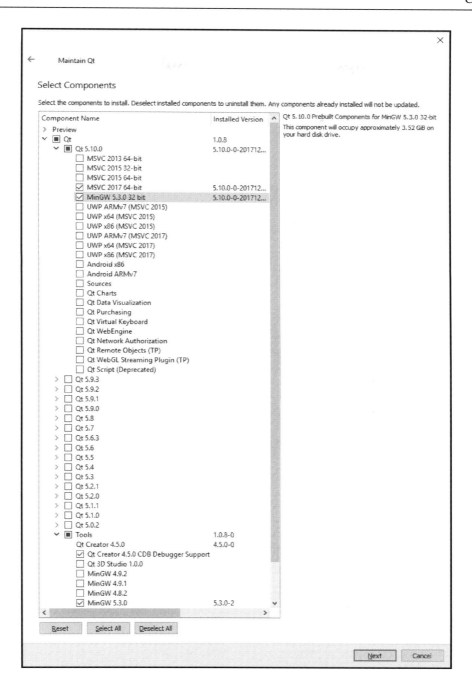

Once you are finished making your selections, click on **Next** and **Update** to kick off the installation.

 It's generally a good idea to leave the installation location as the default for consistency across machines, but feel free to install it wherever you want.

Maintaining your installation

Once installed, you can update, add, and remove components (or even the entire Qt installation) via the `Maintenance Tool` application that is located in the directory you installed Qt to.

Launching this tool provides pretty much the same experience as when we first installed Qt. The **Add or remove components** option is the one you want to add in items you may have previously not needed, including kits and even entirely new releases of the framework. Unless you actively uncheck them, components already installed on your system will not be affected.

Qt Creator

While a detailed overview of Qt Creator is beyond the scope of this book (the Qt Creator manual is accessible via the Help mode as described here), it's worth having a quick whistle stop tour before we get stuck to our first project, so launch the freshly installed application and we'll take a look:

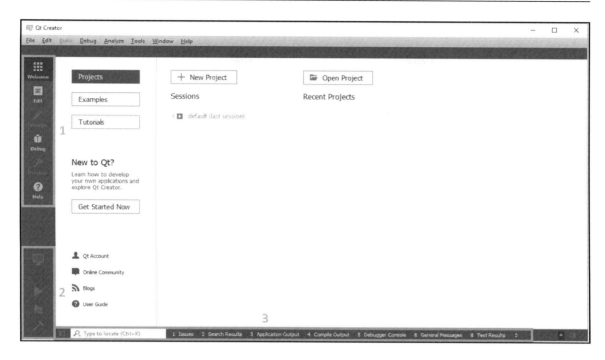

At the upper left-hand side (**1**) are the different areas or modes of the application:

- **Welcome** mode is the default when Qt Creator is launched and is the jumping off point to create or open projects. There is an extensive set of examples that help showcase the various capabilities of the framework as well as a selection of tutorial videos.
- **Edit** mode is where you will be spending the vast majority of your time and is used for editing all the various text-based files.
- **Design** is accessible only when you have a UI file open and is a WYSIWYG editor for views. Although useful for UX design and basic layout work, it can get frustrating quite quickly and we will do all of our QML work in Edit mode instead. Working this way promotes understanding of the QML (as you have to write it) and also has the advantage that the editor is not adding code that you don't want.
- **Debug** mode is used for debugging applications and is beyond the scope of this book.
- **Projects** mode is where configuration for the project is managed, including the build settings. Changes made here will be reflected in the `*.pro.user` file.
- **Help** mode takes you to the Qt Creator manual and Qt library reference.

Pressing *F1* while the cursor is on a recognized Qt symbol will automatically open context sensitive help for that symbol.

Below that, we have the build/run tools (**2**):

- **Kit/Build** lets you select your kit and set the build mode
- **Run** builds and runs the application without debugging
- **Start Debugging** builds and runs the application with a debugger (note that you must have a debugger installed and configured in your selected kit for this to work)
- **Build Project** builds the application without running it

Along the bottom (**3**), we have a search box and then several output windows:

Issues displays any warnings or errors. For compiler errors relating to your code, double-clicking on the item will navigate you to the relevant source code.

- **Search Results** lets you find occurrences of text within various scopes. *Ctrl + F* brings up a quick search, and from there selecting **Advanced...** also brings up the Search Results console.
- **Application Output** is the console window; all output from application code like std::cout and Qt's equivalent qDebug() appears here, along with certain messages from the Qt framework.
- **Compile Output** contains output from the build process, from qmake through to compilation and linking.
- **Debugger Console** contains debugging information that we won't be covering in this book.
- **General Messages** contains other miscellaneous output, the most useful of which is from qmake parsing of *.pro files, which we will look at later.

The search box really is a hidden gem and saves you from clicking through endless files and folders trying to find what you are looking for. You can start typing the name of a file you are looking for in the box and a filtered list appears with all matching files. Simply click on the file you want, and it opens in the editor. Not only that, there are a large number of filters you can apply too. Click your cursor in the empty search box and it displays a list of available filters. The filter m, for example, searches for C++ methods. So, say you remember writing a method called SomeAmazingFunction() but can't remember where it is, just head over to the search box, start typing m Some, and it will appear in the filtered list.

In **Edit** mode, the layout changes slightly and some new panes appear. Initially, they will be empty, but once you have a project open, they will resemble the following:

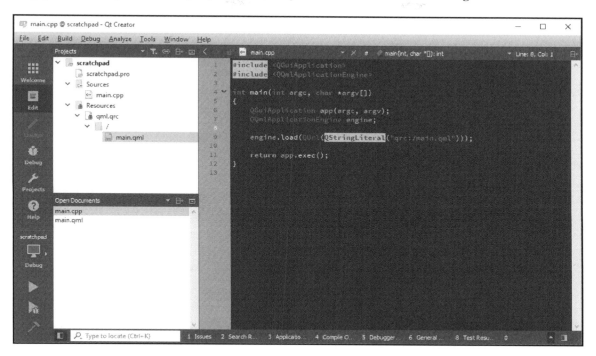

Next to the navigation bar is the project explorer, which you can use to navigate the files and folders of your solution. The lower pane is a list of all of the documents you currently have open. The larger area to the right is the editor pane where you write your code and edit documents.

Double-clicking on a file in the project explorer will generally open it in the editor pane and add it to the open documents list. Clicking on a document in the open documents list will activate it in the editor pane, while clicking on the small **x** to the right of the filename closes it.

Panes can be changed to display different information, resized, split, closed, and possibly filtered or synchronized with the editor using the buttons in the headers. Experiment to get a feel for what they can do.

As you would expect with a modern IDE, the look and feel of the chrome and the text editor is very customizable. Select **Tools > Options...** to see what is available. I generally edit the following:

- Environment > Interface > Theme > Flat
- Text Editor > Fonts & Colors > Color Scheme > My own scheme
- Text Editor > Completion > Surround text selection with brackets > Off
- Text Editor > Completion > Surround text selection with quotes > Off
- C++ > Code Style > Current Settings > Copy... then Edit...
- Edit Code Style > Pointers and References > Bind to Type name > On (other options Off)

Play around and get things how you like them.

Scratchpad project

To demonstrate how minimal a Qt project can be and to give us a programming sandpit to play around in, we'll create a simple scratchpad project. For this project, we won't even use the IDE to do it for us, so you can really see how projects are built up.

First, we need to create a root folder to store all of our Qt projects. On Windows, I use c:\projects\qt, while I use ~/projects/qt on Linux and Mac OS. Create this folder wherever works for you.

Note that file syncing tools (OneDrive, DropBox, and so on) can sometimes cause problems with project folders, so keep your project files in a regular unsynchronized folder and use version control with a remote repository for backups and sharing.

For the remainder of the book, I will loosely refer to this folder as <Qt Projects> or similar. We will also tend toward using the Unix style / separator for file paths, rather than Windows style back slash \. So, for readers using Windows, <Qt Projects>/scratchpad/amazing/code is equivalent to c:\projects\qt\scratchpad\amazing\code. Qt tends to favor this convention too.

Equally, the majority of screenshots in the remainder of the book will be from Windows, so Linux/Mac users should interpret any references to c:\projects\qt as ~/projects/qt.

In our Qt projects folder, create a new folder scratchpad and navigate into it. Create a new plain text file called `scratchpad.pro`, remembering to remove any `.txt` extension the operating system may want to add for you.

Next, simply double-click on the file and it will open in **Qt Creator**:

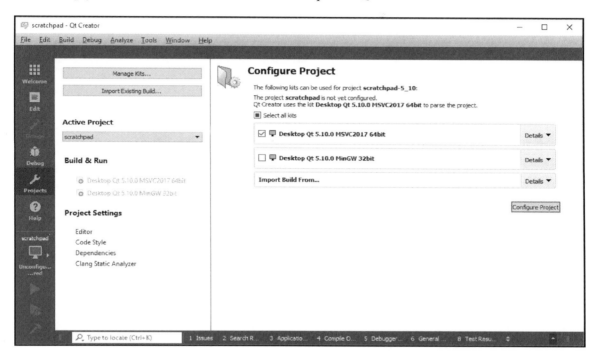

Here, Qt Creator is asking us how we want our project to be configured, namely, which kits we want to use when building and running our code. Pick one or more available kits and click on **Configure Project**. You can easily add and remove kits later, so don't worry about which ones you select.

If you switch back to the `filesystem`, you will see that Qt Creator has created a new file for us called `scratchpad.pro.user`. This is just an XML file containing configuration information. If you delete this file and open the `.pro` file again, you will be prompted to configure the project again. As its name suggests, the configuration settings are relevant to the local user, so often if you load a project created by someone else, you will need to go through the configure project step then too.

With the project successfully configured, you will see the project has been opened, even with a completely empty .pro file. That's about as minimal as a project can get!

Back in the filesystem, create the following plain text files:

- main.cpp
- main.qml
- qml.qrc

I will go through each of these files, explain their purpose, and add their content soon. In a real-world project, we would of course use the IDE to create the files for us. Indeed, that's exactly what we'll do when we create our main solution files. However, the purpose of doing it this way is to show you that when you boil it down, a project is just a bunch of text files. Never be afraid to create and edit files manually. A lot of modern IDEs can confuse and overcomplicate with menu after menu and never-ending option windows. Qt Creator may miss some of the advanced bells and whistles of other IDEs but is refreshingly lean and straightforward.

With those files created, double-click on the scratchpad.pro file in the **Projects** pane and we'll start editing our new project.

qmake

Our project (.pro) files are parsed by a utility called **qmake**, which in turn generates Makefiles that drive the building of the application. We define the type of project output we want, what source files are included as well as the dependencies and much more. Much of this is achieved by simply setting variables as we will do in our project file now.

Add the following to scratchpad.pro:

```
TEMPLATE = app

QT += qml quick

CONFIG += c++14
SOURCES += main.cpp
RESOURCES += qml.qrc
```

Let's run through each of these lines in turn:

```
TEMPLATE = app
```

`TEMPLATE` tells qmake what type of project this is. In our case, it's an executable application that is represented by `app`. Other values we are interested in are `lib` for building library binaries and `subdirs` for multi project solutions. Note that we set a variable with the `=` operator:

```
QT += qml quick
```

Qt is a modular framework that allows you to pull in only the parts you need. The `QT` flag specifies the Qt modules we want to use. The *core* and *gui* modules are included by default. Note that we append additional values to a variable that expects a list with `+=`:

```
CONFIG += c++14
```

`CONFIG` allows you to add project configuration and compiler options. In this case, we are specifying that we want to make use of C++14 features. Note that these language feature flags will have no effect if the compiler you are using does not support them:

```
SOURCES += main.cpp
```

`SOURCES` is a list of all the `*.cpp` source files we want to include in the project. Here, we add our empty `main.cpp` file, where we will implement our `main()` function. We don't have any yet, but when we do, our header files will be specified with a `HEADERS` variable:

```
RESOURCES += qml.qrc
```

`RESOURCES` is a list of all the resource collection files (`*.qrc`) included in the project. Resource collection files are used for managing application resources such as images and fonts, but most crucially for us, our QML files.

With the project file updated, save the changes.

Whenever you save a change to your `*.pro` files, qmake will parse the file. If all is well, you will get a small green bar at the bottom-right of Qt Creator. A red bar indicates some kind of issue, usually a syntax error. Any output from the process will be written out to the **General Messages** window to help you diagnose and fix the problem. White space is ignored, so don't worry about matching up the blank lines exactly.

To get qmake to take a fresh look at your project and generate new `Makefiles`, right-click on your project in the **Projects** pane and select **Run qmake**. It may be slightly tedious, but it's a good habit to manually run qmake in this way on each of your projects before building and running your application. I've found that certain types of code changes can "slip under the radar" and leave you scratching your head when you run your application and they don't seem to have had any effect. If you ever see your application ignoring the changes you've just made, run qmake on each of your projects and try again. The same applies if you get spurious linker errors.

You will see that our other files have now magically appeared in the **Projects** pane:

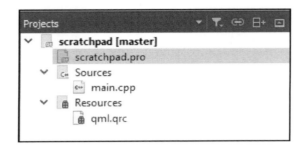

Double-click on `main.cpp` to edit it, and we'll write our first bit of code:

```
#include <QGuiApplication>
#include <QQmlApplicationEngine>

int main(int argc, char *argv[])
{
    QGuiApplication app(argc, argv);
    QQmlApplicationEngine engine;

    engine.load(QUrl(QStringLiteral("qrc:/main.qml")));

    return app.exec();
}
```

All we are doing here is instantiating a Qt GUI application object and asking it to load our `main.qml` file. It's very short and simple because the Qt framework does all the complex low-level work for us. We don't have to worry about platform detection or managing window handles or OpenGL.

Possibly one of the most useful things to learn is that placing the cursor in one of the Qt objects and pressing *F1* will open the help for that type. The same is true for methods and properties on Qt objects. Poke around in the help files to see what QGuiApplication and QQmlApplicationEngine are all about.

To edit the next file in our project—qml.qrc—you need to right-click and select the editor you want to open it with. The default is Resource Editor:

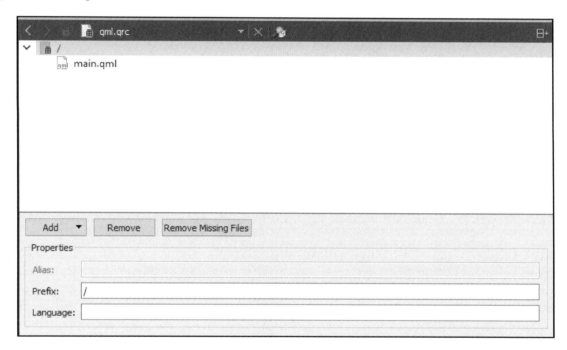

I am personally not a fan of this editor. I don't feel it makes editing any easier than just writing plain text and isn't particularly intuitive. Close this and instead choose Open with > Plain Text Editor.

Add the following content:

```
<RCC>
    <qresource prefix="/">
        <file>main.qml</file>
    </qresource>
</RCC>
```

Back in `main.cpp`, we asked Qt to load the `qrc:/main.qml` file. This essentially breaks down as "look for the file in a `qrc` file with a prefix of `/` and a name of `main.qml`". Now here in our `qrc` file, we have created a `qresource` element with a prefix property of `/`. Inside this element, we have a collection of resources (albeit only one of them) that has the name `main.qml`. Think of `qrc` files as a portable filesystem. Note that the resource files are located relative to the `.qrc` file that references them. In this case, our `main.qml` file is in the same folder as our `qml.qrc` file. If it was in a subfolder called `views`, for example, then the line in `qml.qrc` would read this way:

```
<file>views/main.qml</file>
```

Similarly, the string in `main.cpp` would be `qrc:/views/main.qml`.

Once those changes are saved, you will see our empty `main.qml` file appear as a child of the `qml.qrc` file in the **Projects** pane. Double-click on that file to edit it, and we will finish off our project:

```qml
import QtQuick 2.9
import QtQuick.Window 2.3

Window {
    visible: true
    width: 1024
    height: 768
    title: qsTr("Scratchpad")
    color: "#ffffff"

    Text {
        id: message
        anchors.centerIn: parent
        font.pixelSize: 44
        text: qsTr("Hello Qt Scratchpad!")
        color: "#008000"
    }
}
```

We will cover QML in detail in Chapter 2, *Project Structure*, but in brief, this file represents the screen or view presented to the user when the application launches.

The import lines are similar to `#include` statements in C++, though rather than including a single header file, they import a whole module. In this case, we want the base QtQuick module to give us access to all the core QML types and also the QtQuick window module to give us access to the `Window` component. Modules are versioned and generally, you will want to use the latest version for the release of Qt you are using. The current version numbers can be found in the Qt documentation. Note that although you get code completion when entering the version numbers, the options presented sometimes don't reflect the latest available versions.

As its name suggests, the `Window` element gives us a top-level window, inside which all of our other content will be rendered. We give it a size of 1024 x 765 pixels, a title of "scratchpad" and a background color of white represented as a hex RGB value.

Within that component (QML is a hierarchical markup language), we add a welcome message with the `Text` component. We center the text in the screen and set its font size and color, but other than that, we're not concerned with fancy formatting or anything at this stage, so that's as complicated as we'll make it. Again, we'll cover this in more detail later, so don't worry if it seems a bit alien.

That's it. To build and run our amazing new application, first select the **Kit** and **Build** configuration you want using the monitor icon at the bottom-left:

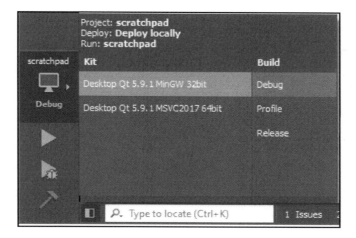

Next, right-click on the project name in the **Projects** pane and select **Run qmake**. When that has completed, **Run** the application using the green play icon:

Summary

In this chapter, we downloaded, installed, and configured Qt. We've taken a whirlwind tour of the Qt Creator IDE, played with its options, and seen how to edit a variety of files with it. We've had a gentle introduction to qmake and seen how absurdly simple creating projects can be, demystifying things in the process. Finally, we built our debut project up from scratch (weak pun intended) and got the obligatory Hello World message on screen.

In Chapter 2, *Project Structure*, we will build on these basics and set up our main solution.

2
Project Structure

In this chapter, we will create a new multiproject solution that will be the foundation of our example application. We will apply a Model View Controller pattern, separating the user interface and business logic. We will also introduce Qt's unit testing framework—QtTest—and demonstrate how to integrate it into our solution. We will cover these things in this chapter:

- Projects, MVC, and unit testing
- Creating a library project
- Creating a unit tests project
- Creating a user interface project
- Mastering MVC
- The QObject base class
- QML
- Controlling project output

Projects, MVC, and unit testing

The scratchpad application we built in the previous chapter is a Qt project, represented by a `.pro` file. In a business environment, technical solutions are generally developed as part of company initiatives, and these initiatives are generally also called **projects**. To try and minimize confusion (and the number of times the word project appears!), we'll use project to mean a Qt project defined by a `.pro` file and the word initiative to refer to projects in the business sense.

The initiative we will work on will be a generic client management system. It will be something that can be tweaked and re purposed for multiple applications—for a supplier managing customers, a health service managing patients, and so on. It will perform common tasks found over and over in real-world **Line of Business** (**LOB**) applications, principally adding, editing, and deleting data.

Our scratchpad application is entirely encapsulated within a single project. For smaller applications, this is perfectly viable. However, with larger code bases, particularly with several developers involved, it often pays to break things up into more manageable pieces.

We will be using a super lightweight implementation of the **Model View Controller** (**MVC**) architectural pattern. If you haven't come across MVC before, it is primarily used to decouple business logic from the user interface. The user interface (View) relays commands to a switchboard style class (Controller) to retrieve the data and perform actions it needs. The controller in turn delegates the responsibility for the data, logic, and rules to data objects (Models):

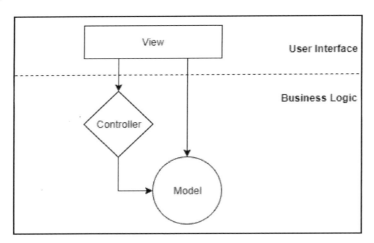

The key is that the **View** knows about the **Controller** and the **Model**, as it needs to send commands to the **Controller** and display the data held in the **Model**. The **Controller** knows about the **Model** as it needs to delegate work to it, but it doesn't know about the **View**. The **Model** knows nothing about either the **Controller** or the **View**.

A key benefit of designing the application this way in a business environment is that dedicated UX specialists can work on the views while programmers work on the business logic. A secondary boon is that because the business logic layer knows nothing about the UI, you add, edit, and even totally replace user interfaces without affecting the logic layer. A great use case would be to have a "full fat" UI for a desktop application and a companion "half fat" UI for a mobile device, both of which can use the same business logic. With all this in mind, we will physically segregate our UI and business logic into separate projects.

We will also look at integrating automated unit tests into our solution. Unit testing and **Test Driven Development (TDD)** has really grown in popularity in recent times and when developing applications in a business environment, you will more than likely be expected to write unit tests alongside your code. If not, you should really propose doing it as it holds a lot of value. Don't worry if you haven't done any unit testing before; it's very straightforward, and we'll discuss it in more detail later in the book.

Finally, we need a way to aggregate these subprojects together so that we don't have to open them individually. We will achieve this with an umbrella solution project that does nothing other than tying the other projects together. This is how we will lay out our projects:

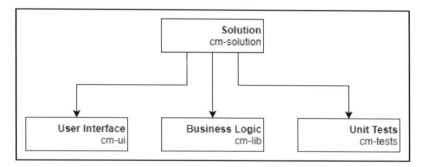

Project creation

In the previous chapter, we saw how easy it is to set up a new project just by creating a few text files. However, we'll create our new solution using Qt Creator. We will use the new project wizard to guide us through creating a top-level solution and a single subproject.

From the top menu, select **File > New File or Project** and then **Projects > Other Project > Subdirs Project** and click on **Choose…**:

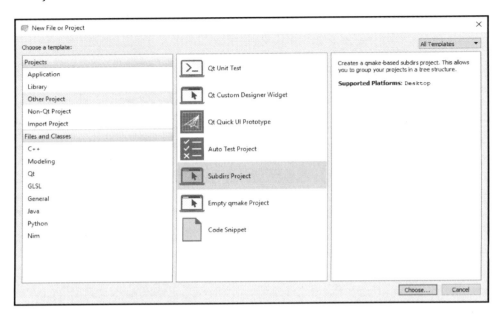

Subdirs Project is the template we need for our top-level solution project. Give it the name cm and create it in our qt projects folder:

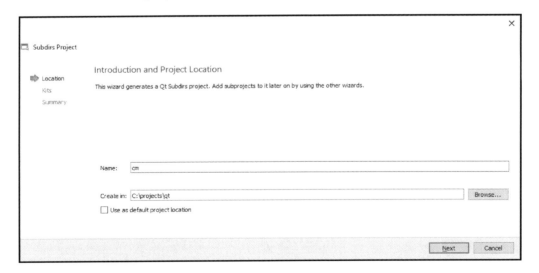

On the **Kit Selection** pane, check the **Desktop Qt 5.10.0 MinGW 32bit** kit we installed. Feel free to select additional kits you want to try out if you have them installed, but it's not necessary. Click on **Next**:

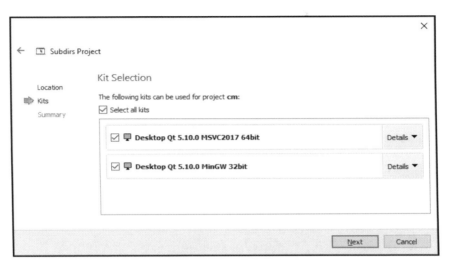

As discussed, version control is beyond the scope of this book, so in the **Project Management** pane, select **None** from the **Add to version control** dropdown. Click on **Finish & Add Subproject**:

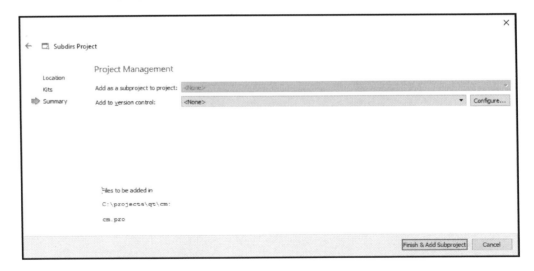

We'll add the user interface project as the first subproject. The wizard follows more or less the same pattern as the steps we've just followed, so perform the following:

1. Select **Projects > Application > Qt Quick Application - Empty** and click on **Choose...**
2. In the **Project Location** dialog, give it the name cm-ui (for Client Management - User Interface), leave the location as our new cm folder, and click on **Next**.
3. In the **Define Build System** dialog, select the build system **qmake** and click on **Next**.
4. In the **Define Project Details** dialog, leave the default minimal Qt version of **QT 5.9** and the **Use Qt Virtual Keyboard** box unchecked then click on **Next**.
5. In the **Kit Selection** dialog, pick the **Desktop Qt 5.10.0 MinGW 32bit** kit plus any other kits you wish to try and click on **Next**.
6. Finally, in the **Project Management** dialog, skip version control (leave it as **<None>**) and click on **Finish**.

Our top-level solution and UI projects are now up and running, so let's add the other subprojects. Add the business logic project next, as follows:

1. In the **Projects** pane, right-click on the top-level cm folder and select **New Subproject....**
2. Select **Projects > Library > C++ Library** and click on **Choose....**
3. In the **Introduction and Project Location** dialog, pick **Shared Library** as the Type, name it cm-lib, create it in <Qt Projects>/cm, and then click on **Next**.
4. In the **Select Required Modules** dialog, just accept the default of **QtCore** and click on **Next**.
5. In the **Class Information** dialog, we get the opportunity to create a new class to get us started. Give the class name Client, with the client.h header file and the client.cpp source file, and then click on **Next**.
6. Finally, in the **Project Management** dialog, skip version control (leave it as **<None>**) and click on **Finish**.

Finally, we will repeat the process to create our unit testing project:

1. **New Subproject....**
2. **Projects > Other Project > Qt Unit Test**.
3. Project name cm-tests.
4. Include **QtCore** and **QtTest**.

5. Create the `ClientTests` test class with the `testCase1` test slot and the `client-tests.cpp` filename. Set the Type as **Test** and check **Generate initialization and cleanup code**.
6. Skip version control and **Finish**.

That was a lot of dialog boxes to get through, but we've now got our skeleton solution in place. Your project folders should look as follows:

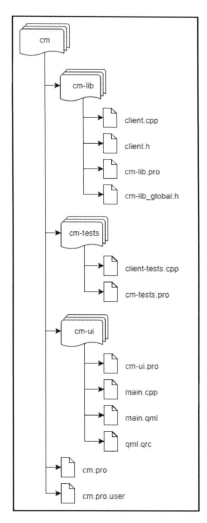

We'll now take a look at each project in turn and make some tweaks before we start adding our content.

cm-lib

First off, head to file explorer and create a new subfolder underneath cm-lib called source; move cm-lib_global.h there. Create another subfolder in source called models and move both the Client class files there.

Next, back in Qt Creator, open up cm-lib.pro and edit it as follows:

```
QT -= gui

TARGET = cm-lib
TEMPLATE = lib

CONFIG += c++14

DEFINES += CMLIB_LIBRARY

INCLUDEPATH += source

SOURCES += source/models/client.cpp

HEADERS += source/cm-lib_global.h \
    source/models/client.h
```

As this is a library project, we do not need to load the default GUI module, so we exclude it using the QT variable. The TARGET variable is the name we wish to give our binary output (for example, cm-lib.dll). It is optional and will default to the project name if not provided, but we'll be explicit. Next, rather than having a TEMPLATE of app as we saw in our scratchpad application, this time we use lib to give us a library. We add c++14 features via the CONFIG variable.

The cm-lib_global.h file is a helpful little bit of preprocessor boilerplate we can use to export our shared library symbols, and you'll see that put to use soon. We use the CMLIB_LIBRARY flag in the DEFINES variable to trigger this export.

Finally, we have slightly rewritten the SOURCES and HEADERS variable lists to account for the new file locations after we moved things around a bit, and we add the source folder (which is where all of our code will live) to the INCLUDEPATH so that the path is searched when we use #include statements.

Right-click on the `cm-lib` folder in the **Projects** pane and select **Run qmake**. When that has finished, right-click again and select **Rebuild**. Everything should be green and happy.

cm-tests

Create new `source/models` subfolders and move `client-tests.cpp` there. Switch back to Qt Creator and edit `cm-tests.pro`:

```
QT += testlib
QT -= gui

TARGET = client-tests
TEMPLATE = app

CONFIG += c++14
CONFIG += console
CONFIG -= app_bundle

INCLUDEPATH += source

SOURCES += source/models/client-tests.cpp
```

This follows pretty much the same approach as with `cm-lib`, with the exception that we want a console app rather than a library. We don't need the GUI module, but we will add the `testlib` module to get access to the Qt Test features.

There really isn't much to this subproject just yet, but you should be able to run qmake and rebuild successfully.

cm-ui

Create two subfolders this time: `source` and `views`. Move `main.cpp` into `source` and `main.qml` into `views`. Rename `qml.qrc` as `views.qrc` and edit `cm-ui.pro`:

```
QT += qml quick

TEMPLATE = app

CONFIG += c++14

INCLUDEPATH += source

SOURCES += source/main.cpp
```

```
RESOURCES += views.qrc

# Additional import path used to resolve QML modules in Qt Creator's code
model
QML_IMPORT_PATH = $$PWD
```

Our UI is written in QML, which requires the qml and quick modules, so we add those. We edit the RESOURCES variable to pick up our renamed resource file and also edit the QML_IMPORT_PATH variable, which we will cover in detail when we get into custom QML modules.

Next, edit views.qrc to account for the fact that we have moved the main.qml file into the views folder. Remember to right-click and **Open With > Plain Text Editor**:

```
<RCC>
    <qresource prefix="/">
        <file>views/main.qml</file>
    </qresource>
</RCC>
```

Finally, we also need to edit a line in main.cpp to account for the file move:

```
engine.load(QUrl(QStringLiteral("qrc:/views/main.qml")));
```

You should now be able to run qmake and rebuild the cm-ui project. Before we run it, let's take a quick look at the build configuration button now that we have multiple projects open:

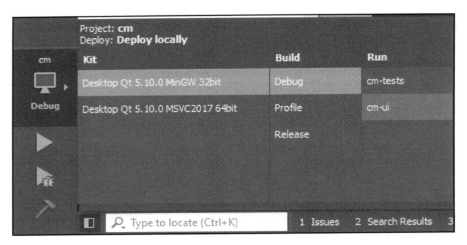

Note that now, along with the **Kit** and **Build** options, we must also select the executable we wish to run. Ensure that cm-ui is selected and then run the application:

Hello World indeed. It's fairly uninspiring stuff, but we have a multiproject solution building and running happily, which is a great start. Close the application when you simply can't take any more fun!

Mastering MVC

Now that our solution structure is in place, we'll get started on the MVC implementation. As you'll see, it is very minimal and incredibly easy to set up.

First, expand cm-ui > Resources > views.qrc > / > views, right-click on main.qml, select **Rename**, and rename the file as MasterView.qml. If you get a message about project editing, just select **Yes** to continue anyway:

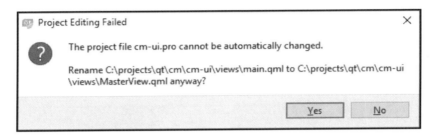

If you do get the error message, the file will still appear as main.qml in the **Projects** pane, but the file will have been renamed in the filesystem.

Next, edit views.qrc (right-click on it and select **Open With > Plain Text Editor**). Replace the content as follows:

```
<RCC>
    <qresource prefix="/views">
        <file alias="MasterView.qml">views/MasterView.qml</file>
    </qresource>
</RCC>
```

If you recall how we load this QML file in main.cpp, the syntax is qrc:<prefix><filename>. We previously had a / prefix and a views/main.qml relative filename. This gave us qrc:/views/main.qml.

A prefix of / isn't terribly descriptive. As you add more and more QML files, it's really helpful to organize them into blocks with meaningful prefixes. Having unstructured resource blocks also makes the **Projects** pane ugly and more difficult to navigate, as you just saw when you had to drill down through views.qrc > / > views. So, the first step is to rename the prefix from / to /views.

However, with a prefix of /views and a relative filename of views/main.qml, our URL is now qrc:/views/views/main.qml.

This is worse than it was before, and we still have a deep folder structure in `views.qrc`. Fortunately, we can add an *alias* for our file to make both of these problems go away. You can use the alias of a resource in place of the relative path, so if we assign an alias of `main.qml`, we can replace `views/main.qml` with simply `main.qml`, giving us `qrc:/views/main.qml`.

That's concise and descriptive, and our **Projects** pane is neater too.

So, going back to our updated version of `views.qrc`, we have simply updated the name of the file from `main.qml` to `MasterView.qml`, consistent with the file rename we performed, and we have also provided a shortcut alias, so we don't have to specify **views** twice.

We now need to update our code in `main.cpp` to reflect these changes:

```
engine.load(QUrl(QStringLiteral("qrc:/views/MasterView.qml")));
```

You should be able to run qmake, and build and run to verify that nothing has broken.

Next, we'll create a `MasterController` class, so right-click on the `cm-lib` project and select **Add New... > C++ > C++ Class > Choose...**:

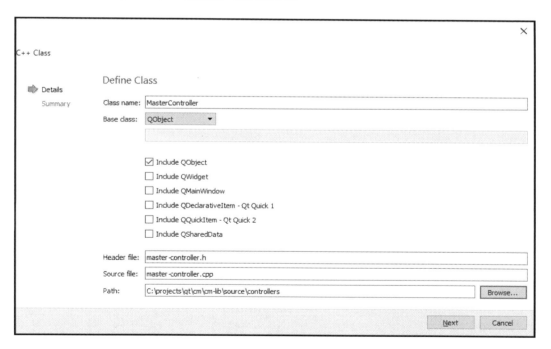

Use the **Browse...** button to create the source/controllers subfolder.

By selecting **QObject** as the base class and including it, Qt Creator will write some of the boilerplate code for us. You can always add it yourself later, so don't feel like it's a necessary part of creating a new class.

Once you've skipped version control and created the class, declare and define it as follows. Our MasterController doesn't do anything particularly exciting just yet, we're just doing the groundwork.

Here's master-controller.h:

```
#ifndef MASTERCONTROLLER_H
#define MASTERCONTROLLER_H

#include <QObject>

#include <cm-lib_global.h>

namespace cm {
namespace controllers {

class CMLIBSHARED_EXPORT MasterController : public QObject
{
    Q_OBJECT

public:
    explicit MasterController(QObject* parent = nullptr);
};

}}

#endif
```

All we've really added to the default implementation Qt Creator gave us is the CMLIBSHARED_EXPORT macro Qt Creator wrote for us in cm-lib_global.h to take care of our shared library exports, and to put the class inside a namespace.

 I always have the project name as a root namespace and then additional namespaces that reflect the physical location of the class files within the source directory, so in this case, I use cm::controllers, as the class is located in the directory source/controllers.

This is `master-controller.cpp`:

```cpp
#include "master-controller.h"

namespace cm {
namespace controllers {

MasterController::MasterController(QObject* parent)
    : QObject(parent)
{
}

}}
```

I use a slightly unorthodox style in the implementation file—most people just add `using namespace cm::controllers;` at the top of the `.cpp` file. I often like to put the code within the scope of namespaces because it becomes collapsible in the IDE. By repeating the innermost namespace scope (*controllers* in this example), you can break your code up into collapsible regions much like you can in C#, which helps with navigation in larger files, as you can collapse the sections you're not interested in. It makes no functional difference, so use whichever style you prefer.

QObject

So, what is this funky **QObject** thingy we are inheriting from which keeps popping up? Well, it's the base class for all Qt objects, and it gives us some powerful features for free.

QObjects organize themselves into object hierarchies with a *parent* object assuming ownership of their *child* objects, which means we don't have to worry (as much!) about memory management. For example, if we have an instance of a Client class derived from QObject that is the parent of an Address also derived from QObject, then the address is automatically destroyed when the client is destroyed.

QObjects carry metadata that allows a degree of type inspection and is the backbone for interaction with QML. They can also communicate with each other via an event subscription mechanism where the events are emitted as *signals* and the subscribed delegates are known as *slots*.

All you need to remember for now is that for any custom classes you write where you want to interact with it in the UI, ensure that it derives from QObject. Whenever you do derive from QObject, ensure that you always add the magical Q_OBJECT macro to your class before you do anything else. It injects a bunch of super complicated boilerplate code that you don't need to understand in order to use QObjects effectively.

We are now at the point where we need to reference code from one subproject (MasterController in cm-lib) in another (cm-ui). We first need to be able to access the declarations for our #include statements. Edit the INCLUDEPATH variable in cm-ui.pro as follows:

```
INCLUDEPATH += source \
    ../cm-lib/source
```

The \ symbol is a "continue on to the next line" indicator, so you can set a variable to multiple values spanning several lines. Just like console commands, '..' means traverse up a level, so here we are stepping up out of the local folder (cm-ui) and then down into the cm-lib folder to get at its source code. You need to be careful that the project folders remain in the same location relative to each other, else this won't work.

Just below this, we'll tell our UI project where to find the implementation (compiled binary) of our library project. If you take a look at the filesystem alongside the top-level cm project folder, you will see one or more build folders, for example, **build-cm-Desktop_Qt_5_9_0_MinGW_32bit-Debug**. Each folder is created when we run qmake for a given kit and configuration and is populated with the output when we build.

Next, navigate to the folder relevant to the kit and configuration you are using, and you will find a **cm-lib** folder with another configuration folder inside it. Copy this file path; for example, I am using the MinGW 32 bit kit in Debug configuration, so my path is <Qt Projects>/build-cm-Desktop_Qt_5_10_0_MinGW_32bit-Debug/cm-lib/debug.

In that folder, you will find the compiled binaries relevant for your OS, for example, cm-lib.dll on Windows. This is the folder we want our cm-ui project to reference for the cm-lib library implementation. To set this up, add the following statement to cm-ui.pro:

```
LIBS += -L$$PWD/../../build-cm-Desktop_Qt_5_10_0_MinGW_32bit-Debug/cm-
lib/debug -lcm-lib
```

LIBS is the variable used to add referenced libraries to the project. The -L prefix denotes a directory, while -l denotes a library file. Using this syntax allows us to ignore the file extensions (.a, .o, .lib) and prefixes (lib...), which can vary between operating systems and let qmake figure it out. We use the special $$ symbol to access the value of the PWD variable, which contains the working directory of the current project (the full path to cm/cm-ui in this case). From that location, we then drill up two directories with ../.. to get us to the Qt projects folder. From there, we drill back down to the location where we know the cm-lib binaries are built.

Now, this is painful to write, ugly as hell, and will fall over as soon as we switch kits or configurations, but we will come back and tidy up all this later. With the project references all wired up, we can head on over to main.cpp in cm-ui.

To be able to use a given class in QML, we need to register it, which we do in main() before we create the QML Application Engine. First, include the MasterController:

```
#include <controllers/master-controller.h>
```

Then, right after the QGuiApplication is instantiated but before the QQmlApplicationEngine is declared, add the following line:

```
qmlRegisterType<cm::controllers::MasterController>("CM", 1, 0,
"MasterController");
```

What we are doing here is registering the type with the QML engine. Note that the template parameter must be fully qualified with all namespaces. We will add the type's metadata into a module called **CM** with a version number **1.0**, and we want to refer to this type as MasterController in QML markup.

Then, we instantiate an instance of MasterController and inject it into the root QML context:

```
cm::controllers::MasterController masterController;
QQmlApplicationEngine engine;
engine.rootContext()->setContextProperty("masterController",
&masterController);
engine.load(QUrl(QStringLiteral("qrc:/views/MasterView")));
```

Note that you need to set the context property before loading the QML file, and you will also need to add the following header:

```
#include <QQmlContext>
```

So, we've created a controller, registered it with the QML engine, and it's good to go. What now? Let's do our first bit of QML.

QML

Qt Modeling Language (QML) is a hierarchical declarative language for user interface layout with a syntax similar to **JavaScript Object Notation (JSON)**. It can bind to C++ objects via Qt's meta object system and also supports inline JavaScript. It's much like HTML or XAML but without the XMLness. If you are someone who likes JSON more than XML, this can only be a good thing!

Go ahead and open up `MasterView.qml`, and we'll see what's going on.

The first thing you'll see is a couple of `import` statements. They are similar to `#include` statements in C++—they bring in pieces of functionality that we want to use in the view. They can be packed and versioned modules as with QtQuick 2.9, or they can be relative paths to local content.

Next, the QML hierarchy begins with a Window object. The scope of the object is represented by the subsequent { }, so everything within the braces is either a property or child of the object.

Properties follow JSON property syntax, of the form key: value. A notable difference is that speech marks are not required unless you are providing a string literal as a value. Here, we are setting the `visible` property of the **Window** object to be `true` and the size of the window to be **640** x **480** pixels, and we are displaying **Hello World** in the title bar.

Let's change the title and add a simple message. Replace the **Hello World** title with **Client Management** and insert a **Text** component inside the body of the **Window**:

```
Window {
    visible: true
    width: 640
    height: 480
    title: qsTr("Client Management")

    Text {
        text: "Welcome to the Client Management system!"
    }
}
```

Save your changes, and **Run qmake** and **Run** the application:

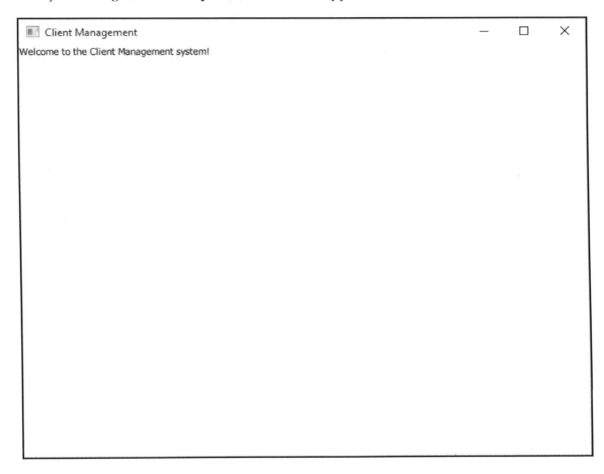

Let's make `MasterController` start earning its keep and rather than hard-coding our welcome message in the UI, we'll obtain it dynamically from our controller.

Edit `master-controller.h` and add a new public property of the `QString` type called `welcomeMessage`, setting it to an initial value:

```
QString welcomeMessage = "This is MasterController to Major Tom";
```

You will also need to #include <QString>.

In order to be able to access this member from QML, we need to configure a new property. After the **Q_OBJECT** macro but before the first public access modifier, add the following:

```
Q_PROPERTY( QString ui_welcomeMessage MEMBER welcomeMessage CONSTANT )
```

Here, we are creating a new property of the **QString** type that QML can access. QML will refer to the property as ui_welcomeMessage and when called, will get (or set) the value in the MEMBER variable called welcomeMessage. We are explicitly setting the value of the variable up front and will not change it, so it will remain CONSTANT.

> You can simply name the property welcomeMessage, rather than ui_welcomeMessage. My personal preference is to explicitly name things that are solely intended for UI consumption with a ui_ prefix to differentiate them from member variables and methods. Do whatever works for you.

Head back to MasterView.qml, and we will put this property to use. Change the text property of the Text component to the following:

```
text: masterController.ui_welcomeMessage
```

Note how the QML editor recognizes masterController and even offers code completion for it. Now, rather than displaying a string literal as the message, the QML will access the ui_welcomeMessage property of the instance of MasterController we injected into the root context in main(), which will, in turn, get the value of the welcomeMessage member variable.

Build and **Run**, and you should now see the message coming from the
`MasterController`:

We now have a working mechanism for QML to call into C++ code and get hold of
whatever data and business logic we want to provide it. Here, an important thing to note is
that our `MasterController` knows nothing about the existence of `MasterView`, and this is
a key part of the MVC pattern.

Project output

In order to let our `cm-ui` project know where to find the implementation of `cm-lib`, we used the `LIBS` variable in our project file. It was a pretty ugly folder name, but it's only one line and everything has worked perfectly well, so it could be tempting to leave things as they are. However, look forward to when we are ready to produce our first build for testing or even production. We've written some really clever code, and everything is building and running beautifully. We switch the configuration from **Debug** to **Release** and...everything falls over. The problem is that we've hard-coded the library path in our project file to look in the `Debug` folder. Change to a different kit or another operating system and the problem is even worse, as you will have binary compatibility issues from using different compilers.

Let's set a few goals:

- Get rid of the unwieldy `build-cm...` folders
- Aggregate all the compiled binary output into one common folder `cm/binaries`
- Hide all temporary build artifacts in their own folders `cm/<project>/build`
- Create separate build and binary folders for different compilers and architectures
- Detect those compilers and architectures automatically

So, where do these funny long folder names come from in the first place? In Qt Creator, click on the **Projects** mode icon in the navigation bar. Down the left-hand side in the **Build & Run** section, select **Desktop Qt 5.9.0 MinGW 32 bit > Build**. Here, you will see the Build Settings for the MinGW kit in this solution and under the **Shadow build** checkbox, you will recognize the long build directory.

We need to leave shadow builds enabled as this gives us the capability to perform builds to alternative locations for different kits. We will control the exact output of our builds in the `.pro` files, but we still need to specify a build directory here to keep Qt Creator happy. Enter **<Qt Projects>/shadow-builds**. Repeat this setting for each build configuration (Debug/Release/Profile) using the dropdown at the top of the pane, and for all the kits you are using:

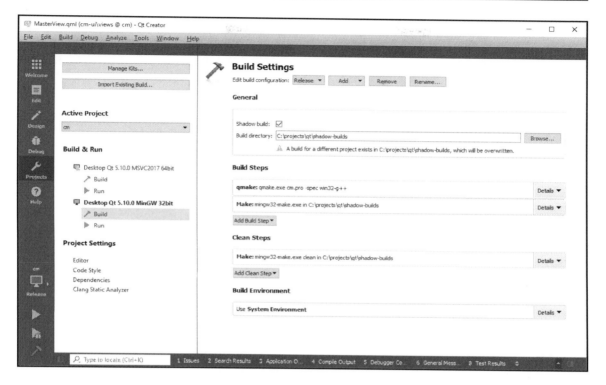

In your filesystem, delete any of the old `build-cm...` folders. Right-click on the solution folder and **Run qmake**. After qmake has finished, you should see that shell `cm-lib`, `cm-tests`, and `cm-ui` folders have been created in **<Qt Projects>/shadow-builds** and that the long `build-cm...` folders have not reappeared.

The first step for dynamically setting any relative path is to know which path you are currently on. We've already seen that in action in qmake when we used `$$PWD` to get the project working directory. To help us visualize what is going on, let's introduce our first qmake function—`message()`.

Add the following line to `cm.pro`—it doesn't matter where in the file it goes:

```
message(cm project dir: $${PWD})
```

Add the following line to `cm-lib.pro`:

```
message(cm-lib project dir: $${PWD})
```

The `message()` is a test function supported by qmake that outputs the supplied string parameter to the console. Note that you don't need to surround the text with double quotes. When you save the changes, you will see the **Project Working Directory (PWD)** of both the solution project and the library project logged out to the **General Messages** console:

```
Project MESSAGE: cm project dir: C:/projects/qt/cm

Project MESSAGE: cm-lib project dir: C:/projects/qt/cm/cm-lib
```

qmake actually takes multiple passes over `.pro` files, so whenever you use `message()`, you may see the same output several times over in the console. You can filter out the majority of duplicates using `message()` in conjunction with a scope—`!build_pass:message(Here is my message)`. This prevents the `message()` method from being called during the build pass.

If we look back at the default behavior of Qt Creator for shadow builds, we'll see that the aim was to allow multiple builds to sit alongside each other. This is achieved by constructing distinct folder names containing the kit, platform, and build configuration:

```
build-cm-solution-Desktop_Qt_5_10_0_MinGW_32bit-Debug
```

You can see just by looking at the folder name that the contents are from a build of the **cm** project using the **Qt 5.10.0 for Desktop MinGW 32bit** kit in **Debug** mode. We'll now reimplement this approach in a cleaner and more flexible way.

Rather than concatenating the information into one long folder name, we'll prefer a hierarchical structure consisting of the `Operating System > Compiler > Processor Architecture > Build Configuration` folders.

Let's first hard-code this path and then move on to automating it. Edit `cm-lib.pro` and add this:

```
DESTDIR = $$PWD/../binaries/windows/gcc/x86/debug
message(cm-lib output dir: $${DESTDIR})
```

This is to reflect that we are building with the **MinGW 32bit** kit on **Windows** in **Debug** mode. Replace *Windows* with *osx* or *Linux* if you are on a different OS. We've added another call to `message()` to output this destination directory in the **General Messages** console. Remember that `$$PWD` extracts the working directory of the `.pro` file being processed (`cm-lib.pro` in this case), so this gives us `<Qt Projects>/cm/cm-lib`.

Right-click on the cm-lib project, run qmake, and build. Ensure that you have the MinGW kit selected, along with Debug mode.

Navigate to <Qt Projects>/cm/binaries/<OS>/gcc/x86/debug in the filesystem, and you will see our library binaries without the associated clutter of build artifacts. This is a good first step, but if you now change the build configuration to Release or switch kits, the destination directory will remain the same, which is not what we want.

The technique we are about to implement will be used in all three of our projects, so rather than having to duplicate the configuration in all of our .pro files, let's extract the configuration to a shared file and include it instead.

In the root cm folder, create two new empty text files called qmake-target-platform.pri and qmake-destination-path.pri. In cm-lib.pro, cm-tests.pro, and cm-ui.pro, add these lines:

```
include(../qmake-target-platform.pri)
include(../qmake-destination-path.pri)
```

Add these lines somewhere near the top of the *.pro files. The exact order doesn't matter too much as long as they are before the DESTDIR variable is set.

Edit qmake-target-platform.pri as follows:

```
win32 {
    CONFIG += PLATFORM_WIN
    message(PLATFORM_WIN)
    win32-g++ {
        CONFIG += COMPILER_GCC
        message(COMPILER_GCC)
    }
    win32-msvc2017 {
        CONFIG += COMPILER_MSVC2017
        message(COMPILER_MSVC2017)
        win32-msvc2017:QMAKE_TARGET.arch = x86_64
    }
}

linux {
    CONFIG += PLATFORM_LINUX
    message(PLATFORM_LINUX)
    # Make QMAKE_TARGET arch available for Linux
    !contains(QT_ARCH, x86_64){
        QMAKE_TARGET.arch = x86
    } else {
        QMAKE_TARGET.arch = x86_64
```

```
    }
    linux-g++{
        CONFIG += COMPILER_GCC
        message(COMPILER_GCC)
    }
}

macx {
    CONFIG += PLATFORM_OSX
    message(PLATFORM_OSX)
    macx-clang {
        CONFIG += COMPILER_CLANG
        message(COMPILER_CLANG)
        QMAKE_TARGET.arch = x86_64
    }
    macx-clang-32{
        CONFIG += COMPILER_CLANG
        message(COMPILER_CLANG)
        QMAKE_TARGET.arch = x86
    }
}

contains(QMAKE_TARGET.arch, x86_64) {
    CONFIG += PROCESSOR_x64
    message(PROCESSOR_x64)
} else {
    CONFIG += PROCESSOR_x86
    message(PROCESSOR_x86)
}

CONFIG(debug, release|debug) {
    CONFIG += BUILD_DEBUG
    message(BUILD_DEBUG)
} else {
    CONFIG += BUILD_RELEASE
    message(BUILD_RELEASE)
}
```

Here, we are leveraging the platform detection capabilities of qmake to inject personalized flags into the CONFIG variable. On each operating system, different platform variables become available. For example, on Windows, the win32 variable is present, Linux is represented by linux, and Mac OS X by macx. We can use these platform variables with curly braces to act like if statements:

```
win32 {
    # This block will execute on Windows only...
}
```

We can consider different combinations of platform variables to figure out what compiler and processor architecture the currently selected kit is using, and then add developer-friendly flags to the `CONFIG`, which we can use later in our `.pro` files. Remember that we are trying to construct a build path—`Operating System > Compiler > Processor Architecture > Build Configuration`.

When you save these changes, you should see the flags similar to the following in the **General Message** console:

```
Project MESSAGE: PLATFORM_WIN
Project MESSAGE: COMPILER_GCC
Project MESSAGE: PROCESSOR_x86
Project MESSAGE: BUILD_DEBUG
```

Try switching kits or changing the build configuration, and you should see different output. When I switch my kit to Visual Studio 2017 64 bit in Release mode, I now get this:

```
Project MESSAGE: PLATFORM_WIN
Project MESSAGE: COMPILER_MSVC2017
Project MESSAGE: PROCESSOR_x64
Project MESSAGE: BUILD_RELEASE
```

With the same project on a Linux machine with the MinGW 64 bit kit, I get this:

```
Project MESSAGE: PLATFORM_LINUX
Project MESSAGE: COMPILER_GCC
Project MESSAGE: PROCESSOR_x64
Project MESSAGE: BUILD_DEBUG
```

On a Mac using Clang 64 bit, I get the following:

```
Project MESSAGE: PLATFORM_OSX
Project MESSAGE: COMPILER_CLANG
Project MESSAGE: PROCESSOR_x64
Project MESSAGE: BUILD_DEBUG
```

 To get this to work on Windows, I had to make an assumption as `QMAKE_TARGET.arch` is not correctly detected for MSVC2017, so I assumed that if the compiler is MSVC2017, then it must be x64 as there was no 32 bit kit available.

Now that all the platform detection is done, we can construct the destination path dynamically. Edit qmake-destination-path.pri:

```
platform_path = unknown-platform
compiler_path = unknown-compiler
processor_path = unknown-processor
build_path = unknown-build

PLATFORM_WIN {
    platform_path = windows
}
PLATFORM_OSX {
    platform_path = osx
}
PLATFORM_LINUX {
    platform_path = linux
}

COMPILER_GCC {
    compiler_path = gcc
}
COMPILER_MSVC2017 {
    compiler_path = msvc2017
}
COMPILER_CLANG {
    compiler_path = clang
}

PROCESSOR_x64 {
    processor_path = x64
}
PROCESSOR_x86 {
    processor_path = x86
}

BUILD_DEBUG {
    build_path = debug
} else {
    build_path = release
}

DESTINATION_PATH =
$$platform_path/$$compiler_path/$$processor_path/$$build_path
message(Dest path: $${DESTINATION_PATH})
```

Here, we create four new variables—*platform_path, compiler_path, processor_path,* and *build_path*—and assign default values to them all. We then use the CONFIG flags we created in the previous file and construct our folder hierarchy, storing it in a variable of our own, called DESTINATION_PATH. For example, if we detect Windows as the operating system, we add the PLATFORM_WIN flag to CONFIG and as a result of that, set platform_path to windows. Switching between kits and configurations on Windows, I now get these messages:

```
Dest path: windows/gcc/x86/debug
```

Alternatively, I get this:

```
Dest path: windows/msvc2017/x64/release
```

On Linux, I get the following:

```
Dest path: linux/gcc/x64/debug
```

On Mac OS, this is what I get:

```
Dest path: osx/clang/x64/debug
```

You can just combine these platform detection and destination path creation tricks in one file, but by keeping them separate, you can use the flags elsewhere in your project files. In any case, we are now dynamically creating a path based on our build environment and storing it in a variable for later use.

The next thing to do is to plug this DESTINATION_PATH variable into our project files. While we're here, we can also structure our build artifacts using the same mechanism by adding a few more lines. Add the following to all three *.pro files, replacing the DESTDIR statement already in cm-lib.pro:

```
DESTDIR = $$PWD/../binaries/$$DESTINATION_PATH
OBJECTS_DIR = $$PWD/build/$$DESTINATION_PATH/.obj
MOC_DIR = $$PWD/build/$$DESTINATION_PATH/.moc
RCC_DIR = $$PWD/build/$$DESTINATION_PATH/.qrc
UI_DIR = $$PWD/build/$$DESTINATION_PATH/.ui
```

Temporary build artifacts will now be placed into discreet directories within the build folder.

Finally, we can fix the problem that brought us here in the first place. In `cm-tests` and `cm-ui`, we can now set the `LIBS` variable using our new dynamic destination path:

```
LIBS += -L$$PWD/../binaries/$$DESTINATION_PATH -lcm-lib
```

You can now right-click on the `cm` project, run qmake, and build to automatically build all three subprojects in one step. All the output will be sent to the correct place and the library binaries can be easily located by the other projects. You can switch kits and configurations and not have to worry about referencing the wrong libraries.

Summary

In this chapter, we took our project creation skills up to the next level, and our solution is now starting to take shape. We implemented an MVC pattern and bridged the gap between our UI and business logic projects. We dabbled with our first bit of QML and took a look at the cornerstone of the Qt framework, QObject.

We removed all those unsightly `build-cm...` folders, flexed our qmake muscles, and took control of where all of our files go. All binaries are now placed in the `cm/binaries` folder, organized by platform, compiler, processor architecture, and build configuration. All temporary build artifacts that aren't required by the end user are now hidden away. We can freely switch kits and build configurations, and have our output automatically rerouted to the correct location.

In `Chapter 3`, *User Interface*, we will design our UI and get stuck in some more QML.

3

User Interface

In this chapter, we will take a more detailed look at QML and sketch out our user interface layout. We'll create placeholder views for all of our screens and implement a framework to navigate between them. We will also discuss the content within those views, specifically how to anchor and size elements in a flexible and responsive way. We will cover these topics:

- User interface design
- Creating views
- The StackView component
- Anchoring elements
- Sizing elements
- Navigating between views

UX

If you've ever worked with other declarative UI technologies like HTML and XAML, they often take a parent/child approach to UI, that is, there is a parent or root view that is ever present and contains global functionality, such as top-level navigation. It then has dynamic content or child views, which switch in and out as needed and present context sensitive commands where necessary.

We will take the same approach, with our MasterView being the root of our UI. We will add a global navigation bar and a content pane where we can add and remove content as needed. Child views will optionally present a command bar for performing actions, for example, saving a record to a database.

Let's take a look at the basic layout we are aiming for:

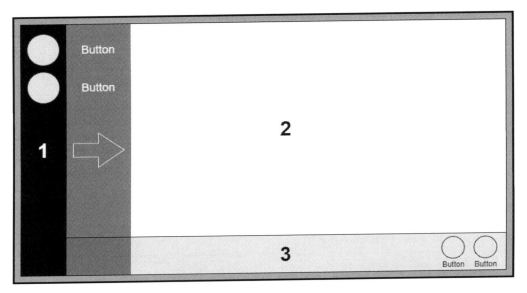

The Navigation Bar (**1**) will be ever present and contain buttons that will navigate the user to key areas within the application. By default, the bar will be narrow and the commands associated with the buttons will be represented by icons; however, pressing a toggle button will expand the bar to display accompanying descriptive text for each button.

The Content Pane (**2**) will be a stack of child views. Navigating to different areas of the application will be achieved by replacing the child view in the content pane. For example, if we add a **New Client** button on the navigation bar and press it, we will push the **New Client View** onto the content frame stack.

The Command Bar (**3**) is an optional element that will be used to present further command buttons to the user. The key difference to the navigation bar is that these commands will be context sensitive relating to the current view. For example, when creating a new client, we will need a Save button, but when we are searching for clients, a Save button makes no sense. Each child view will optionally present its own command bar. The commands will be presented by icons with a short description underneath.

Now let's plan the flow of screens, or views as we'll call them:

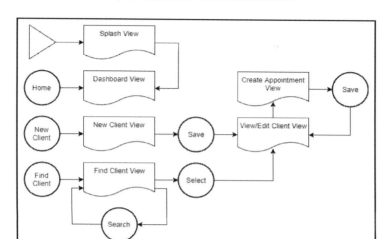

Creating views

In **cm-ui**, right-click on `views.qrc` and select **Add New...**. Select **Qt > QML File** and click on **Choose...**:

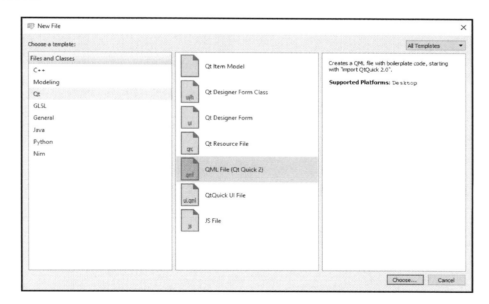

Create the `SplashView.qml` file in `cm-ui/ui/views`. Repeat this process until you've created all the following views:

File	Purpose
`SplashView.qml`	Placeholder view displayed while the UI is loading.
`DashboardView.qml`	The central "home" view.
`CreateClientView.qml`	View for entering details of a new client.
`EditClientView.qml`	View for reading/updating the existing client details.
`FindClientView.qml`	View for searching for the existing clients.

Edit `views.qrc` in the **Plain Text Editor** as we have done previously. You will see that our new views have been added to a new `qresource` block with the default prefix of the following:

```
<RCC>
    <qresource prefix="/views">
        <file alias="MasterView">views/MasterView.qml</file>
    </qresource>
    <qresource prefix="/">
        <file>views/SplashView.qml</file>
        <file>views/DashboardView.qml</file>
        <file>views/CreateClientView.qml</file>
        <file>views/EditClientView.qml</file>
        <file>views/FindClientView.qml</file>
    </qresource>
</RCC>
```

Also note that the **Projects** navigator is a bit of a mess:

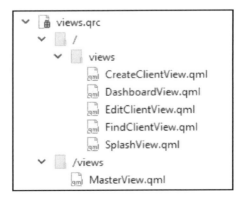

Move all the new files into the "/views" prefix block and remove the "/" block. Add an alias for each of the new files:

```
<RCC>
    <qresource prefix="/views">
        <file alias="MasterView.qml">views/MasterView.qml</file>
        <file alias="SplashView.qml">views/SplashView.qml</file>
        <file alias="DashboardView.qml">views/DashboardView.qml</file>
        <file
alias="CreateClientView.qml">views/CreateClientView.qml</file>
        <file alias="EditClientView.qml">views/EditClientView.qml</file>
        <file
alias="CreateAppointmentView.qml">views/CreateAppointmentView.qml</file>
        <file alias="FindClientView.qml">views/FindClientView.qml</file>
    </qresource>
</RCC>
```

As soon as you save these changes, you should see the navigator clean right up:

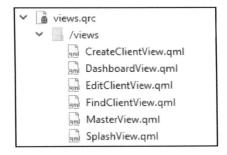

StackView

Our child views will be presented via a **StackView** component, which provides a stack-based navigation model with built-in history. New views (and views in this context means pretty much any QML) are pushed onto the stack when they are to be displayed and can be popped off the stack in order to go back to the previous view. We won't need to use the history capabilities, but they are a very useful feature.

To gain access to the component, we first need to reference the module, so add the import to **MasterView**:

```
import QtQuick.Controls 2.2
```

With that done, let's replace our **Text** element containing our welcome message with a
`StackView`:

```
StackView {
    id: contentFrame
    initialItem: "qrc:/views/SplashView.qml"
}
```

We assign the component a unique identifier `contentFrame` so that we can reference it
elsewhere in the QML, and we specify which child view we want to load by default—the
new `SplashView`.

Next, edit `SplashView`. Update the `QtQuick` module version to 2.9 so that it matches
MasterView (do this for all further QML files if not explicitly stated). This is not strictly
necessary, but it's a good practice to avoid inconsistencies across views. There is generally
not much in the way of breaking changes in minor releases of Qt, but the same code on two
views referencing different versions of QtQuick may exhibit different behavior that can
cause problems.

All we'll do with this view, for now, is to make a rectangle 400 pixels wide by 200 pixels
high, which has a "vibrant" background color so that we can see that it has loaded:

```
import QtQuick 2.9

Rectangle {
    width: 400
    height: 200
    color: "#f4c842"
}
```

Colors can be specified using hexadecimal RGB values as we did here, or named SVG
colors. I generally find hex easier as I can never remember the names of the colors!

 If you hover your cursor over the hex string in Qt Creator, you get a really
useful little pop-up color swatch.

Now run the application, and you should see that the welcome message no longer displays and instead, you are presented with a glorious orange-yellow rectangle, which is our **SplashView**.

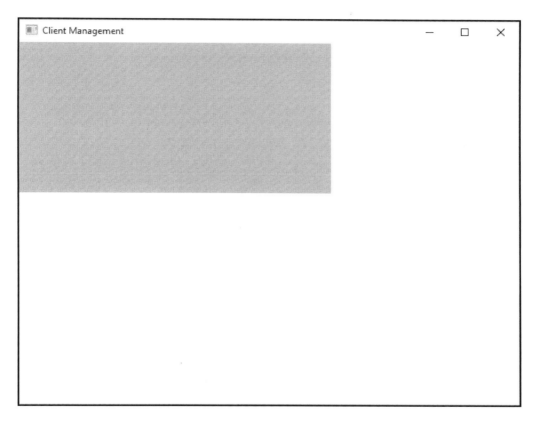

Anchors

One slight problem with our wonderful new **SplashView** is that it doesn't actually fill the window. Sure, we can change the 400 x 200 dimensions to 1024 x 768 so that it matches **MasterView**, but then what happens if the user resizes the window? Modern UI is all about responsive design—dynamic content that can adapt to the display it's being presented on, so hard-coding properties appropriate for only one platform aren't ideal. Fortunately, anchors come to our rescue.

Let's put our trusty old **scratchpad** project to use and take a look at anchors in action.

Right-click on qml.qrc and add a new AnchorsDemo.qml QML file alongside the existing main.qml file in the scratchpad folder. Don't worry about subfolders or .qrc prefixes, aliases, or any of that jazz.

Dip into main.cpp and load our new file instead of main.qml:

```
engine.load(QUrl(QStringLiteral("qrc:/AnchorsDemo.qml")));
```

Next, paste the following code into AnchorsDemo:

```
import QtQuick 2.9
import QtQuick.Window 2.2

Window {
    visible: true
    width: 1024
    height: 768
    title: qsTr("Scratchpad")
    color: "#ffffff"
    Rectangle {
        id: paleYellowBackground
        anchors.fill: parent
        color: "#cece9e"
    }
    Rectangle {
        id: blackRectangleInTheCentre
        width: 120
        height: 120
        anchors.centerIn: parent
        color: "#000000"
    }
    Rectangle {
        id: greenRectangleInTheCentre
        width: 100
        height: 100
        anchors.centerIn: parent
        anchors.verticalCenterOffset: 20
        color: "#008000"
    }
    Rectangle {
        id: redRectangleTopLeftCorner
        width: 100
        height: 100
        anchors {
            top: parent.top
```

```
            left: parent.left
        }
        color: "#800000"
    }
    Rectangle {
        id: blueRectangleTopLeftCorner
        width: 100
        height: 100
        anchors{
            top: redRectangleTopLeftCorner.bottom
            left: parent.left
        }
        color: "#000080"
    }
    Rectangle {
        id: purpleRectangleTopLeftCorner
        width: 100
        height: 100
        anchors{
            top: blueRectangleTopLeftCorner.bottom
            left: parent.left
            leftMargin: 20
        }
        color: "#800080"
    }
    Rectangle {
        id: turquoiseRectangleBottomRightCorner
        width: 100
        height: 100
        anchors{
            bottom: parent.bottom
            right: parent.right
            margins: 20
        }
        color: "#008080"
    }
}
```

Build and run the application, and you'll be presented with this rather bewildering sight:

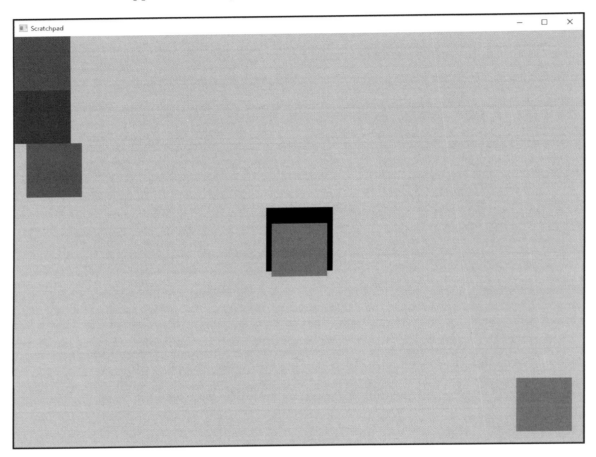

This may all look a bit confusing at first and I apologize if your color perception is suboptimal, but all we've done is draw a sequence of gaudily colored rectangles with differing anchors values. Let's walk through each rectangle one by one and see what is going on:

```
Rectangle {
    id: paleYellowBackground
    anchors.fill: parent
    color: "#cece9e"
}
```

Our first rectangle is the dull yellow brown background; `anchors.fill: parent` tells the rectangle to fill its parent, however big that may be. The parent of any given QML component is the QML component that contains it—the next level up in the hierarchy. In this case, it is the **Window** element. The **Window** element is 1024 x 768 pixels, so that's how big the rectangle is. Note that we don't need to specify width and height properties for the rectangle because they are inferred from the anchors.

This is exactly the behavior we want for our **SplashView**, but let's look at some other capabilities of anchors before we return to our main project:

```
Rectangle {
    id: blackRectangleInTheCentre
    width: 120
    height: 120
    anchors.centerIn: parent
    color: "#000000"
}
Rectangle {
    id: greenRectangleInTheCentre
    width: 100
    height: 100
    anchors.centerIn: parent
    anchors.verticalCenterOffset: 20
    color: "#008000"
}
```

We'll look at the next two rectangles together. First, we have a black rectangle that is 120 pixels square; `anchors.centerIn: parent` positions it at the center of its parent. We must specify the **width** and **height** because we are only positioning it, not sizing it.

Next, we have a slightly smaller green rectangle, also centered in its parent. We then use the `anchors.verticalCenterOffset` property to move it 20 pixels further down the screen. The x, y coordinate system used for positioning has its root (0, 0) at the top-left of the screen; `verticalCenterOffset` adds to the y coordinate. Positive numbers move the item down the screen, and negative numbers move the item up the screen. Its sister property—`horizontalCenterOffset`—is used for adjustments in the x axis.

One last thing to note here is that the rectangles overlap, and it is the green rectangle that wins out and is displayed in full. The black rectangle is pushed back and obscured. Similarly, all of our small rectangles sit in front of the large background rectangle. QML is rendered in a top-down fashion, so when the root element (**Window**) gets painted, its children are processed one by one from the top of the file to the bottom. So, items at the bottom of the file will be rendered in front of those rendered at the top of the file. The same is true if you paint a wall white and then paint it black, the wall will appear black because that's what was painted (rendered) last:

```
Rectangle {
    id: redRectangleTopLeftCorner
    width: 100
    height: 100
    anchors {
        top: parent.top
        left: parent.left
    }
    color: "#800000"
}
```

Next, we draw a red rectangle and rather than positioning or sizing the whole rectangle at once, we just anchor certain sides. We take the anchor on its **top** side and align it to the anchor on the **top** side of its parent (**Window**). We anchor its **left** side to its parent's **left** side. Hence, it becomes "attached" to the top-left corner.

We have to type the following:

```
anchors.top: parent.top
anchors.left: parent.left
```

Another helpful piece of syntactic sugar at work here is rather than doing that, we can remove the duplication and set the subproperties of the anchors group within curly braces:

```
anchors {
    top: parent.top
    left: parent.left
}
```

Next, the blue rectangle:

```
Rectangle {
    id: blueRectangleTopLeftCorner
    width: 100
    height: 100
    anchors{
        top: redRectangleTopLeftCorner.bottom
```

```
        left: parent.left
    }
    color: "#000080"
}
```

This follows the same pattern, though this time rather than attaching only to its parent, we also anchor to a sibling (the red rectangle), which we can reference though the id property:

```
Rectangle {
    id: purpleRectangleTopLeftCorner
    width: 100
    height: 100
    anchors{
        top: blueRectangleTopLeftCorner.bottom
        left: parent.left
        leftMargin: 20
    }
    color: "#800080"
}
```

The purple rectangle anchors to the bottom of the blue rectangle and to the left-hand side of the Window, but here we introduce our first margin. Each side has its own margin and in this case, we use leftMargin to give us an offset from the left anchor in exactly the same way as we saw with verticalCenterOffset earlier:

```
Rectangle {
    id: turquoiseRectangleBottomRightCorner
    width: 100
    height: 100
    anchors{
        bottom: parent.bottom
        right: parent.right
        margins: 20
    }
    color: "#008080"
}
```

Finally, our turquoise rectangle uses some of that empty space over on the right-hand side of the screen and demonstrates how we can set the margin on all four sides simultaneously using the margins property.

Note that all of these bindings are dynamic. Try resizing the window, and all the rectangles will adapt automatically. Anchors are a great tool for responsive UI design.

Let's head back to our `SplashView` in our `cm-ui` project and apply what we've just learned. Replace the fixed **width** and **height** attributes with the more dynamic `anchors.fill` property:

```
Rectangle {
    anchors.fill: parent
    color: "#f4c842"
}
```

Now, the `SplashView` will fill whatever its parent element is. Build and run, and you'll see that rather than our lovely colorful rectangle filling the screen as we expected, it has disappeared altogether. Let's take a look at why that is.

Sizing

Our rectangle will fill its parent, so the size of the rectangle depends entirely on the size of its parent. Walking up the QML hierarchy, the component that contains the rectangle is the `StackView` element back in **MasterView**:

```
StackView {
    id: contentFrame
    initialItem: Qt.resolvedUrl("qrc:/views/SplashView.qml")
}
```

Often, QML components are clever enough to size themselves based on their children. Previously, we had set our rectangle to a fixed size of 400 x 200. The `StackView` could look at that and say "I need to contain a single **Rectangle** that is 400 x 200, so I'll make myself 400 x 200 too. Easy!". We can always overrule that and set it to some other size using its **width** and **height** properties, but it can work out what size it wanted to be.

Back in `scratchpad`, create a new `SizingDemo.qml` view and edit `main.cpp` to load it on startup, just like we did with `AnchorsDemo`. Edit `SizingDemo` as follows:

```
import QtQuick 2.9
import QtQuick.Window 2.2

Window {
    visible: true
    width: 1024
    height: 768
    title: qsTr("Scratchpad")
    color: "#ffffff"
    Column {
```

```
            id: columnWithText
            Text {
                id: text1
                text: "Text 1"
            }
            Text {
                id: text2
                text: "Text 2"
                width: 300
                height: 20
            }
            Text {
                id: text3
                text: "Text 3 Text 3 Text 3 Text 3 Text 3 Text 3 Text 3 Text 3
Text 3 Text 3 Text 3 Text 3 Text 3 Text 3 Text 3 Text 3 Text 3 Text
3 Text 3 Text 3 Text 3 Text 3 Text 3 Text 3 Text 3 Text 3 Text 3
Text 3 Text 3 Text 3 Text 3 Text 3 Text 3 Text 3 Text 3"
            }
            Text {
                id: text4
                text: "Text 4 Text 4 Text 4 Text 4 Text 4 Text 4 Text 4 Text 4
Text 4 Text 4 Text 4 Text 4 Text 4 Text 4 Text 4 Text 4 Text 4 Text
4 Text 4 Text 4 Text 4 Text 4 Text 4 Text 4 Text 4 Text 4 Text 4
Text 4 Text 4 Text 4 Text 4 Text 4 Text 4 Text 4 Text 4"
                width: 300
            }
            Text {
                id: text5
                text: "Text 5 Text 5 Text 5 Text 5 Text 5 Text 5 Text 5 Text 5
Text 5 Text 5 Text 5 Text 5 Text 5 Text 5 Text 5 Text 5 Text 5 Text
5 Text 5 Text 5 Text 5 Text 5 Text 5 Text 5 Text 5 Text 5 Text 5
Text 5 Text 5 Text 5 Text 5 Text 5 Text 5 Text 5 Text 5"
                width: 300
                wrapMode: Text.Wrap
            }
        }
        Column {
            id: columnWithRectangle
            Rectangle {
                id: rectangle
                anchors.fill: parent
            }
        }
        Component.onCompleted: {
            console.log("Text1 - implicitWidth:" + text1.implicitWidth + "
implicitHeight:" + text1.implicitHeight + " width:" + text1.width + "
height:" + text1.height)
            console.log("Text2 - implicitWidth:" + text2.implicitWidth + "
```

```
implicitHeight:" + text2.implicitHeight + " width:" + text2.width + "
height:" + text2.height)
        console.log("Text3 - implicitWidth:" + text3.implicitWidth + "
implicitHeight:" + text3.implicitHeight + " width:" + text3.width + "
height:" + text3.height)
        console.log("Text4 - implicitWidth:" + text4.implicitWidth + "
implicitHeight:" + text4.implicitHeight + " width:" + text4.width + "
height:" + text4.height)
        console.log("Text5 - implicitWidth:" + text5.implicitWidth + "
implicitHeight:" + text5.implicitHeight + " width:" + text5.width + "
height:" + text5.height)
        console.log("ColumnWithText - implicitWidth:" +
columnWithText.implicitWidth + " implicitHeight:" +
columnWithText.implicitHeight + " width:" + columnWithText.width + "
height:" + columnWithText.height)
        console.log("Rectangle - implicitWidth:" + rectangle.implicitWidth
+ " implicitHeight:" + rectangle.implicitHeight + " width:" +
rectangle.width + " height:" + rectangle.height)
        console.log("ColumnWithRectangle - implicitWidth:" +
columnWithRectangle.implicitWidth + " implicitHeight:" +
columnWithRectangle.implicitHeight + " width:" + columnWithRectangle.width
+ " height:" + columnWithRectangle.height)
    }
}
```

Run this, and you'll get another screen full of nonsense:

Of far more interest to us here is what is output to the console:

```
qml: Text1 - implicitWidth:30 implicitHeight:13 width:30 height:13

qml: Text2 - implicitWidth:30 implicitHeight:13 width:300 height:20

qml: Text3 - implicitWidth:1218 implicitHeight:13 width:1218 height:13

qml: Text4 - implicitWidth:1218 implicitHeight:13 width:300 height:13

qml: Text5 - implicitWidth:1218 implicitHeight:65 width:300 height:65

qml: ColumnWithText - implicitWidth:1218 implicitHeight:124 width:1218
height:124

qml: Rectangle - implicitWidth:0 implicitHeight:0 width:0 height:0

qml: ColumnWithRectangle - implicitWidth:0 implicitHeight:0 width:0
height:0
```

So, what's going on? We've created two **Column** elements, which are invisible layout components that arrange their child elements vertically. We've stuffed the first column with various **Text** elements and added a single **Rectangle** to the second. At the bottom of the view is a JavaScript function that will execute when the **Window** component has completed (that is, finished loading). All the function does is write out the implicitWidth, implicitHeight, width, and height properties of various elements on the view.

Let's walk through the elements and the corresponding console lines:

```
Text {
    id: text1
    text: "Text 1"
}
```

```
qml: Text1 - implicitWidth:30 implicitHeight:13 width:30 height:13
```

This **Text** element contains a short piece of text, and we have not specified any sizes. Its `implicitWidth` and `implicitHeight` properties are the sizes the element wants to be based on its content. Its `width` and `height` properties are the sizes the element actually is. In this case, it will size itself however it wants to, because we haven't specified otherwise, so its `width`/`height` are the same as its `implicitWidth`/`implicitHeight`:

```
Text {
    id: text2
    text: "Text 2"
    width: 300
    height: 20
}
```

```
qml: Text2 - implicitWidth:30 implicitHeight:13 width:300 height:20
```

With `text2`, the implicit sizes are the same as `text1` as the content is virtually identical. However, this time, we have explicitly told it to be 300 wide and 20 high. The console tells us that the element is doing as it's told and is indeed that size:

```
Text {
    id: text3
    text: "Text 3 Text 3 Text 3 Text 3 Text 3 Text 3 Text 3 Text 3 Text 3
    Text 3 Text 3 Text 3 Text 3 Text 3 Text 3 Text 3 Text 3 Text 3 Text
    3 Text 3 Text 3 Text 3 Text 3 Text 3 Text 3 Text 3 Text 3 Text 3
    Text 3 Text 3 Text 3 Text 3 Text 3 Text 3 Text 3"
}
```

```
qml: Text3 - implicitWidth:1218 implicitHeight:13 width:1218 height:13
```

This `text3` takes the same hands-off approach as `text1`, but with a much longer piece of text as its content. This time, `implicitWidth` is much larger as that is the amount of space it needs to fit the long text in. Note that this is actually wider than the window and the text gets cut off. Again, we haven't instructed it otherwise, so it sizes itself:

```
Text {
    id: text4
    text: "Text 4 Text 4 Text 4 Text 4 Text 4 Text 4 Text 4 Text 4 Text 4
    Text 4 Text 4 Text 4 Text 4 Text 4 Text 4 Text 4 Text 4 Text 4 Text
    4 Text 4 Text 4 Text 4 Text 4 Text 4 Text 4 Text 4 Text 4 Text 4
    Text 4 Text 4 Text 4 Text 4 Text 4 Text 4 Text 4"
    width: 300
}
```

```
qml: Text4 - implicitWidth:1218 implicitHeight:13 width:300 height:13
```

The `text4` has the same lengthy block of text, but we've told it what width we want this time. You'll notice on screen that even though the element is only 300 pixels wide, the text is visible all the way across the window. The content is overflowing the bounds of its container. You can set the `clip` property to `true` to prevent this, but we're not too concerned with that here:

```
Text {
    id: text5
    text: "Text 5 Text 5 Text 5 Text 5 Text 5 Text 5 Text 5 Text 5 Text
    5 Text 5 Text 5 Text 5 Text 5 Text 5 Text 5 Text 5 Text 5 Text 5
    Text 5 Text 5 Text 5 Text 5 Text 5 Text 5 Text 5 Text 5 Text 5 Text
    5 Text 5 Text 5 Text 5 Text 5 Text 5 Text 5 Text 5 Text 5 Text 5"
    width: 300
    wrapMode: Text.Wrap
}
```

```
qml: Text5 - implicitWidth:1218 implicitHeight:65 width:300 height:65
```

The `text5` repeats the same long block of text and constrains the width to 300, but this time, we bring a bit of order to proceedings by setting the `wrapMode` property to `Text.Wrap`. With this setting, the enabled behavior is much more like what you would expect from a block of text—it fills up the available width and then wraps onto the next line. The `implicitHeight` and, consequently, the `height` of the element has increased to accommodate the contents. Note, however, that the `implicitHeight` is still the same as earlier; this is still the width the control wants to be in order to fit all of its content in, given the constraints we have defined, and we have defined no height constraint.

We then print out the properties of the column containing all this text:

```
qml: ColumnWithText - implicitWidth:1218 implicitHeight:124 width:1218
height:124
```

The important thing to note is that the column is able to figure out how wide and high it needs to be to accommodate all of its children.

Next, we get to the issue we encountered back in `SplashView`:

```
Column {
    id: columnWithRectangle
    Rectangle {
        id: rectangle
        anchors.fill: parent
    }
}
```

Here, we have a chicken and egg scenario. The `Column` tries to work out how large it needs to be to contain its children, so it takes a look at `Rectangle`. `Rectangle` has no explicit size information and no children of its own, it is just set to fill its parent, the `Column`. Neither element can figure out how big they are supposed to be, so they both default to 0x0, which renders them invisible.

`qml: Rectangle – implicitWidth:0 implicitHeight:0 width:0 height:0`

`qml: ColumnWithRectangle – implicitWidth:0 implicitHeight:0 width:0 height:0`

Sizing of elements is probably the thing that has caught me out the most with QML over the years. As a general guideline, if you write some QML but then can't see it rendered on screen, it's probably a sizing issue. I usually find that giving everything an arbitrary fixed **width** and **height** is a good start when debugging, and then one by one, make the sizes dynamic until you recreate the problem.

Armed with this knowledge, let's head back to `MasterView` and fix our earlier problem.

Add `anchors.fill: parent` to the `StackView` component:

```
StackView {
    id: contentFrame
    anchors.fill: parent
    initialItem: Qt.resolvedUrl("qrc:/views/SplashView.qml")
}
```

The `StackView` will now fill its parent **Window**, which we have explicitly given a fixed size of 1024 x 768. Run the app again, and you should now have a lovely orange-yellow `SplashView` that fills the screen and happily resizes itself if you resize the window:

Navigation

Lets make a quick addition to our `SplashView`:

```
Rectangle {
    anchors.fill: parent
    color: "#f4c842"
    Text {
        anchors.centerIn: parent
        text: "Splash View"
    }
}
```

This just adds the name of the view to the screen, so when we start moving between views, we know which one we are looking at. With that done, copy the content of `SplashView` into all the other new views, updating the text in each to reflect the name of the view, for example, in `DashboardView`, the text could say "Dashboard View".

The first piece of navigation we want to do is when the `MasterView` has finished loading and we're ready for action, load the `DashboardView`. We achieve this using one of the QML component slots we've just seen—`Component.onCompleted()`.

Add the following line to the root `Window` component in `MasterView`:

```
Component.onCompleted:
contentFrame.replace("qrc:/views/DashboardView.qml");
```

Now when you build and run, as soon as the `MasterView` has finished loading, it switches the child view to `DashboardView`. This probably happens so fast that you no longer even see `SplashView`, but it is still there. Having a splash view like this is great if you've got an application with quite a lot of initialization to do, and you can't really have non-blocking UI. It's a handy place to put the company logo and a "Reticulating splines..." loading message. Yes, that was a Sims reference!

The StackView is just like the history in your web browser. If you visit `www.google.com` and then `www.packtpub.com`, you are *pushing* `www.packtpub.com` onto the stack. If you click on **Back** on the browser, you return to `www.google.com`. This history can consist of several pages (or views), and you can navigate backward and forward through them. Sometimes you don't need the history and sometimes you actively don't want users to be able to go back. The `replace()` method we called, as its name suggests, pushes a new view onto the stack and clears any history so that you can't go back.

In the `Component.onCompleted` slot, we've seen an example of how to navigate between views directly from QML. We can use this approach for all of our application navigation. For example, we can add a button for the user to create a new client and when it's clicked on, push the `CreateClientView` straight on to the stack, as follows:

```
Button {
    onClicked: contentFrame.replace("qrc:/views/CreateClientView.qml")
}
```

For UX designs or simple UI heavy applications with little business logic, this is a perfectly valid approach. The trouble is that your QML views and components become very tightly coupled, and the business logic layer has no visibility of what the user is doing. Quite often, moving to a new screen of the application isn't as simple as just displaying a new view. You may need to update a state machine, set some models up, or clear out some data from the previous view. By routing all of our navigation requests through our **MasterController** switchboard, we decouple our components and gain an intercept point for our business logic to take any actions it needs to as well as validate that the requests are appropriate.

We will request navigation to these views by emitting signals from our business logic layer and having our **MasterView** respond to them and perform the transition. Rather than cluttering up our **MasterController**, we'll delegate the responsibility for navigation to a new controller in cm-lib, so create a new header file (there is no implementation as such, so we don't need a .cpp file) called `navigation-controller.h` in `cm/cm-lib/source/controllers` and add the following code:

```
#ifndef NAVIGATIONCONTROLLER_H
#define NAVIGATIONCONTROLLER_H

#include <QObject>

#include <cm-lib_global.h>
#include <models/client.h>

namespace cm {
namespace controllers {

class CMLIBSHARED_EXPORT NavigationController : public QObject
{
    Q_OBJECT

public:
    explicit NavigationController(QObject* _parent = nullptr)
        : QObject(_parent)
    {}

signals:
    void goCreateClientView();
    void goDashboardView();
    void goEditClientView(cm::models::Client* client);
    void goFindClientView();
};

}
}
```

```
#endif
```

We have created a minimal class that inherits from QObject and implements a signal for each of our new views. Note that we don't need to navigate to the **MasterView** or the **SplashView**, so there is no corresponding signal for those. When we navigate to the EditClientView, we will need to inform the UI which **Client** we want to edit, so we will pass it through as a parameter. Calling one of these methods from anywhere within our business logic code fires a request into the ether saying "I want to go to the so-and-so view, please". It is then up to the **MasterView** over in the UI layer to monitor those requests and respond accordingly. Note that the business logic layer still knows nothing about the UI implementation. It's fine if nobody responds to the signal; it is not a two-way communication.

Whenever you inherit from QObject, always remember the Q_OBJECT macro and also an overloaded constructor that takes a QObject parent. As we want to use this class outside of this project (in the UI project), we must also remember the **CMLIBSHARED_EXPORT** macro.

We've looked forward a little bit here and assumed that our Client class will be in the cm::models namespace, but the default Client class that Qt added for us when we created the project is not, so let's fix that before we move on:

client.h:

```
#ifndef CLIENT_H
#define CLIENT_H

#include "cm-lib_global.h"

namespace cm {
namespace models {

class CMLIBSHARED_EXPORT Client
{
public:
    Client();
};

}}

#endif
```

client.cpp:

```
#include "client.h"
```

```
namespace cm {
namespace models {

Client::Client()
{
}


}}
```

We need to be able to create an instance of a NavigationController and have our UI interact with it. For unit testing reasons, it is good practice to hide object creation behind some sort of object factory interface, but we're not concerned with that at this stage, so we'll simply create the object in **MasterController**. Let's take this opportunity to add the Private Implementation (PImpl) idiom to our **MasterController** too. If you haven't come across PImpl before, it is simply a technique to move all private implementation details out of the header file and into the definition. This helps keep the header file as short and clean as possible, with only the includes necessary for consumers of the public API. Replace the declaration and implementation as follows:

`master-controller.h`:

```
#ifndef MASTERCONTROLLER_H
#define MASTERCONTROLLER_H

#include <QObject>
#include <QScopedPointer>
#include <QString>

#include <cm-lib_global.h>
#include <controllers/navigation-controller.h>

namespace cm {
namespace controllers {

class CMLIBSHARED_EXPORT MasterController : public QObject
{
    Q_OBJECT
    Q_PROPERTY( QString ui_welcomeMessage READ welcomeMessage CONSTANT )
    Q_PROPERTY( cm::controllers::NavigationController*
ui_navigationController READ navigationController CONSTANT )

public:
    explicit MasterController(QObject* parent = nullptr);
    ~MasterController();
    NavigationController* navigationController();
    const QString& welcomeMessage() const;
```

```
    private:
        class Implementation;
        QScopedPointer<Implementation> implementation;
    };

    }}
    #endif
```

master-controller.cpp:

```
    #include "master-controller.h"

    namespace cm {
    namespace controllers {

    class MasterController::Implementation
    {
    public:
        Implementation(MasterController* _masterController)
            : masterController(_masterController)
        {
            navigationController = new NavigationController(masterController);
        }

        MasterController* masterController{nullptr};
        NavigationController* navigationController{nullptr};
        QString welcomeMessage = "This is MasterController to Major Tom";
    };

    MasterController::MasterController(QObject* parent)
        : QObject(parent)
    {
        implementation.reset(new Implementation(this));
    }

    MasterController::~MasterController()
    {
    }

    NavigationController* MasterController::navigationController()
    {
        return implementation->navigationController;
    }

    const QString& MasterController::welcomeMessage() const
    {
        return implementation->welcomeMessage;
    }
```

```
} }
```

You may have noted that we don't specify the **cm::controllers** namespace for the NavigationController accessor method, but we do for the Q_PROPERTY. This is because the property is accessed by the UI QML, which is not executing within the scope of the cm namespace, so we have to explicitly specify the fullyqualified name. As a general rule of thumb, be explicit about namespaces for anything that QML interacts with directly, including parameters in signals and slots.

Next, we need to register the new NavigationController class with the QML system in the **cm-ui** project, so in main.cpp, add the following registration next to the existing one for **MasterController**:

```
qmlRegisterType<cm::controllers::NavigationController>("CM", 1, 0,
"NavigationController");
```

We're now ready to wire up **MasterView** to react to these navigation signals. Add the following element before the StackView:

```
Connections {
    target: masterController.ui_navigationController
    onGoCreateClientView:
contentFrame.replace("qrc:/views/CreateClientView.qml")
    onGoDashboardView: contentFrame.replace("qrc:/views/DashboardView.qml")
    onGoEditClientView:
contentFrame.replace("qrc:/views/EditClientView.qml", {selectedClient:
client})
    onGoFindClientView:
contentFrame.replace("qrc:/views/FindClientView.qml")
}
```

We are creating a connection component bound to our new instance of **NavigationController**, which reacts to each of the go signals we added and navigates to the relevant view via the contentFrame, using the same replace() method we used previously to move to the Dashboard. So whenever the goCreateClientView() signal gets fired on the **NavigationController**, the onGoCreateClientView() slot gets called on our Connections component and the CreateClientView is loaded into the **StackView** named contentFrame. In the case of onGoEditClientView where a client parameter is passed from the signal, we pass that object along to a property named selectedClient, which we will add to the view later.

Some signals and slots in QML components are automatically generated and connected for us and are convention based. Slots are named on[CapitalisedNameOfRelatedSignal]. So, for example, if you have a signal called mySplendidSignal(), then the corresponding slot will be named onMySplendidSignal. These conventions are in play with our NavigationController and Connections components.

Next, let's add a navigation bar to **MasterView** with some placeholder buttons so that we can try these signals out.

Add a Rectangle to form the background for our bar:

```
Rectangle {
    id: navigationBar
    anchors {
        top: parent.top
        bottom: parent.bottom
        left: parent.left
    }
    width: 100
    color: "#000000"
}
```

This draws a black strip 100 pixels wide anchored to the left-hand side of the view.

We also need to adjust our `StackView` so that it allows some space for our bar. Rather than filling its parent, let's anchor three of its four sides to its parent, but attach the left-hand side to the right-hand side of our bar:

```
StackView {
    id: contentFrame
    anchors {
        top: parent.top
        bottom: parent.bottom
        right: parent.right
        left: navigationBar.right
    }
    initialItem: Qt.resolvedUrl("qrc:/views/SplashView.qml")
}
```

Now, let's add some buttons to our navigation `Rectangle`:

```
Rectangle {
    id: navigationBar
    ...

    Column {
        Button {
            text: "Dashboard"
            onClicked:
masterController.ui_navigationController.goDashboardView()
        }
        Button {
            text: "New Client"
            onClicked:
masterController.ui_navigationController.goCreateClientView()
        }
        Button {
            text: "Find Client"
            onClicked:
masterController.ui_navigationController.goFindClientView()
        }
    }

}
```

We use the `Column` component to lay out our buttons for us, rather than having to individually anchor the buttons to each other. Each button displays some text and when clicked on, calls a signal on the **NavigationController**. Our `Connection` component reacts to the signals and performs the view transition for us:

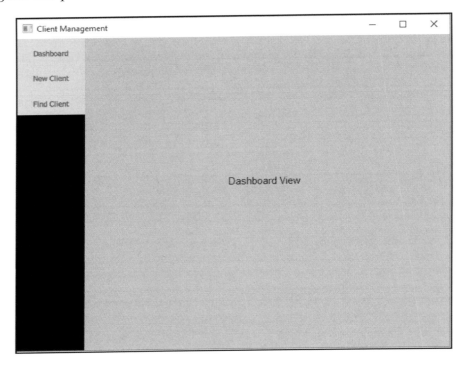

Great stuff, we have a functional navigation framework! However, when you click on one of the navigation buttons, the navigation bar disappears momentarily and comes back again. We are also getting "conflicting anchors" messages in our **Application Output** console, which suggest that we're doing something that's not quite right. Let's address those issues before we move on.

Fixing conflicts

The navigation bar problem is a simple one. As explained previously, QML is hierarchical in structure. This bears out in the way the elements are rendered—child elements that appear first are rendered first. In our case, we draw the navigation bar and then we draw the content frame. When the **StackView** component loads new content, by default it applies funky transitions to make it look nice. Those transitions can result in content moving out of bounds of the control and drawing over any content below it. There are a couple of ways to address this.

Firstly, we can rearrange the order that the components are rendered in and put the navigation bar after the content frame. This will draw the navigation bar over the top of the StackView, regardless of what was going on with it. The second option and the one we will implement is to simply set the `clip` property of the **StackView**:

```
clip: true
```

This clips any content that overlaps the boundary of the control and doesn't render it.

The next problem is a little more esoteric. As we've discussed, the number one cause of confused head scratching I've encountered over the past few years of QML development is the sizing of components. Some components we've used, such as **Rectangle**, are intrinsically visual elements. If their size is not defined, either directly with the `width`/`height` properties or indirectly with **anchors**, then they will not render. Other elements such as **Connections** are not visual at all and size properties are redundant. Layout elements such as **Column** may have a fixed size in one axis, but be dynamic in the other by nature.

One thing that most components have in common is that they inherit from **Item**, which in turn inherits directly from **QtObject**, which is just a plain **QObject**. In much the same way that the Qt Framework on the C++ side implements a lot of default behavior for plain old **QObject***, QML components often implement default behavior for **Item** components that we can leverage here.

In our child views, we have used **Rectangle** as our root object. This makes sense as we want to display a rectangle of a fixed size and color. However, this causes problems for the **StackView** as it doesn't know what size it should be. To provide this information, we try and anchor it to its parent (the **StackView**), but then that causes problems of its own by conflicting with the transitions the **StackView** is trying to perform when we switch views.

Our way out of this dilemma is to instead have the root of our child views be a plain old **Item**. **StackView** components have internal logic to handle **Item** components and will just size it for us. Our **Rectangle** component then becomes the child of an **Item** component that has already been sized automatically, and we can anchor to that instead:

```
Item {
    Rectangle {
        ...
    }
}
```

This is all a bit confusing and feels like Voodoo, but the takeaway here is that having **Item** as the root element in your custom QML is often a good thing. Go ahead and add a root **Item** component in this way to all the child views (but not **MasterView**).

Run the application again, and you should now have nice smooth transitions and no warning messages in the console.

Summary

We have a flexible, decoupled navigation mechanism in place and are successfully transitioning between different views. We have the basics of a navigation bar in place and a working content pane as designed at the beginning of the chapter.

Having the UI call the business logic layer to emit a signal that the UI then reacts to may seem like a bit of a roundabout way of navigating between views, but this business logic signal/UI slot design brings benefits. It keeps the UI modular as the views don't need to know about each other. It keeps the logic for navigation in the business logic layer and enables that layer to request that the UI navigate the user to a particular view without needing to know anything about the UI or the view itself. Crucially, it also gives us intercept points so that when the user requests navigation to a given view, we can handle it and perform any additional processing we need, such as state management or cleanup.

In Chapter 4, *Style*, we will introduce a shared style component, and QML modules and icons before we complete our UI design with a dynamic command bar.

4
Style

It's generally a good idea to aim for function before form in the development process, but the UI is the part of the application our users interact with and is a key ingredient of a successful solution. In this chapter, we will introduce a CSS-like style resource and build on the responsive design principles we introduced in the last chapter.

We will create custom QML components and modules to maximize code reuse. We will integrate Font Awesome into our solution to provide us with a suite of scalable icons and help give our UI a modern graphical look. We will tidy up the navigation bar, introduce the concept of commands, and build the framework for a dynamic, context-sensitive command bar.

We will cover the following topics in this chapter:

- Custom style resource
- Font Awesome
- Custom components
- Navigation bar styling
- Commands

Style resource

First off, let's create a new resource file to contain the non-QML visual elements we will need. In the cm-ui project, **Add New... > Qt > Qt Resource File**:

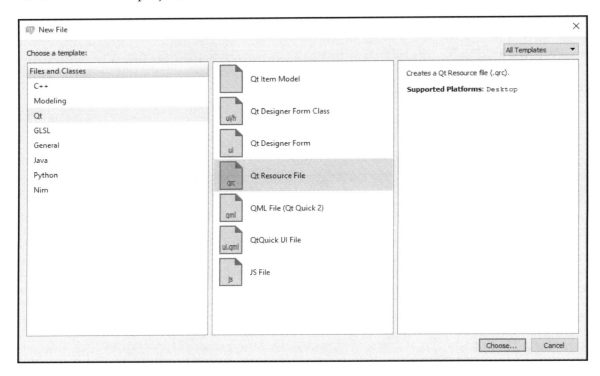

Name the file assets.qrc and place it in cm/cm-ui. Your new file will automatically open in the **Resource Editor**, which I don't find to be a particularly helpful editor, so close it. You will see that the assets.qrc file has been added to the **Resources** section of the cm-ui project. Right-click on it and select **Add New... > Qt > QML File**. Call the file Style.qml and save it to cm/cm-ui/assets.

Edit the assets.qrc file in the **Plain Text Editor** in the same way we did for the views:

```
<RCC>
    <qresource prefix="/assets">
        <file alias="Style.qml">assets/Style.qml</file>
    </qresource>
</RCC>
```

Now, edit `Style.qml` and we'll add a single style property to use for the background color of our views:

```
pragma Singleton
import QtQuick 2.9

Item {
    readonly property color colourBackground: "#f4c842"
}
```

What we are doing here in C++ terms is creating a singleton class with a public member variable of type const color called `colourBackground` with an initialized value of a hex RGB code for (very) light grey.

Now, we need to perform a little bit of a manual fudge to wire this up. We need to create a Module Definition file named `qmldir` (with no file extension) in the same folder as `Style.qml` (`cm/cm-ui/assets`). There is no built-in template for this type of file, so we need to create it ourselves. File Explorer in older versions of Windows used to make this a painful exercise as it always insisted on a file extension. A console command was required to forcibly rename the file. Windows 10 will happily create the file without an extension. In the Unix world, files without an extension are more common.

With the `qmldir` file created, edit `assets.qrc` and insert a new entry for it right next to `Style.qml` inside the `/assets` prefix:

```
<file alias="qmldir">assets/qmldir</file>
```

Double-click on the newly added `qmldir` file and enter the following lines:

```
module assets
singleton Style 1.0 Style.qml
```

We have already seen modules when we **import QtQuick 2.9**. This makes version 2.9 of the QtQuick module available for use in our views. In our `qmldir` file, we are defining a new module of our own called `assets` and telling Qt that there is a **Style** object within version **1.0** of that module, for which the implementation is in our `Style.qml` file.

With our new style module created and wired up, let's now put that modern off-white color to use. Start with the first child view we see, `SplashView`, and add the following to get access to our new module:

```
import assets 1.0
```

You'll note that we're presented with an angry red underline, suggesting that all is not well. Hover over the line with the mouse pointer, and a tooltip will tell us that we need to add the import path to our new `qmldir` definition file.

There are a couple of ways to do this. The first option is to go to the **Projects** mode and select the current kit's **Build** settings and then **Debug** mode. At the bottom in the **Build Environment** section, click on **Details**. Here, you can see a list of all the environment variables for the current kit and configuration. **Add** a new variable called **QML2_IMPORT_PATH** and set its value to the `cm-ui` folder:

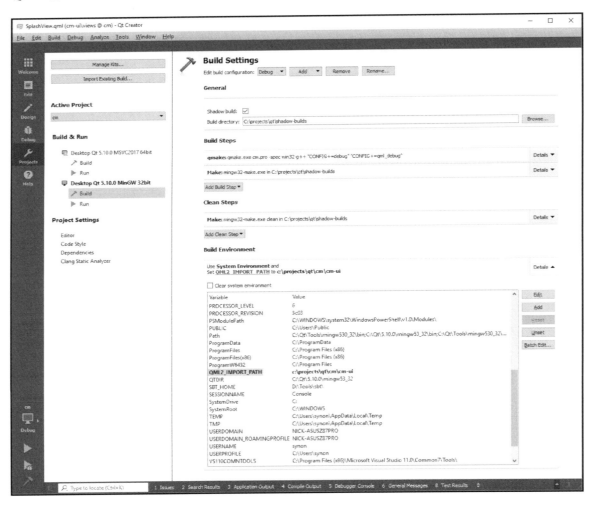

This adds the project working directory of the `cm-ui` project (`/projects/qt/cm/cm-ui`) to the QML Import Path. Note that our module name must reflect the relative path to the `qmldir` file from this import path.

The problem with this approach is that this environment variable is tied to the `cm.pro.user` file. If you share the project with other developers, they will have their own `cm.pro.user` files, and they will have to remember to add this variable too. Furthermore, it's tied to an absolute path and if you copy the project code to another machine, it may not be at that location.

The second, and preferred, option is to add the following line to `main.cpp` immediately after instantiating **QQmlApplicationEngine**:

```
engine.addImportPath("qrc:/");
```

So why `qrc:/` and not the absolute path to our `qmldir` file? You'll remember that we added our `views.qrc` resource bundle to a `RESOURCES` variable in `cm-ui.pro`. What this does is it takes all the files from `views.qrc` and compiles them into the application binary in a kind of virtual filesystem, where the prefixes act as virtual folders. The root of this virtual filesystem is referenced as `qrc:/` and by using this in the import path, we are essentially asking Qt to look inside all of our bundled resource files for any modules. Head over to `cm-ui.pro` and ensure that our new `assets.qrc` has also been added to `RESOURCES`:

```
RESOURCES += views.qrc \
    assets.qrc
```

This can be a bit confusing, so to reiterate, we have added the following folder to search for new modules, either using the **QML2_IMPORT_PATH** environment variable to search our `cm-ui` project folder on our local physical filesystem, or the `addImportPath()` method to search the root of our virtual resource filesystem at runtime.

In both cases, our `qmldir` file that defines our new module is in a folder called `assets` a level below that, that is, either `<Qt Projects>/cm/cm-ui/assets` in the physical filesystem or `qrc:/assets` in the virtual.

This gives us the module name `assets`. If our folder structure was deeper, like stuff/badgers/assets, then our module would need to be called `stuff.badgers.assets`, as that is the path relative to our defined import path. Similarly, if we wanted to add another module for our existing views, we would create a `qmldir` file in `cm-ui/views` and call the module `views`.

If you see that Qt Creator is still a bit confused and the red line still persists, ensure that `cm-ui.pro` contains the `QML_IMPORT_PATH +=` `$$PWD` line.

With all this in place, we can now use our new module. Including the module means we can now access our singleton `Style` object and read properties from it. Replace the `color` property of our `SplashView`:

```
Rectangle {
    ...
    color: Style.colourBackground
    ...
}
```

Repeat this to set the background color for all of our views except `MasterView`. Remember to `include ui.assets 1.0` in each view too.

When you build and run the application, you may wonder why we've gone through all of that rigmarole when the views look exactly the same as they did before. Well, let's say that we've just had a meeting with the guys from marketing where they told us that yellowy orange is not a good fit for the brand any more, and we need to change all the views to be a clean off-white color. We would previously have had to go into every view and change the color from `#f4c842` to `#efefef`. Now, there are only seven of them, so it's not a big deal, but imagine if we had to change all the colors for all the components in 50 complex views; that would be a very painful exercise.

However, go to `Style.qml` and change the `colourBackground` property from `#f4c842` to `#efefef`. Build and run the application and bask in the glory of our rebranded app! By setting up our shared style component early, we can add the properties as we go and then restyling our app later becomes much easier. We can add properties of all types here, not just colors, so we'll be adding sizes, fonts, and other things as we progress further through our development.

Font Awesome

With our styling framework in place, let's review what our navigation bar looks like and figure out what we want to achieve:

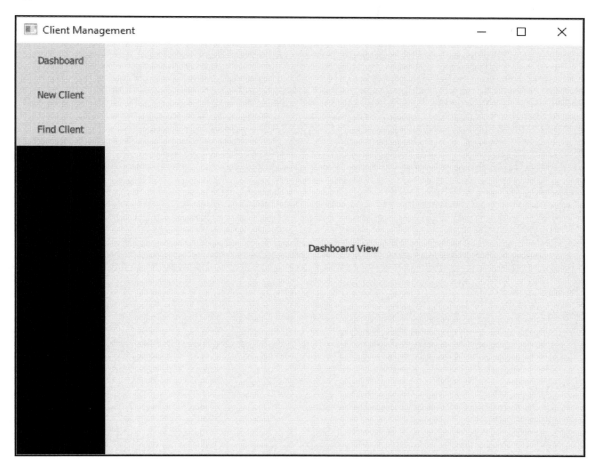

The buttons we want to display on our navigation bar are **Dashboard View** (the Home view), **New Client View**, and **Find Client View**, along with a toggle button at the top to expand and collapse the bar.

A common UI design pattern is to represent simple commands with icons. Further information about the command can be obtained by a variety of means; for example, when you hover over the button, information can be displayed in a tooltip or a status bar at the bottom of the screen. Our approach will be to have a collapsible bar. The default state of the bar will be collapsed and will display an icon representing each command. In expanded state, the bar will display both the icon and a textual description of the command. The user will be able to toggle the states with an additional button. This is a pattern particularly prevalent in mobile application development, where you want to consume as little screen space as possible by default.

There are a few options for displaying the icons for our buttons. Older desktop applications would more than likely use image files of some description. This gives you full artistic control over how your icons look, but carries several drawbacks. Image files tend to be comparatively large in size, and they are a fixed size. If you need to draw them at a different size, then they can look bad, particularly if they are scaled up or if the aspect ratio changes.

Scalable Vector Graphics (SVG) are much smaller files and scale very well. They are more difficult to create and can be a bit more limited artistically, but they can be very useful for the purpose of icons. However, from experience, they can be quite tricky to work with in Qt/QML.

The third option that gives you the small file size and scalability benefits of SVG but are much easier to work with are symbol font files. This is a very common solution in web development, and this is the approach we will take.

There are numerous symbol fonts available but perhaps the most popular for development is **Font Awesome**. It provides a wide range of terrific symbols and has a very helpful website; check out: http://fontawesome.io/.

 Check any licensing applicable for fonts you choose to use, especially if you are using them commercially.

Download the kit and open up the archive file. The file we are interested in is fonts/fontawesome-webfont.ttf. Copy this file into our project folder in cm/cm-ui/assets.

In our `cm-ui` project, edit `assets.qrc` and add the font to our resources:

```
<file alias="fontawesome.ttf">assets/fontawesome-webfont.ttf</file>
```

Remember that our alias doesn't have to be the same as the original filename, and we've taken the opportunity to shorten it a bit.

Next up, edit `Style.qml` and we'll wire the font up to our custom style for easy use. We first need the font to be loaded and made available for use, which we achieve using a `FontLoader` component. Add the following inside the root **Item** element:

```
FontLoader {
    id: fontAwesomeLoader
    source: "qrc:/assets/fontawesome.ttf"
}
```

In the `source` property, we use the `/assets` prefix (or virtual folder) we defined in our `assets.qrc` file along with the `fontawesome.ttf` alias. Now, we have loaded the font but as it stands, we won't be able to reference it from outside of `Style.qml`. This is because only properties at root component level are accessible outside of the file. Child components are deemed effectively private. The way we get around this is by creating a `property alias` for the element we want to expose:

```
Item {
    property alias fontAwesome: fontAwesomeLoader.name
    readonly property color colourBackground: "#efefef"
    FontLoader {
        id: fontAwesomeLoader
        source: "qrc:/assets/fontawesome.ttf"
    }
}
```

This creates a publicly available property called `fontAwesome`, which when called, simply redirects the caller to the `name` property of the internal `fontAwesomeLoader` element.

With the wiring done, let's find the icons we want to use. Back on the Font Awesome website, navigate to the **Icons** page. Here, you can see all the available icons. Clicking on one will display further information about it, and it is from here that we can get the key piece of information we need in order to display it, and that is the unicode character. I'll select the following icons for our menu, but feel free to choose whichever icons you want:

Command	Icon	Unicode character
Toggle Menu	bars	f0c9
Dashboard	home	f015
New Client	user-plus	f234
Find Client	search	f002

Now, let's replace the `Button` components on our `MasterView` with a `Text` component for each of our icons:

```
Column {
    Text {
        font {
            family: Style.fontAwesome
            pixelSize: 42
        }
        color: "#ffffff"
        text: "\uf0c9"
    }
    Text {
        font {
            family: Style.fontAwesome
            pixelSize: 42
        }
        color: "#ffffff"
        text: "\uf015"
    }
    Text {
        font {
            family: Style.fontAwesome
            pixelSize: 42
        }
        color: "#ffffff"
        text: "\uf234"
    }
    Text {
        font {
```

```
        family: Style.fontAwesome
        pixelSize: 42
    }
    color: "#ffffff"
    text: "\uf002"
    }
}
```

You will also need to add the **assets 1.0** import if you haven't already:

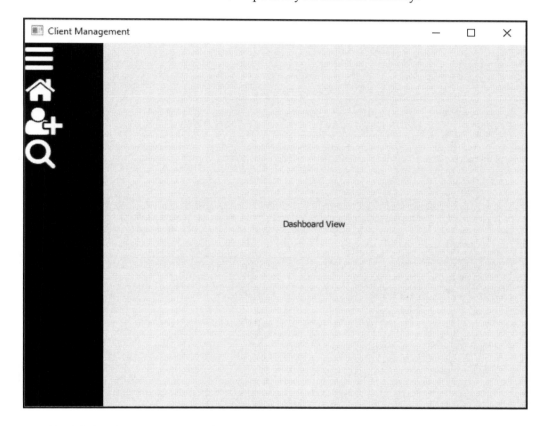

Next, we'll add the descriptive text for the client commands. Wrap each of the `Text` components in a `Row` and add a further `Text` component for the description, as follows:

```
Row {
    Text {
        font {
            family: Style.fontAwesome
            pixelSize: 42
```

```
        }
        color: "#ffffff"
        text: "\uf234"
    }
    Text {
        color: "#ffffff"
        text: "New Client"
    }
}
}
```

The Row component will lay out its children horizontally—first the icon and then the descriptive text. Repeat this for the other commands. Add the descriptions **Dashboard** and **Find Client** for the other buttons and simply an empty string for the toggle command:

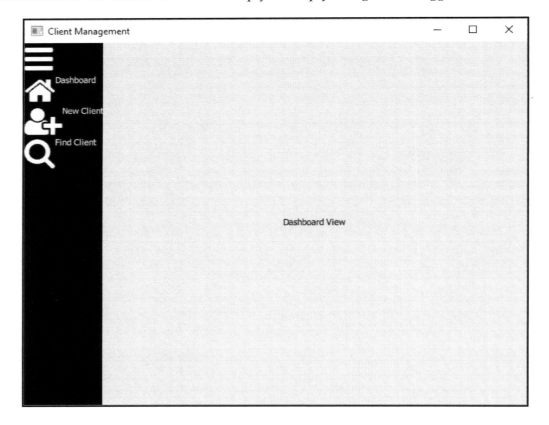

Before we get too carried away making further changes, we'll take a breath, do some refactoring, and look at introducing components.

Components

The QML, what we've just written, is functional enough, but it's already becoming difficult to maintain. Our `MasterView` is getting a little long and difficult to read. When we come to change how our command buttons look, for example, aligning the icon and text, we will have to change it in four places. If we want to add a fifth button, we have to copy, paste, and edit a whole bunch of QML to do so. This is where reusable components come into play.

Components are exactly the same as the views we have already created—just snippets of QML. The difference is purely semantic. Throughout this book, views represent screens that lay out content while components are the content.

The easiest way to create a new component is when you have already written the QML that you want to form the basis for your component, which we have done. Right-click on any of the `Row` elements we added for our commands and select **Refactoring > Move Component into Separate File**.

Name the new component `NavigationButton` and save it to a new folder—`cm/cm-ui/components`:

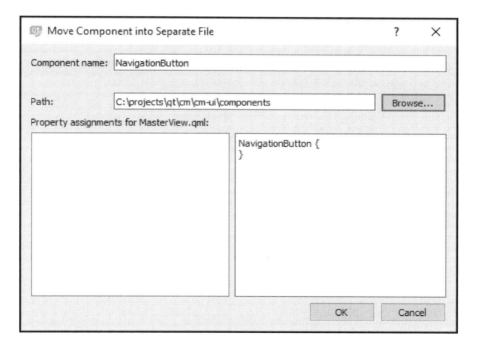

The Row element will be moved to our new file and in `MasterView`, you will be left with an empty `NavigationButton` component:

```
NavigationButton {
}
```

Unfortunately, it comes with a big red squiggly, and our app will no longer run. While the refactoring step has happily created a new `NavigationButton.qml` file for us, it's not actually included in our project anywhere, so Qt doesn't know where it is. It's easy enough to resolve though, and we just need to set up our resources bundle as we did with our views and assets:

1. Create a new `Qt Resource File` called `components.qrc` in the `cm/cm-ui` folder

2. Create an empty `qmldir` file in `cm/cm-ui/components` as we did for our assets

3. Edit `components.qrc` to include both of our new files within a `/components` prefix:

```
<RCC>
    <qresource prefix="/components">
        <file alias="qmldir">components/qmldir</file>
        <file
alias="NavigationButton.qml">components/NavigationButton.qml</file>
    </qresource>
</RCC>
```

4. Edit `qmldir` to set up our module and add our `NavigationButton` component to it:

```
module components
NavigationButton 1.0 NavigationButton.qml
```

5. Ensure that `components.qrc` has been added to the RESOURCES variable in `cm-ui.pro`

6. In `MasterView`, include our new components module to get access to our new component:

```
import components 1.0
```

 Sometimes, getting our module to be fully recognized and banishing the red squigglies may only be accomplished by restarting Qt Creator, as that forces the reload of all the QML modules.

We now have a reusable component that hides away the implementation details, reduces code duplication, and makes it much easier to add new commands and maintain the old ones. However, there are a few changes we need to make to it before we can leverage it for our other commands.

Currently, our `NavigationButton` has hard-coded icon and description text values that will be the same whenever we use the component. We need to expose both the text properties so that we can set them to be different for each of our commands. As we saw, we can achieve this using property aliases, but we need to add unique identifiers to our `Text` elements for that to work. Let's set the default values to be something generic and also implement advice from earlier in the book to have an `Item` component as the root element:

```
import QtQuick 2.9
import assets 1.0

Item {
    property alias iconCharacter: textIcon.text
    property alias description: textDescription.text

    Row {
        Text {
            id: textIcon
            font {
                family: Style.fontAwesome
                pixelSize: 42
            }
            color: "#ffffff"
            text: "\uf11a"
        }
        Text {
            id: textDescription
            color: "#ffffff"
            text: "SET ME!!"
        }
    }
}
```

Now that our component is configurable with properties, we can replace our commands in `MasterView`:

```
Column {
    NavigationButton {
        iconCharacter: "\uf0c9"
        description: ""
    }
    NavigationButton {
```

```
        iconCharacter: "\uf015"
        description: "Dashboard"
    }
    NavigationButton {
        iconCharacter: "\uf234"
        description: "New Client"
    }
    NavigationButton {
        iconCharacter: "\uf002"
        description: "Find Client"
    }
}
```

This is much more concise and manageable than all of the duplicated QML we had earlier. Now, if you run the application, you'll see that while we've taken a couple of steps forward, and that we've also taken one step back:

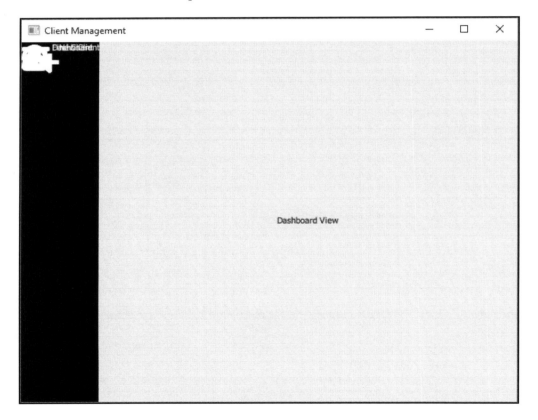

As you can see, all of our components are drawn on top of each other. The root cause of this is the issue we've touched on previously regarding sizing. We have a visual component with a root Item element, and we haven't explicitly defined its size. Another thing we are neglecting is our custom style. Let's fix those next.

Styling the navigation bar

Starting with the easy part, let's first move our hard-coded colors and icon pixel size from NavigationButton into Style.qml:

```
readonly property color colourNavigationBarBackground: "#000000"
readonly property color colourNavigationBarFont: "#ffffff"
readonly property int pixelSizeNavigationBarIcon: 42
```

We now need to think about how we want to size the elements of our button. We have an icon which we want to be square, so the width and height will be the same. Next, to that, we have a text description that will be the same height as the icon but will be wider:

The width of the entire component is the width of the icon plus the width of the description. The height of the entire component is the same as both the height of the icon and description; however, it gives us more flexibility to make the height the same as whichever is the larger of the two. That way, if we ever decide to make one item larger than the other, we know that the component will be large enough to contain them both. Let's pick starter sizes of 80 x 80 for the icon and 80 x 240 for the description and define the properties:

```
readonly property real widthNavigationButtonIcon: 80
readonly property real heightNavigationButtonIcon:
widthNavigationButtonIcon
readonly property real widthNavigationButtonDescription: 240
readonly property real heightNavigationButtonDescription:
heightNavigationButtonIcon
readonly property real widthNavigationButton: widthNavigationButtonIcon +
widthNavigationButtonDescription
readonly property real heightNavigationButton:
Math.max(heightNavigationButtonIcon, heightNavigationButtonDescription)
```

There are a couple of things to note here. Properties can be bound directly to other properties, which reduces the amount of duplication and makes the whole setup much more dynamic. We know that we want our icon to be square, so by binding the height to be the same as the width, if we want to change the total size of the icon, we just need to update the width, and the height will automatically update. QML also has strong integration with a JavaScript engine, so we can use the `Math.max()` function to help us figure out which is the larger height.

Another thing we would like the navigation buttons to do is to provide some kind of visual cue when the user hovers the mouse over a button to indicate that it is an interactive element. To do that, we need each button to have its own background rectangle.

In the `NavigationButton`, wrap the `Row` element in a new `Rectangle` and plug the sizes into our component:

```
Item {
    property alias iconCharacter: textIcon.text
    property alias description: textDescription.text

    width: Style.widthNavigationButton
    height: Style.heightNavigationButton

    Rectangle {
        id: background
        anchors.fill: parent
        color: Style.colourNavigationBarBackground

        Row {
            Text {
                id: textIcon
                width: Style.widthNavigationButtonIcon
                height: Style.heightNavigationButtonIcon
                font {
                    family: Style.fontAwesome
                    pixelSize: Style.pixelSizeNavigationBarIcon
                }
                color: Style.colourNavigationBarFont
                text: "\uf11a"
            }
            Text {
                id: textDescription
                width: Style.widthNavigationButtonDescription
                height: Style.heightNavigationButtonDescription
                color: Style.colourNavigationBarFont
                text: "SET ME!!"
            }
```

```
            }
        }
    }
```

Run again, and you'll see a slight improvement:

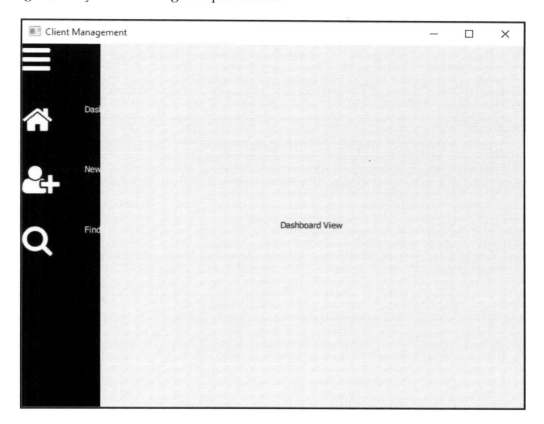

We're getting part of the description cut off because our navigation bar is hard-coded to be 100 pixels wide. We need to change this and also implement the toggle expanded/collapsed functionality. We have already calculated the sizes we need, so let's prepare by adding a couple of new properties to Style.qml:

```
readonly property real widthNavigationBarCollapsed:
widthNavigationButtonIcon
readonly property real heightNavigationBarExpanded: widthNavigationButton
```

The collapsed state will be just wide enough for the icon, while the expanded state will contain the entire button, including description.

Next, let's encapsulate our navigation bar in a new component. There won't be any reuse benefits in this case as there will only ever be one, but it helps keep our QML organized and makes `MasterView` more concise and easy to read.

You can right-click on the `Rectangle` component in `MasterView` and refactor our navigation bar into a new QML file, as we did for our `NavigationButton`. However, let's do it manually so that you are comfortable with both approaches. Right-click on `components.qrc` and select **Add New... > Qt > QML File**. Add `NavigationBar.qml` to `cm/cm-ui/components`:

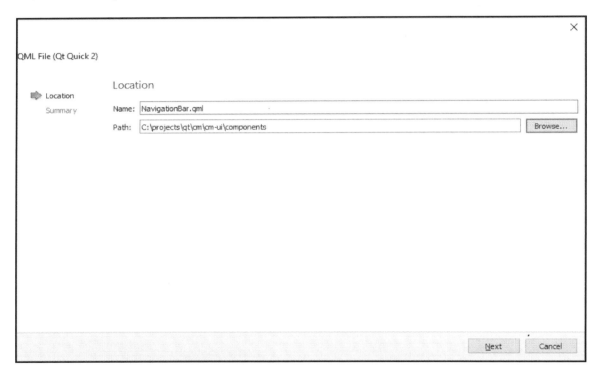

Edit `components.qrc` and move our new `NavigationBar` into the `/components` prefix section with an alias:

```
<file alias="NavigationBar.qml">components/NavigationBar.qml</file>
```

Add the component to our components module by editing `qmldir`:

```
NavigationBar 1.0 NavigationBar.qml
```

Cut the `Rectangle` and its child elements from `MasterView` and paste it into
`NavigationBar.qml` inside the root `Item` element. Update the `QtQuick` module import to
version 2.9 if it has been initialized to some older version. Add an import for our assets
module to gain access to our Style object. Move the Rectangle's `anchors` and `width`
properties to the root `Item` and set the `Rectangle` to fill its parent:

```
import QtQuick 2.9
import assets 1.0

Item {
    anchors {
        top: parent.top
        bottom: parent.bottom
        left: parent.left
    }
    width: 100

    Rectangle {
        anchors.fill: parent
        color: "#000000"

        Column {
            NavigationButton {
                iconCharacter: "\uf0c9"
                description: ""
            }
            NavigationButton {
                iconCharacter: "\uf015"
                description: "Dashboard"
            }
            NavigationButton {
                iconCharacter: "\uf234"
                description: "New Client"
            }
            NavigationButton {
                iconCharacter: "\uf002"
                description: "Find Client"
            }
        }
    }
}
```

Back in `MasterView`, you can now add the new `NavigationBar` component in where the `Rectangle` used to be:

```
NavigationBar {
    id: navigationBar
}
```

Although you get the dreaded red squigglies again, you will actually be able to run the application and verify that the refactoring hasn't broken anything.

The anchoring of our new `NavigationBar` component is fine, but the `width` is a little more complicated—how do we know whether it should be `Style.widthNavigationBarCollapsed` or `Style.heightNavigationBarExpanded`? We'll control this with a publicly accessible Boolean property that indicates whether the bar is collapsed or not. We can then use the value of this property to decide which width we want using the conditional `?` operator syntax. Set the property to be true initially, so the bar will render in its collapsed state by default:

```
property bool isCollapsed: true
```

With that in place, replace the hard-coded `width` of 100, as follows:

```
width: isCollapsed ? Style.widthNavigationBarCollapsed :
Style.heightNavigationBarExpanded
```

Next, update the `color` property of `Rectangle` to `Style.colourNavigationBarBackground`:

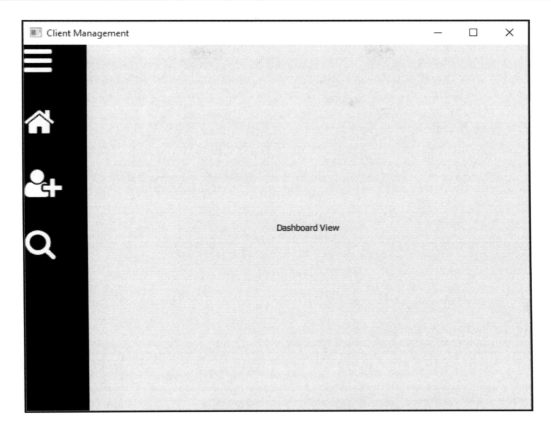

We're getting there now, but one key thing we've missed along the way is that clicking on the buttons now doesn't actually do anything anymore. Let's fix that next.

Clicking

Early on in this book, we looked at a component called MouseArea. This was soon superseded by our use of Button components, which provide the clicking functionality for us. However, now that we are rolling our own form of buttons, we need to implement the clicking functionality ourselves. Much like the Button components, our NavigationButton shouldn't really do anything when they are clicked on, other than informing their parent that the event has occurred. Components should be as generic and ignorant about context as possible so that you can use them in multiple places. What we need to do is add a MouseArea component and simply pass on the onClicked event via a custom signal.

In NavigationButton, we first add the signal that we want to emit whenever the component has been clicked on. Add this just after the properties:

```
signal navigationButtonClicked()
```

 Try and give the signals quite specific names, even if they are a little long. If you simply call everything clicked(), then things can get a little confusing and sometimes you may find yourself referencing a different signal to the one you intended.

Next, we'll add another property to support some mouse hover magic we'll implement. This will be a color type, and we'll default it to be the regular background color:

```
property color hoverColour: Style.colourNavigationBarBackground
```

We'll use this color in conjunction with the states property of Rectangle:

```
states: [
    State {
        name: "hover"
        PropertyChanges {
            target: background
            color: hoverColour
        }
    }
]
```

Think of each state in the array as a named configuration. The default configuration has no name ("") and consists of the properties we have already set within the `Rectangle` element. The "hover" state applies changes to the properties specified in the `PropertyChanges` element, that is, it will change the `color` property of the element with ID `background` to be whatever the value of `hoverColour` is.

Next, inside the `Rectangle` but below the `Row`, add our `MouseArea`:

```
MouseArea {
    anchors.fill: parent
    cursorShape: Qt.PointingHandCursor
    hoverEnabled: true
    onEntered: background.state = "hover"
    onExited: background.state = ""
    onClicked: navigationButtonClicked()
}
```

We use the `anchors` property to fill the whole button background area, including icon and description. Next, we'll jazz things up a bit by changing the mouse cursor to a pointing hand when it enters the button area and enabling hovering with the `hoverEnabled` flag. When enabled, the **entered** and **exited** signals are emitted when the cursor enters and exits the area, and we can use the corresponding slots to change the appearance of our background `Rectangle` by switching between the hover state we've just implemented and the default (""). Finally, we respond to the `clicked()` signal of `MouseArea` with the `onClicked()` slot and simply emit our own signal.

We can now react to the `navigationButtonClicked()` signal in our `NavigationBar` component and add some hover colors while we're at it. Implement the toggle button first:

```
NavigationButton {
    iconCharacter: "\uf0c9"
    description: ""
    hoverColour: "#993333"
    onNavigationButtonClicked: isCollapsed = !isCollapsed
}
```

We implement the `<MyCapitalisedSignalName>` convention to create a slot for our signal and when it fires, we simply toggle the value of `isCollapsed` between `true` and `false`.

You can now run the application. Click on the Toggle button to expand and collapse the navigation bar:

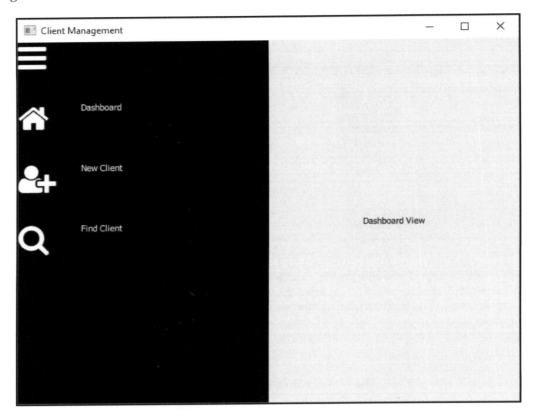

Note how because of our use of anchors, the child views dynamically resize themselves to accommodate the navigation bar. You will also see the pointing hand cursor and a flash of color when you hover over the button, which helps the user understand that it is an interactive element and visualizes the boundaries.

For the remaining navigation buttons, what we want to do in reaction to the clicked event is to emit the `goDashboardView()`, `goCreateClientView()`, and `goFindClientView()` signals on the `NavigationCoordinator`.

Add the `onNavigationButtonClicked` slots to the other buttons and drill down through the `masterController` object to get to the signals we want to call. Add some fancy colors of your choice too:

```
NavigationButton {
    iconCharacter: "\uf015"
    description: "Dashboard"
    hoverColour: "#dc8a00"
    onNavigationButtonClicked:
masterController.ui_navigationController.goDashboardView();
}
NavigationButton {
    iconCharacter: "\uf234"
    description: "New Client"
    hoverColour: "#dccd00"
    onNavigationButtonClicked:
masterController.ui_navigationController.goCreateClientView();
}
NavigationButton {
    iconCharacter: "\uf002"
    description: "Find Client"
    hoverColour: "#8aef63"
    onNavigationButtonClicked:
masterController.ui_navigationController.goFindClientView();
}
```

You can now click on the buttons to navigate to the different child views.

A few last little tweaks to finish the navigation bar are to align the content of our buttons a little better and resize a few things.

The description text should align vertically with the center of the icon rather than the top, and our icons should be centered rather than pinned up against the edge of the window. The first issue is easy to solve, because we've already been consistent and explicit with our sizings. Simply add the following property to both the `Text` components in `NavigationButton`:

```
verticalAlignment: Text.AlignVCenter
```

Both the `Text` elements were sized to take up the full height of the button, so we simply need to align the text vertically within that space.

Fixing the alignment of the icons is just the same, but this time in the horizontal axis. Add the following to the Text component of the icon:

```
horizontalAlignment: Text.AlignHCenter
```

As for the sizings, our description text is a little small and there is a lot of empty space after the text. Add a new property to our Style object:

```
readonly property int pixelSizeNavigationBarText: 22
```

Use the new property in the description Text element:

```
font.pixelSize: Style.pixelSizeNavigationBarText
```

Next, reduce the widthNavigationButtonDescription property in Style to 160.

Run the app and we're nearly there. The sizing and alignment is much better now:

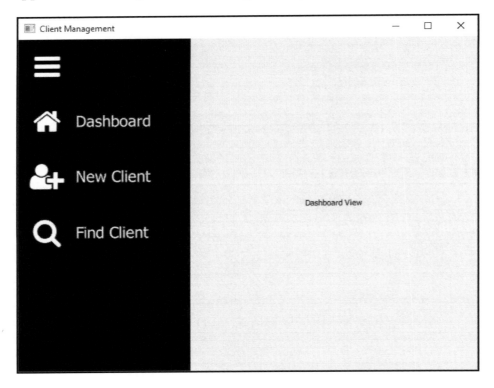

However, one thing you may not note is that when the bar is collapsed and only the icon is displayed, the `MouseArea` is still the full width of the button including the description. Try moving the mouse where the description would be, and you can see the pointing hand cursor appear. You can even click on the components and the transition happens. What we need to do to fix this is rather than the root `Item` element in `NavigationButton` being a fixed width (`Style.widthNavigationButton`), we need to make it dynamic and set it to `parent.width` instead. In order for that to work, we then need to walk up the QML hierarchy and ensure that its parent has a width too. Its parent is the `Column` element in `NavigationBar`. Set the `width` property of `Column` to be `parent.width` too.

With those changes in place, the navigation bar now behaves as expected.

Commands

The next thing on our to-do list is to implement a context-sensitive command bar. While our navigation bar is a constant presence with the same buttons regardless of what the user is doing, the command bar will come and go and will contain different buttons depending on the context. For example, if the user is adding or editing a client, we will need a **Save** button to commit any changes to the database. However, if we are searching for a client, then saving makes no sense and a **Find** button is more relevant. While the techniques for creating our command bar are broadly similar to the navigation bar, the additional flexibility required poses more of a challenge.

To help us overcome these obstacles, we will implement commands. An additional benefit of this approach is that we get to move the logic out of the UI layer and into the business logic layer. I like the UI to be as dumb and as generic as possible. This makes your application more flexible, and bugs in C++ code are easier to identify and resolve than those in QML.

A command object will encapsulate an icon, descriptive text, a function to determine whether the button is enabled or not, and finally, an `executed()` signal that will be emitted when the related button is pressed. Each button in our command bar will then be bound to a command object.

Each of our child view may have a list of commands and an associated command bar. For the views that do, we will present the list of commands to the UI via a command controller.

Create two new C++ classes in the cm-lib project, both of which should inherit from QObject:

- **Command** in a new folder cm-lib/source/framework
- **Command Controller** in the existing folder cm-lib/source/controllers

command.h:

```
#ifndef COMMAND_H
#define COMMAND_H

#include <functional>

#include <QObject>
#include <QScopedPointer>
#include <QString>

#include <cm-lib_global.h>

namespace cm {
namespace framework {

class CMLIBSHARED_EXPORT Command : public QObject
{
    Q_OBJECT
    Q_PROPERTY( QString ui_iconCharacter READ iconCharacter CONSTANT )
    Q_PROPERTY( QString ui_description READ description CONSTANT )
    Q_PROPERTY( bool ui_canExecute READ canExecute NOTIFY canExecuteChanged
)

public:
    explicit Command(QObject* parent = nullptr,
                     const QString& iconCharacter = "",
                     const QString& description = "",
                     std::function<bool()> canExecute = [](){ return
                                                      true; });
    ~Command();

    const QString& iconCharacter() const;
    const QString& description() const;
    bool canExecute() const;

signals:
    void canExecuteChanged();
    void executed();

private:
```

```
    class Implementation;
    QScopedPointer<Implementation> implementation;
};

}}

#endif
```

command.cpp:

```
#include "command.h"

namespace cm {
namespace framework {

class Command::Implementation
{
public:
    Implementation(const QString& _iconCharacter, const QString&
     _description, std::function<bool()> _canExecute)
        : iconCharacter(_iconCharacter)
        , description(_description)
        , canExecute(_canExecute)
    {
    }

    QString iconCharacter;
    QString description;
    std::function<bool()> canExecute;
};

Command::Command(QObject* parent, const QString& iconCharacter, const
QString& description, std::function<bool()> canExecute)
    : QObject(parent)
{
    implementation.reset(new Implementation(iconCharacter, description,
canExecute));
}

Command::~Command()
{
}

const QString& Command::iconCharacter() const
{
    return implementation->iconCharacter;
}
```

```
const QString& Command::description() const
{
    return implementation->description;
}

bool Command::canExecute() const
{
    return implementation->canExecute();
}


}
}
```

The QObject, namespaces, and dll export code should be familiar by now. We represent the icon character and description values we want to display on the UI buttons as strings. We hide the member variables away in the private implementation and provide `accessor` methods for them. We could have represented the `canExecute` member as a simple `bool` member that calling code could set to `true` or `false` as required; however, a much more elegant solution is to pass in a method that calculates the value for us on the fly. By default, we set it to a lambda that returns `true`, which means that the button will be enabled. We provide a `canExecuteChanged()` signal to go along with this, which we can fire whenever we want the UI to reassess whether the button is enabled or not. The last element is the `executed()` signal that will be fired by the UI when the corresponding button is pressed.

`command-controller.h`:

```
#ifndef COMMANDCONTROLLER_H
#define COMMANDCONTROLLER_H

#include <QObject>
#include <QtQml/QQmlListProperty>
#include <cm-lib_global.h>
#include <framework/command.h>

namespace cm {
namespace controllers {

class CMLIBSHARED_EXPORT CommandController : public QObject
{
    Q_OBJECT
    Q_PROPERTY(QQmlListProperty<cm::framework::Command>
     ui_createClientViewContextCommands READ
     ui_createClientViewContextCommands CONSTANT)

public:
    explicit CommandController(QObject* _parent = nullptr);
```

```
    ~CommandController();

    QQmlListProperty<framework::Command>
    ui_createClientViewContextCommands();

public slots:
    void onCreateClientSaveExecuted();

private:
    class Implementation;
    QScopedPointer<Implementation> implementation;
};

}}

#endif
```

command-controller.cpp:

```
#include "command-controller.h"

#include <QList>
#include <QDebug>

using namespace cm::framework;

namespace cm {
namespace controllers {

class CommandController::Implementation
{
public:
    Implementation(CommandController* _commandController)
        : commandController(_commandController)
    {
        Command* createClientSaveCommand = new Command(
          commandController, QChar( 0xf0c7 ), "Save" );
        QObject::connect( createClientSaveCommand, &Command::executed,
    commandController, &CommandController::onCreateClientSaveExecuted );
        createClientViewContextCommands.append( createClientSaveCommand );
    }

    CommandController* commandController{nullptr};

    QList<Command*> createClientViewContextCommands{};
};

CommandController::CommandController(QObject* parent)
```

```
                    : QObject(parent)
    {
         implementation.reset(new Implementation(this));
    }

    CommandController::~CommandController()
    {
    }

    QQmlListProperty<Command>
    CommandController::ui_createClientViewContextCommands()
    {
         return QQmlListProperty<Command>(this,
    implementation->createClientViewContextCommands);
    }

    void CommandController::onCreateClientSaveExecuted()
    {
         qDebug() << "You executed the Save command!";
    }

    }}
```

Here, we introduce a new type—QQmlListProperty. It is essentially a wrapper that enables QML to interact with a list of custom objects. Remember that we need to fully qualify the templated type in the Q_PROPERTY statements. The private member that actually holds the data is a QList, and we have implemented an accessor method that takes the QList and converts it into a QQmlListProperty of the same templated type.

As per the documentation for QQmlListProperty, this method of object construction should not be used in production code, but we'll use it to keep things simple.

We have created a single command list for our CreateClientView. We'll add command lists for other views later. Again, we'll keep things simple for now; we just create a single command to save a newly created client. When creating the command, we parent it to the command coordinator so that we don't have to worry about memory management. We assign it a floppy disk icon (unicode f0c7) and the **Save** label. We leave the canExecute function as the default for now so it will always be enabled. Next, we connect the executed() signal of the command to the onCreateClientSaveExecuted() slot of the CommandController. With the wiring done, we then add the command to the list.

The intention is that we present the user with a command button bound to a `Command` object. When the user presses the button, we will fire the `executed()` signal from the UI. The connection we've set up will cause the slot on the command controller to be called, and we will execute our business logic. For now, we'll simply print out a line to the console when the button is pressed.

Next, let's register both of our new types in `main.cpp` (remember the `#includes`):

```
qmlRegisterType<cm::controllers::CommandController>("CM", 1, 0,
"CommandController");
qmlRegisterType<cm::framework::Command>("CM", 1, 0, "Command");
```

Finally, we need to add the `CommandCoordinator` property to `MasterController`:

```
Q_PROPERTY( cm::controllers::CommandController* ui_commandController READ
commandController CONSTANT )
```

Then, we add an `accessor` method:

```
CommandController* commandController();
```

Finally, in `master-controller.cpp`, instantiate the object in the private implementation and implement the `accessor` method in exactly the same way as we did for `NavigationController`.

We now have a (very short!) list of commands ready for our `CreateClientView` to consume.

Command bar

Let's begin by adding some more properties to Style for our command components:

```
readonly property color colourCommandBarBackground: "#cecece"
readonly property color colourCommandBarFont: "#131313"
readonly property color colourCommandBarFontDisabled: "#636363"
readonly property real heightCommandBar: heightCommandButton
readonly property int pixelSizeCommandBarIcon: 32
readonly property int pixelSizeCommandBarText: 12

readonly property real widthCommandButton: 80
readonly property real heightCommandButton: widthCommandButton
```

Next, create two new QML components in our UI project: CommandBar.qml and CommandButton.qml in cm-ui/components. Update components.qrc and move the new components into the /components prefix with aliases. Edit qmldir and append the new components:

```
CommandBar 1.0 CommandBar.qml
CommandButton 1.0 CommandButton.qml
```

For our button design, we want to lay out the description below the icon. The icon should be positioned slightly above centre. The component should be square, as follows:

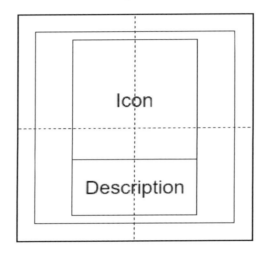

CommandButton.qml:

```
import QtQuick 2.9
import CM 1.0
import assets 1.0

Item {
    property Command command
    width: Style.widthCommandButton
    height: Style.heightCommandButton

    Rectangle {
        id: background
        anchors.fill: parent
        color: Style.colourCommandBarBackground

        Text {
            id: textIcon
```

```
        anchors {
            centerIn: parent
            verticalCenterOffset: -10
        }
        font {
            family: Style.fontAwesome
            pixelSize: Style.pixelSizeCommandBarIcon
        }
        color: command.ui_canExecute ? Style.colourCommandBarFont :
                                colourCommandBarFontDisabled
        text: command.ui_iconCharacter
        horizontalAlignment: Text.AlignHCenter
    }

    Text {
        id: textDescription
        anchors {
            top: textIcon.bottom
            bottom: parent.bottom
            left: parent.left
            right: parent.right
        }
        font.pixelSize: Style.pixelSizeNavigationBarText
        color: command.ui_canExecute ? Style.colourCommandBarFont :
                                colourCommandBarFontDisabled
        text: command.ui_description
        horizontalAlignment: Text.AlignHCenter
        verticalAlignment: Text.AlignVCenter
    }

    MouseArea {
        anchors.fill: parent
        cursorShape: Qt.PointingHandCursor
        hoverEnabled: true
        onEntered: background.state = "hover"
        onExited: background.state = ""
        onClicked: if(command.ui_canExecute) {
                    command.executed();
                }
    }

    states: [
        State {
            name: "hover"
            PropertyChanges {
                target: background
                color: Qt.darker(Style.colourCommandBarBackground)
            }
```

```
                }
            ]
        }
    }
```

This is largely similar to our `NavigationButton` component. We pass in a `Command` object, which is where we will obtain the icon character and description to display in the **Text** elements as well as the signal to emit when the button is pressed, so long as the command can execute.

We use an alternative to the **Row/Column** based layout and use anchors to position our icon and description instead. We center the icon in the parent `Rectangle` and then apply a vertical offset to move it up and allow space for the description. We anchor the top of the description to the bottom of the icon.

Rather than propagating a signal when the button is pressed, we emit the `executed()` signal of the `Command` object, first verifying that the command can execute. We also use this flag to selectively color our text elements, using a paler grey font if the command is disabled.

We implement some more hover functionality with our `MouseArea`, but rather than exposing a property to pass in the hover color, we simply take the default and darken it a few shades using the built-in `Qt.darker()` method. We also only apply the state change in the `onEntered()` slot of the `MouseArea` if the command can be executed.

`CommandBar.qml`:

```
import QtQuick 2.9
import assets 1.0

Item {
    property alias commandList: commandRepeater.model

    anchors {
        left: parent.left
        bottom: parent.bottom
        right: parent.right
    }
    height: Style.heightCommandBar

    Rectangle {
        anchors.fill: parent
        color: Style.colourCommandBarBackground

        Row {
```

```
anchors {
    top: parent.top
    bottom: parent.bottom
    right: parent.right
}

Repeater {
    id: commandRepeater
    delegate: CommandButton {
        command: modelData
    }
}
        }
    }
}
```

Again, this is largely the same as NavigationBar, but with a dynamic list of commands rather than hard-coded QML buttons. We introduce another new component—the Repeater. Given a list of objects via the model property, Repeater will instantiate a QML component defined in the delegate property for each item in the list. The object from the list is made available via the built-in modelData variable. Using this mechanism, we can automatically generate a CommandButton element for each command we have in a given list. We use another property alias so that the caller can set the command list.

Let's put this to use in CreateClientView. First, import components 1.0, and then add the following inside the root Item and after the Rectangle:

```
CommandBar {
    commandList:
masterController.ui_commandController.ui_createClientViewContextCommands
}
```

We drill down through our property hierarchy to get the command list for the create client view and pass that list to the command bar which takes care of the rest. Don't worry if the CommandBar has red squiggles, Qt Creator just needs to catch up with our blistering pace.

Run the app and navigate to **Create Client View**:

Click on the button, and you will see the message output to the console. Adding new commands is as simple as appending a new Command object to the QList inside CommandController—no UI changes needed! The command bar will automatically create a new button for every command it finds in the list. Also note that this command bar is only present on the CreateClientView, so it is context sensitive. We can easily add command bars to other views by simply adding extra lists and properties to the CommandController, as we will later.

Summary

In this chapter, we gave the navigation bar a much needed overhaul. We added our first few components and leveraged our new custom style object, with Font Awesome providing some lovely scalable graphics for us. We also introduced commands and have the framework in place to be able to add context-sensitive command buttons to our views.

In Chapter 5, *Data*, we'll get stuck into the business logic layer and flesh out our first data models.

5
Data

In this chapter, we will implement classes to handle the most critical part of any Line of Business application—the data. We will introduce self-aware data entities, which can automatically serialize to and from **JavaScript Object Notation (JSON)**, a popular serialization format used a lot in web communications. We will create the core models we need for our application and wire them up to our UI for reading and writing via custom controls. We will cover the following topics:

- JSON
- Data decorators
- Abstract data entities
- Collections of data entities
- Concrete data models
- UI controls and data binding

JSON

In case you have never come across JSON before, let's have a quick crash course. It is a simple and lightweight way to express hierarchies of objects and their properties. It is a very popular choice when sending data in HTTP requests. It is similar to XML in intent but is much less verbose.

A JSON object is encapsulated in curly braces { }, while properties are denoted in the format key: value. Strings are delimited with double quotes "". We can represent a single client object as follows:

```
{
    "reference": "CLIENT0001",
    "name": "Dale Cooper"
}
```

Note that white space and control characters such as tab and newline are ignored—the indented properties are to simply make things more readable.

> It's usually a good idea to strip extraneous characters out of JSON when transmitting over the network (for example, in an HTTP request) in order to reduce the size of the payload; every byte counts!

Property values can be one of the following types: String, Number, JSON Object, JSON Array, and the literal values true, false, and null.

We can add the supply address and billing address to our client as child JSON objects, providing a unique key for each. While keys can be in any format as long as they are unique, it is common practice to use camel case, for example, myAwesomeJsonKey. We can express an empty address object with null:

```
{
    "reference": "CLIENT0001",
    "name": "Dale Cooper",
    "supplyAddress": {
        "number": 7,
        "name": "White Lodge",
        "street": "Lost Highway",
        "city": "Twin Peaks",
        "postcode": "WS119"
    },
    "billingAddress": null
}
```

A collection (array) of objects is enclosed in square brackets `[]` separated by commas. We can express no scheduled appointments by simply leaving the square brackets empty:

```
{
    "reference": "CLIENT0001",
    "name": "Dale Cooper",
    "supplyAddress": {
        "number": 7,
        "name": "White Lodge",
        "street": "Lost Highway",
        "city": "Twin Peaks",
        "postcode": "WS119"
    },
    "billingAddress": null,
    "contacts": [
        {
            "type": 1,
            "address": "+12345678"
        },
        {
            "type": 2,
            "address": "dale.cooper@fbi.com"
        }
    ],
    "appointments": []
}
```

Object hierarchy

Most real-world applications represent data in a hierarchical or relational manner, with the data rationalized into discrete objects. There is often a central "root" object, which parents several other child objects, either as singular objects or as a collection. Each discrete object has its own set of data items that can be any number of types. The key principles we want to cover are as listed:

- A range of data types (`string`, `integer`, `datetime`) and an enumerated value
- Object hierarchy
- Multiple single child entities of the same type
- Collections of entities

Balancing these goals with simplicity, the data diagram we will work toward is as follows:

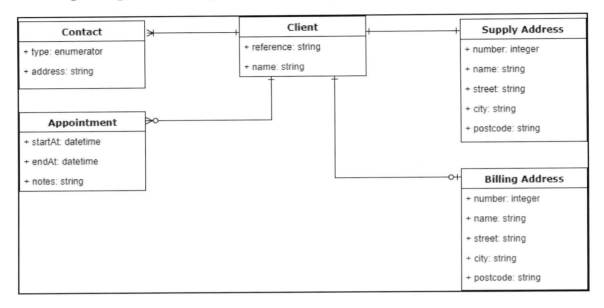

The purpose of each of these models is described in the following table:

Model	Description
Client	This is the root of our object hierarchy and represents an individual or party our company has a relationship with, for example, a customer or a patient.
Contact	A collection of addresses that we can use to contact the client. The possible types of contact will be a telephone, email, and fax. There may be one or more contacts per client.
Appointment	A collection of scheduled appointments with the client, for example, a site visit or consultation. There may be zero or more appointments per client.
Supply address	The address central to the relationship with the client, for example, the site our company supplies energy to or the home address of a patient. There must be one supply address per client.
Billing address	An optional address different to the supply address used for invoicing, for example, the head office of a corporation. There may be zero or one billing address per client.

Another perfectly valid approach would be to aggregate the addresses into a collection, much like we have done with our contacts, but I want to demonstrate using the same type of object (Address) in multiple properties.

With the high-level design in place, we are now in a position to write our classes. However, before we start on our data entities, let's take a look at the data items.

DataDecorators

A simple implementation of the name property of our client model would be to add it as a QString; however, this approach has some shortcomings. Whenever we display this property in the UI, we will probably want to display an informative label next to the textbox so that the user knows what it is for, saying "Name" or something similar. Whenever we want to validate a name entered by the user, we have to manage that in the code somewhere else. Finally, if we want to serialize the value to or from JSON, again there needs to be some other component that does it for us.

To solve all of these problems we will introduce the concept of a DataDecorator, which will lift a given base data type and give us a label, validation capabilities, and JSON serialization out of the box. Our models will maintain a collection of DataDecorators, allowing them to validate and serialize themselves to JSON too by simply walking through the data items and performing the relevant action.

In our cm-lib project, create the following classes in a new folder cm-lib/source/data:

Class	Purpose
DataDecorator	Base class for our data items
StringDecorator	Derived class for string properties
IntDecorator	Derived class for integer properties
DateTimeDecorator	Derived class for date/time properties
EnumeratorDecorator	Derived class for enumerated properties

Our DataDecorator base class will house the features shared across all of our data items.

data-decorator.h:

```
#ifndef DATADECORATOR_H
#define DATADECORATOR_H

#include <QJsonObject>
#include <QJsonValue>
#include <QObject>
#include <QScopedPointer>

#include <cm-lib_global.h>

namespace cm {
namespace data {

class Entity;

class CMLIBSHARED_EXPORT DataDecorator : public QObject
{
    Q_OBJECT
    Q_PROPERTY( QString ui_label READ label CONSTANT )

public:
    DataDecorator(Entity* parent = nullptr, const QString& key =
                "SomeItemKey", const QString& label = "");
                                virtual ~DataDecorator();

    const QString& key() const;
    const QString& label() const;
    Entity* parentEntity();

    virtual QJsonValue jsonValue() const = 0;
    virtual void update(const QJsonObject& jsonObject) = 0;

private:
    class Implementation;
    QScopedPointer<Implementation> implementation;
};

}}

#endif
```

We inherit from QObject, add our `dllexport` macro and wrap the whole thing in namespaces as usual. Also, because this is an abstract base class, we ensure that we've implemented a virtual destructor.

We know that because we are inheriting from QObject, we want to receive a pointer to a parent in our constructor. We also know that all data items will be children of an **Entity** (which we will write soon and have forward declared here), which will itself be derived from QObject. We can leverage these two facts to parent our `DataDecorator` directly to an Entity.

We construct the decorator with a couple of strings. All of our data decorators must have a key that will be used when serializing to and from JSON, and they will also share a `label` property that the UI can use to display descriptive text next to the data control. We tuck these members away in the private implementation and implement some accessor methods for them.

Finally, we begin implementing our JSON serialization by declaring virtual methods to represent the value as a `QJsonValue` and to update the value from a provided `QJsonObject`. As the value is not known in the base class and will instead be implemented in the derived classes, both these methods are pure virtual functions.

`data-decorator.cpp`:

```
#include "data-decorator.h"

namespace cm {
namespace data {

class DataDecorator::Implementation
{
public:
    Implementation(Entity* _parent, const QString& _key, const QString&
                                                          _label)
        : parentEntity(_parent)
        , key(_key)
        , label(_label)
    {
    }
    Entity* parentEntity{nullptr};
    QString key;
    QString label;
};

DataDecorator::DataDecorator(Entity* parent, const QString& key, const
QString& label)
```

```
     : QObject((QObject*)parent)
{
    implementation.reset(new Implementation(parent, key, label));
}

DataDecorator::~DataDecorator()
{
}

const QString& DataDecorator::key() const
{
    return implementation->key;
}

const QString& DataDecorator::label() const
{
    return implementation->label;
}

Entity* DataDecorator::parentEntity()
{
    return implementation->parentEntity;
}


}}
```

The implementation is very straightforward, essentially just managing some data members.

Next, we'll implement our derived decorator class for handling strings.

```
string-decorator.h:

    #ifndef STRINGDECORATOR_H
    #define STRINGDECORATOR_H

    #include <QJsonObject>
    #include <QJsonValue>
    #include <QObject>
    #include <QScopedPointer>
    #include <QString>

    #include <cm-lib_global.h>
    #include <data/data-decorator.h>

    namespace cm {
    namespace data {

    class CMLIBSHARED_EXPORT StringDecorator : public DataDecorator
```

```
{
    Q_OBJECT
    Q_PROPERTY( QString ui_value READ value WRITE setValue NOTIFY
            valueChanged )
public:
    StringDecorator(Entity* parentEntity = nullptr, const QString& key =
"SomeItemKey", const QString& label = "", const QString& value = "");
    ~StringDecorator();

    StringDecorator& setValue(const QString& value);
    const QString& value() const;

    QJsonValue jsonValue() const override;
    void update(const QJsonObject& jsonObject) override;

signals:
    void valueChanged();

private:
    class Implementation;
    QScopedPointer<Implementation> implementation;
};

}}

#endif
```

There isn't much else going on here—we're just adding a strongly typed QString value property to hold our value. We also override the virtual JSON-related methods.

When deriving from a class that inherits from QObject, you need to add the Q_OBJECT macro to the derived class as well as the base class if the derived class implements its own signals or slots.

string-decorator.cpp:

```
#include "string-decorator.h"

#include <QVariant>

namespace cm {
namespace data {

class StringDecorator::Implementation
{
public:
```

```
    Implementation(StringDecorator* _stringDecorator, const QString&
                                                  _value)
        : stringDecorator(_stringDecorator)
        , value(_value)
    {
    }

    StringDecorator* stringDecorator{nullptr};
    QString value;
};

StringDecorator::StringDecorator(Entity* parentEntity, const QString& key,
const QString& label, const QString& value)
    : DataDecorator(parentEntity, key, label)
{
    implementation.reset(new Implementation(this, value));
}

StringDecorator::~StringDecorator()
{
}

const QString& StringDecorator::value() const
{
    return implementation->value;
}

StringDecorator& StringDecorator::setValue(const QString& value)
{
    if(value != implementation->value) {
        // ...Validation here if required...
        implementation->value = value;
        emit valueChanged();
    }
    return *this;
}

QJsonValue StringDecorator::jsonValue() const
{
    return QJsonValue::fromVariant(QVariant(implementation->value));
}

void StringDecorator::update(const QJsonObject& _jsonObject)
{
    if (_jsonObject.contains(key())) {
        setValue(_jsonObject.value(key()).toString());
    } else {
        setValue("");
```

```
        }
    }
}}
```

Again, there is nothing particularly complicated here. By using the READ and WRITE property syntax rather than the simpler MEMBER keyword, we now have a way of intercepting values being set by the UI, and we can decide whether or not we want to apply the change to the member variable. The mutator can be as complex as you need it to be, but all we're doing for now is setting the value and emitting the signal to tell the UI that it has been changed. We wrap the operation in an equality check, so we don't take any action if the new value is the same as the old one.

> Here, the mutator returns a reference to self (*this), which is helpful because it enables method chaining, for example, myName.setValue("Nick").setSomeNumber(1234).setSomeOtherProperty(true). However, this is not necessary for the property bindings, so feel free to use the more common void return type if you prefer.

We use a two-step conversion process, converting our QString value into a QVariant before converting it into our target QJsonValue type. The QJsonValue will be plugged into the parent Entity JSON object using the key from the DataDecorator base class. We will cover that in more detail when we write the **Entity** related classes.

> An alternative approach would be to simply represent the value of our various data items as a QVariant member in the DataDecorator base class, removing the need to have separate classes for QString, int, and so on. The problem with this approach is that you end up having to write lots of nasty code that says "if you have a QVariant containing a string then run this code if it contains an int then run this code...". I prefer the additional overhead of writing the extra classes in exchange for having known types and cleaner, simpler code. This will become particularly helpful when we look at data validation. Validating a string is completely different from validating a number and different again from validating a date.

`IntDecorator` and `DateTimeDecorator` are virtually identical to `StringDecorator`, simply substituting `QString` values for int or `QDateTime`. However, we can supplement `DateTimeDecorator` with a few additional properties to help us out. Add the following properties and an accessor method to go with each:

```
Q_PROPERTY( QString ui_iso8601String READ toIso8601String NOTIFY
valueChanged )
Q_PROPERTY( QString ui_prettyDateString READ toPrettyDateString NOTIFY
valueChanged )
Q_PROPERTY( QString ui_prettyTimeString READ toPrettyTimeString NOTIFY
valueChanged )
Q_PROPERTY( QString ui_prettyString READ toPrettyString NOTIFY valueChanged
)
```

The purpose of these properties is to make the UI easily access the date/time value as a `QString` preformatted to a few different styles. Let's run through the implementation for each of the accessors.

Qt has inbuilt support for ISO8601 format dates, which is a very common format when transmitting datetime values between systems, for example, in HTTP requests. It is a flexible format that supports several different representations but generally follows the format yyyy-MM-ddTHH:mm:ss.zt, where T is a string literal, z is milliseconds, and t is the timezone information:

```
QString DateTimeDecorator::toIso8601String() const
{
    if (implementation->value.isNull()) {
        return "";
    } else {
        return implementation->value.toString(Qt::ISODate);
    }
}
```

Next, we provide a method to display a full datetime in a long human readable format, for example, Sat 22 Jul 2017 @ 12:07:45:

```
QString DateTimeDecorator::toPrettyString() const
{
    if (implementation->value.isNull()) {
        return "Not set";
    } else {
        return implementation->value.toString( "ddd d MMM yyyy @ HH:mm:ss"
);
    }
}
```

The final two methods display either the date or time component, for example, 22 Jul 2017 or 12:07 pm:

```
QString DateTimeDecorator::toPrettyDateString() const
{
    if (implementation->value.isNull()) {
        return "Not set";
    } else {
        return implementation->value.toString( "d MMM yyyy" );
    }
}

QString DateTimeDecorator::toPrettyTimeString() const
{
    if (implementation->value.isNull()) {
        return "Not set";
    } else {
        return implementation->value.toString( "hh:mm ap" );
    }
}
```

Our final type, `EnumeratorDecorator`, is broadly the same as `IntDecorator`, but it also accepts a mapper. This container helps us map the stored int value to a string representation. If we consider the `Contact.type` enumerator we plan to implement, the enumerated value will be 0, 1, 2, so on; however, when it comes to the UI, that number won't mean anything to the user. We really need to present `Email`, `Telephone`, or some other string representation, and the map allows us to do just that.

enumerator-decorator.h:

```
#ifndef ENUMERATORDECORATOR_H
#define ENUMERATORDECORATOR_H

#include <map>

#include <QJsonObject>
#include <QJsonValue>
#include <QObject>
#include <QScopedPointer>

#include <cm-lib_global.h>
#include <data/data-decorator.h>

namespace cm {
namespace data {
```

```
class CMLIBSHARED_EXPORT EnumeratorDecorator : public DataDecorator
{
    Q_OBJECT
    Q_PROPERTY( int ui_value READ value WRITE setValue NOTIFY
                                            valueChanged )
    Q_PROPERTY( QString ui_valueDescription READ valueDescription
                                        NOTIFY valueChanged )

public:
    EnumeratorDecorator(Entity* parentEntity = nullptr, const QString&
    key = "SomeItemKey", const QString& label = "", int value = 0,
    const std::map<int, QString>& descriptionMapper = std::map<int,
     QString>());
    ~EnumeratorDecorator();

    EnumeratorDecorator& setValue(int value);
    int value() const;
    QString valueDescription() const;

    QJsonValue jsonValue() const override;
    void update(const QJsonObject& jsonObject) override;

signals:
    void valueChanged();

private:
    class Implementation;
    QScopedPointer<Implementation> implementation;
};

}}

#endif
```

We store the map as another member variable in our private implementation class and then use it to provide the string representation of the enumerated value:

```
QString EnumeratorDecorator::valueDescription() const
{
    if (implementation->descriptionMapper.find(implementation->value)
                    != implementation->descriptionMapper.end()) {
        return implementation->descriptionMapper.at(implementation-
                                            >value);
    } else {
        return {};
    }
}
```

Now that we have covered the data types we need for our entities, let's move on to the entities themselves.

Entities

As we have a lot of functionality we want to share across our data models, we'll implement an **Entity** base class. We need to be able to represent parent/child relationships so that a client can have supply and billing addresses. We also need to support collections of entities for our contacts and appointments. Finally, each entity hierarchy must be able to serialize itself to and from a JSON object.

Create a new class Entity in `cm-lib/source/data`.

`entity.h`:

```
#ifndef ENTITY_H
#define ENTITY_H

#include <map>

#include <QObject>
#include <QScopedPointer>

#include <cm-lib_global.h>
#include <data/data-decorator.h>

namespace cm {
namespace data {

class CMLIBSHARED_EXPORT Entity : public QObject
{
    Q_OBJECT

public:
    Entity(QObject* parent = nullptr, const QString& key =
                                        "SomeEntityKey");
    Entity(QObject* parent, const QString& key, const QJsonObject&
      jsonObject);
    virtual ~Entity();

public:
    const QString& key() const;
    void update(const QJsonObject& jsonObject);
    QJsonObject toJson() const;
```

```
    signals:
        void childEntitiesChanged();
        void dataDecoratorsChanged();

    protected:
        Entity* addChild(Entity* entity, const QString& key);
        DataDecorator* addDataItem(DataDecorator* dataDecorator);

    protected:
        class Implementation;
        QScopedPointer<Implementation> implementation;
    };

    }}

    #endif
```

entity.cpp:

```
    #include "entity.h"

    namespace cm {
    namespace data {

    class Entity::Implementation
    {
    public:
        Implementation(Entity* _entity, const QString& _key)
            : entity(_entity)
            , key(_key)
        {
        }
        Entity* entity{nullptr};
        QString key;
        std::map<QString, Entity*> childEntities;
        std::map<QString, DataDecorator*> dataDecorators;
    };

    Entity::Entity(QObject* parent, const QString& key)
        : QObject(parent)
    {
        implementation.reset(new Implementation(this, key));
    }

    Entity::Entity(QObject* parent, const QString& key, const QJsonObject&
                jsonObject) : Entity(parent, key)
    {
        update(jsonObject);
```

```
}

Entity::~Entity()
{
}

const QString& Entity::key() const
{
    return implementation->key;
}

Entity* Entity::addChild(Entity* entity, const QString& key)
{
    if(implementation->childEntities.find(key) ==
        std::end(implementation->childEntities)) {
        implementation->childEntities[key] = entity;
        emit childEntitiesChanged();
    }
    return entity;
}

DataDecorator* Entity::addDataItem(DataDecorator* dataDecorator)
{
    if(implementation->dataDecorators.find(dataDecorator->key()) ==
        std::end(implementation->dataDecorators)) {
        implementation->dataDecorators[dataDecorator->key()] =
        dataDecorator;
        emit dataDecoratorsChanged();
    }
    return dataDecorator;
}

void Entity::update(const QJsonObject& jsonObject)
{
    // Update data decorators
    for (std::pair<QString, DataDecorator*> dataDecoratorPair :
        implementation->dataDecorators) {
        dataDecoratorPair.second->update(jsonObject);
    }
    // Update child entities
    for (std::pair<QString, Entity*> childEntityPair : implementation-
    >childEntities)
{childEntityPair.second>update(jsonObject.value(childEntityPair.first).toOb
ject());
    }
}

QJsonObject Entity::toJson() const
```

```
{
    QJsonObject returnValue;
    // Add data decorators
    for (std::pair<QString, DataDecorator*> dataDecoratorPair :
                        implementation->dataDecorators) {
        returnValue.insert( dataDecoratorPair.first,
        dataDecoratorPair.second->jsonValue() );
    }
    // Add child entities
    for (std::pair<QString, Entity*> childEntityPair :
implementation->childEntities) {
        returnValue.insert( childEntityPair.first,
childEntityPair.second->toJson() );
    }
    return returnValue;
}

}}
```

Much like our `DataDecorator` base class, we assign all entities a unique key, which will be used in JSON serialization. We also add an overloaded constructor to which we can pass a `QJsonObject` so that we can instantiate an entity from JSON. On a related note, we also declare a pair of methods to serialize an existing instance to and from JSON.

Our entity will maintain a few collections—a map of data decorators representing the properties of the model, and a map of entities representing individual children. We map the key of each item to the instance.

We expose a couple of protected methods that are derived classes will use to add its data items and children; for example, our client model will add a name data item along with the `supplyAddress` and `billingAddress` children. To complement these methods, we also add signals to tell any interested observers that the collections have changed.

In both cases, we check that the key doesn't already exist on the map before adding it. We then return the supplied pointer so that the consumer can use it for further actions. You'll see the value of this when we come to implement the data models.

We use our populated maps for the JSON serialization methods. We've already declared an `update()` method on our `DataDecorator` base class, so we simply iterate through all the data items and pass the JSON object down to each in turn. Each derived decorator class has its own implementation to take care of the parsing. Similarly, we recursively call `Entity::update()` on each of the child entities.

Serializing to a JSON object follows the same pattern. Each data item can convert its value to a `QJsonValue` object, so we get each value in turn and append it to a root JSON object using the key of each item. We recursively call `Entity::toJson()` on each of the children, and this cascades down the hierarchy tree.

Before we can finish off our **Entity**, we need to declare a group of classes to represent an entity collection.

Entity collections

To implement entity collections, we need to leverage some more advanced C++ techniques, and we will take a brief break from our conventions so far, implementing multiple classes in a single header file.

Create `entity-collection.h` in `cm-lib/source/data`, and in it, add our namespaces as normal and forward declare Entity:

```
#ifndef ENTITYCOLLECTION_H
#define ENTITYCOLLECTION_H

namespace cm {
namespace data {
    class Entity;
}}

#endif
```

Next, we'll walk through the necessary classes in turn, each of which must be added in order inside the namespaces.

We first define the root class, which does nothing more than inheriting from `QObject` and giving us access to all the goodness that it brings, such as object ownership and signals. This is required because classes deriving directly from `QObject` cannot be templated:

```
class CMLIBSHARED_EXPORT EntityCollectionObject : public QObject
{
    Q_OBJECT

public:
    EntityCollectionObject(QObject* _parent = nullptr) : QObject(_parent)
{}
    virtual ~EntityCollectionObject() {}

signals:
    void collectionChanged();
};
```

You will need to add includes for `QObject` and our DLL export macros. Next, we need a type agnostic interface to use with our entities, much the same as we have with the `DataDecorator` and Entity maps we've implemented. However, things are a little more complicated here, as we will not derive a new class for each collection we have, so we need some way of getting typed data. We have two requirements. Firstly, the UI needs a `QList` of derived types (for example, **Client***) so that it can access all the properties specific to a client and display all the data. Secondly, our **Entity** class needs a vector of base types (**Entity***) so that it can iterate its collections without caring exactly which type it is dealing with. The way we achieve this is to declare two template methods but delay defining them until later. `derivedEntities()` will be used when the consumer wants a collection of the derived type, while `baseEntities()` will be used when the consumer just wants access to the base interface:

```
class EntityCollectionBase : public EntityCollectionObject
{
public:
    EntityCollectionBase(QObject* parent = nullptr, const QString& key
                                          = "SomeCollectionKey")
        : EntityCollectionObject(parent)
        , key(key)
    {}

    virtual ~EntityCollectionBase()
    {}

    QString getKey() const
    {
        return key;
```

```
    }

    virtual void clear() = 0;
    virtual void update(const QJsonArray& json) = 0;
    virtual std::vector<Entity*> baseEntities() = 0;

    template <class T>
    QList<T*>& derivedEntities();

    template <class T>
    T* addEntity(T* entity);

private:
    QString key;
};
```

Next, we declare a full template class where we store our collection of derived types and implement all of our methods, except for the two template methods we just discussed:

```
template <typename T>
class EntityCollection : public EntityCollectionBase
{
public:
    EntityCollection(QObject* parent = nullptr, const QString& key =
            "SomeCollectionKey")
        : EntityCollectionBase(parent, key)
    {}

    ~EntityCollection()
    {}

    void clear() override
    {
        for(auto entity : collection) {
            entity->deleteLater();
        }
        collection.clear();
    }

    void update(const QJsonArray& jsonArray) override
    {
        clear();
        for(const QJsonValue& jsonValue : jsonArray) {
            addEntity(new T(this, jsonValue.toObject()));
        }
    }

    std::vector<Entity*> baseEntities() override
```

```
    {
        std::vector<Entity*> returnValue;
        for(T* entity : collection) {
            returnValue.push_back(entity);
        }
        return returnValue;
    }

    QList<T*>& derivedEntities()
    {
        return collection;
    }

    T* addEntity(T* entity)
    {
        if(!collection.contains(entity)) {
            collection.append(entity);
            EntityCollectionObject::collectionChanged();
        }
        return entity;
    }

private:
    QList<T*> collection;
};
```

 You will need `#include <QJsonValue>` and `<QJsonArray>` for these classes.

The `clear()` method simply empties the collection and tidies up the memory; `update()` is conceptually the same as the JSON methods we implemented in Entity, except that we are dealing with a collection of entities, so we take a JSON array instead of an object. `addEntity()` adds an instance of a derived class to the collection, and `derivedEntities()` returns the collection; `baseEntities()` does a little more work, creating a new vector on request and populating it with all the items in the collection. It is just implicitly casting pointers, so we're not concerned about expensive object instantiation.

Finally, we provide the implementation for our magic templated methods:

```
template <class T>
QList<T*>& EntityCollectionBase::derivedEntities()
{
    return dynamic_cast<const
EntityCollection<T>&>(*this).derivedEntities();
}

template <class T>
T* EntityCollectionBase::addEntity(T* entity)
{
    return dynamic_cast<const
EntityCollection<T>&>(*this).addEntity(entity);
}
```

What we've achieved by delaying our implementation of these methods is that we've now fully declared our templated `EntityCollection` class. We can now "route" any calls to the templated methods through to the implementation in the templated class. It's a tricky technique to wrap your head around, but it will hopefully make more sense when we start implementing these collections in our real-world models.

With our entity collections now ready, we can return to our Entity class and add them to the mix.

In the header, `#include <data/entity-collection.h>`, add the signal:

```
void childCollectionsChanged(const QString& collectionKey);
```

Also, add the protected method:

```
EntityCollectionBase* addChildCollection(EntityCollectionBase*
entityCollection);
```

In the implementation file, add the private member:

```
std::map<QString, EntityCollectionBase*> childCollections;
```

Then, add the method:

```
EntityCollectionBase* Entity::addChildCollection(EntityCollectionBase*
entityCollection)
{
    if(implementation->childCollections.find(entityCollection-
      >getKey()) == std::end(implementation->childCollections)) {
        implementation->childCollections[entityCollection->getKey()] =
                                    entityCollection;
        emit childCollectionsChanged(entityCollection->getKey());
    }
    return entityCollection;
}
```

This works in exactly the same way as the other maps, associating a key with a pointer to a base class.

Next, add the collections to the `update()` method:

```
void Entity::update(const QJsonObject& jsonObject)
{
    // Update data decorators
    for (std::pair<QString, DataDecorator*> dataDecoratorPair :
          implementation->dataDecorators) {
        dataDecoratorPair.second->update(jsonObject);
    }

    // Update child entities
    for (std::pair<QString, Entity*> childEntityPair : implementation-
        >childEntities) { childEntityPair.second-
        >update(jsonObject.value(childEntityPair.first).toObject());
    }

    // Update child collections
    for (std::pair<QString, EntityCollectionBase*> childCollectionPair
        : implementation->childCollections) {
            childCollectionPair.second-
        >update(jsonObject.value(childCollectionPair.first).toArray());
    }
}
```

Finally, add the collections to the `toJson()` method:

```
QJsonObject Entity::toJson() const
{
    QJsonObject returnValue;

    // Add data decorators
```

```
for (std::pair<QString, DataDecorator*> dataDecoratorPair :
    implementation->dataDecorators) {
    returnValue.insert( dataDecoratorPair.first,
    dataDecoratorPair.second->jsonValue() );
}

// Add child entities
for (std::pair<QString, Entity*> childEntityPair : implementation-
    >childEntities) {
    returnValue.insert( childEntityPair.first,
    childEntityPair.second->toJson() );
}

// Add child collections
for (std::pair<QString, EntityCollectionBase*> childCollectionPair
    : implementation->childCollections) {
    QJsonArray entityArray;
        for (Entity* entity : childCollectionPair.second-
        >baseEntities()) {
        entityArray.append( entity->toJson() );
    }
    returnValue.insert( childCollectionPair.first, entityArray );
}

return returnValue;
}
```

 You will need `#include <QJsonArray>` for that last snippet.

We use the `baseEntities()` method to give us a collection of `Entity*`. We then append the JSON object from each entity to a JSON array and when complete, add that array to our root JSON object with the collection's key.

The past few sections have been quite long and complex and may seem like a lot of work just to implement some data models. However, it's all code that you write once, and it gives you a lot of functionality for free with every entity you go on and make, so it's worth the investment in the long run. We'll go ahead and look at how to implement these classes in our data models.

Data models

Now that we have the infrastructure in place to be able to define data objects (entities and entity collections) and properties of various types (data decorators), we can move on and build the object hierarchy we laid out earlier in the chapter. We already have a default **Client** class created by Qt Creator, so supplement that in `cm-lib/source/models` with the following new classes:

Class	Purpose
Address	Represents a supply or billing address
Appointment	Represents an appointment with a client
Contact	Represents a method of contacting a client

We'll start with the simplest of the models—the address.

`address.h`:

```cpp
#ifndef ADDRESS_H
#define ADDRESS_H

#include <QObject>

#include <cm-lib_global.h>
#include <data/string-decorator.h>
#include <data/entity.h>

namespace cm {
namespace models {

class CMLIBSHARED_EXPORT Address : public data::Entity
{
    Q_OBJECT
    Q_PROPERTY(cm::data::StringDecorator* ui_building MEMBER building
                                          CONSTANT)
    Q_PROPERTY(cm::data::StringDecorator* ui_street MEMBER street
                                          CONSTANT)
    Q_PROPERTY(cm::data::StringDecorator* ui_city MEMBER city CONSTANT)
    Q_PROPERTY(cm::data::StringDecorator* ui_postcode MEMBER postcode
                                          CONSTANT)
    Q_PROPERTY(QString ui_fullAddress READ fullAddress CONSTANT)

public:
    explicit Address(QObject* parent = nullptr);
```

```
    Address(QObject* parent, const QJsonObject& json);

    data::StringDecorator* building{nullptr};
    data::StringDecorator* street{nullptr};
    data::StringDecorator* city{nullptr};
    data::StringDecorator* postcode{nullptr};

    QString fullAddress() const;
};

}}

#endif
```

We define the properties we designed at the beginning of the chapter, but instead of using regular QString objects, we use our new StringDecorators. To protect the integrity of our data, we should really use the READ keyword and return a StringDecorator* const via an accessor method, but for simplicity, we'll use MEMBER instead. We also provide an overloaded constructor that we can use to construct an address from a QJsonObject. Finally, we add a helper fullAddress() method and property to concatenate the address elements into a single string for use in the UI.

address.cpp:

```
#include "address.h"

using namespace cm::data;

namespace cm {
namespace models {

Address::Address(QObject* parent)
        : Entity(parent, "address")
{
    building = static_cast<StringDecorator*>(addDataItem(new
StringDecorator(this, "building", "Building")));
    street = static_cast<StringDecorator*>(addDataItem(new
StringDecorator(this, "street", "Street")));
    city = static_cast<StringDecorator*>(addDataItem(new
StringDecorator(this, "city", "City")));
    postcode = static_cast<StringDecorator*>(addDataItem(new
StringDecorator(this, "postcode", "Post Code")));
}

Address::Address(QObject* parent, const QJsonObject& json)
        : Address(parent)
```

```
{
    update(json);
}

QString Address::fullAddress() const
{
    return building->value() + " " + street->value() + "\n" + city->value()
+ "\n" + postcode->value();
}

}}
```

This is where all of our hard work starts to come together. We need to do two things with each of our properties. Firstly, we need a pointer to the derived type (StringDecorator), which we can present to the UI in order to display and edit the value. Secondly, we need to make the base Entity class aware of the base type (DataDecorator) so that it can iterate the data items and perform the JSON serialization work for us. We can use the addDataItem() method to achieve both these goals in a one-line statement:

```
building = static_cast<StringDecorator*>(addDataItem(new
StringDecorator(this, "building", "Building")));
```

Breaking this down, we create a new StringDecorator* with the building key and Building UI label. This is immediately passed to addDataItem(), which adds it to the dataDecorators collection in the **Entity** and returns the data item as a DataDecorator*. We can then cast it back to a StringDecorator* before storing it in the building member variable.

The only other piece of implementation here is to take a JSON object, construct the address as normal by calling the default constructor, and then update the model using the update() method.

The Appointment and Contact models follow the same pattern, just with different properties and the appropriate variation of DataDecorator for each of their data types. Where Contact varies more significantly is in its use of an EnumeratorDecorator for the contactType property. To support this, we first define an enumerator in the header file that contains all the possible values we want:

```
enum eContactType {
    Unknown = 0,
    Telephone,
    Email,
    Fax
};
```

Note that we have a default value of `Unknown` represented by 0. This is important as it allows us to accommodate an initial unset value. Next, we define a mapper container that allows us to map each of the enumerated types to a descriptive string:

```
std::map<int, QString> Contact::contactTypeMapper = std::map<int, QString>
{
    { Contact::eContactType::Unknown, "" }
    , { Contact::eContactType::Telephone, "Telephone" }
    , { Contact::eContactType::Email, "Email" }
    , { Contact::eContactType::Fax, "Fax" }
};
```

When creating the new `EnumeratorDecorator`, we supply the default value (0 for `eContactType::Unknown`) along with the mapper:

```
contactType = static_cast<EnumeratorDecorator*>(addDataItem(new
EnumeratorDecorator(this, "contactType", "Contact Type", 0,
contactTypeMapper)));
```

Our client model is a little more complex, as it not only has data items but has child entities and collections too. However, the way we create and expose these things is very similar to what we have already seen.

client.h:

```
#ifndef CLIENT_H
#define CLIENT_H

#include <QObject>
#include <QtQml/QQmlListProperty>

#include <cm-lib_global.h>
#include <data/string-decorator.h>
#include <data/entity.h>
#include <data/entity-collection.h>
#include <models/address.h>
#include <models/appointment.h>
#include <models/contact.h>

namespace cm {
namespace models {

class CMLIBSHARED_EXPORT Client : public data::Entity
{
    Q_OBJECT
    Q_PROPERTY( cm::data::StringDecorator* ui_reference MEMBER
                                           reference CONSTANT )
```

```
    Q_PROPERTY( cm::data::StringDecorator* ui_name MEMBER name CONSTANT )
    Q_PROPERTY( cm::models::Address* ui_supplyAddress MEMBER
                                    supplyAddress CONSTANT )
    Q_PROPERTY( cm::models::Address* ui_billingAddress MEMBER
                                    billingAddress CONSTANT )
    Q_PROPERTY( QQmlListProperty<Appointment> ui_appointments READ
                        ui_appointments NOTIFY appointmentsChanged )
    Q_PROPERTY( QQmlListProperty<Contact> ui_contacts READ ui_contacts
                                        NOTIFY contactsChanged )

public:
    explicit Client(QObject* parent = nullptr);
    Client(QObject* parent, const QJsonObject& json);

    data::StringDecorator* reference{nullptr};
    data::StringDecorator* name{nullptr};
    Address* supplyAddress{nullptr};
    Address* billingAddress{nullptr};
    data::EntityCollection<Appointment>* appointments{nullptr};
    data::EntityCollection<Contact>* contacts{nullptr};

    QQmlListProperty<cm::models::Appointment> ui_appointments();
    QQmlListProperty<cm::models::Contact> ui_contacts();

signals:
    void appointmentsChanged();
    void contactsChanged();
};

}}

#endif
```

We expose the child entities as pointers to the derived type and the collections as pointers to a templated `EntityCollection`.

`client.cpp`:

```
#include "client.h"

using namespace cm::data;

namespace cm {
namespace models {

Client::Client(QObject* parent)
    : Entity(parent, "client")
```

```
{
    reference = static_cast<StringDecorator*>(addDataItem(new
                StringDecorator(this, "reference", "Client Ref")));
    name = static_cast<StringDecorator*>(addDataItem(new
                StringDecorator(this, "name", "Name")));
    supplyAddress = static_cast<Address*>(addChild(new Address(this),
                                "supplyAddress"));
    billingAddress = static_cast<Address*>(addChild(new Address(this),
                                "billingAddress"));
    appointments = static_cast<EntityCollection<Appointment>*>
    (addChildCollection(new EntityCollection<Appointment>(this,
                                "appointments")));
    contacts =
static_cast<EntityCollection<Contact>*>(addChildCollection(new
EntityCollection<Contact>(this, "contacts")));
}

Client::Client(QObject* parent, const QJsonObject& json)
    : Client(parent)
{
    update(json);
}

QQmlListProperty<Appointment> Client::ui_appointments()
{
    return QQmlListProperty<Appointment>(this,
appointments->derivedEntities());
}

QQmlListProperty<Contact> Client::ui_contacts()
{
    return QQmlListProperty<Contact>(this, contacts->derivedEntities());
}

}}
```

Adding child entities follows the same pattern as data items, but using the addChild() method. Note that we add more than one child of the same address type, but ensure that they have different key values to avoid duplicates and invalid JSON. Entity collections are added with addChildCollection() and other than being templated, they follow the same approach.

While it was a lot of work to create our entities and data items, creating models is really quite straightforward and now they all come packed with features that we wouldn't otherwise have had.

Before we can use our fancy new models in the UI, we need to register the types in `main.cpp` in `cm-ui`, including the data decorators that represent the data items. Remember to add the relevant `#include` statements first:

```
qmlRegisterType<cm::data::DateTimeDecorator>("CM", 1, 0,
"DateTimeDecorator");
qmlRegisterType<cm::data::EnumeratorDecorator>("CM", 1, 0,
"EnumeratorDecorator");
qmlRegisterType<cm::data::IntDecorator>("CM", 1, 0, "IntDecorator");
qmlRegisterType<cm::data::StringDecorator>("CM", 1, 0, "StringDecorator");

qmlRegisterType<cm::models::Address>("CM", 1, 0, "Address");
qmlRegisterType<cm::models::Appointment>("CM", 1, 0, "Appointment");
qmlRegisterType<cm::models::Client>("CM", 1, 0, "Client");
qmlRegisterType<cm::models::Contact>("CM", 1, 0, "Contact");
```

With that done, we'll create an instance of a client in `MasterController`, which we will use to populate data for new clients. This follows exactly the same pattern that we've used for adding the other controllers.

First, add the member variable to the private implementation of `MasterController`:

```
Client* newClient{nullptr};
```

Then, initialize it in the `Implementation` constructor:

```
newClient = new Client(masterController);
```

Third, add the accessor method:

```
Client* MasterController::newClient()
{
    return implementation->newClient;
}
```

Finally, add `Q_PROPERTY`:

```
Q_PROPERTY( cm::models::Client* ui_newClient READ newClient CONSTANT )
```

We now have an empty instance of a client available for consumption by the UI, specifically `CreateClientView`, which we will edit next. Begin by adding a shortcut property for the new client instance:

```
property Client newClient: masterController.ui_newClient
```

Remember that the properties should all be defined at the root Item level and that you need to `import CM 1.0` to get access to the registered types. This just enables us to use `newClient` as shorthand to access the instance rather than having to type out `masterController.ui_newClient` every time.

At this point, everything is hooked up ready for use, and you should be able to run the application and navigate to the new client view with no problems. The view isn't doing anything with the new client instance just yet, but it's happily sitting there ready for action. Now, let's look at how we can interact with it.

Custom TextBox

We'll start with the `name` data item of our client. Back when we worked with another `QString` property in our UI with the welcome message, we displayed it with the basic text component. This component is read only, so to view and edit our property, we will need to reach for something else. There are a couple of options in the base `QtQuick` module: `TextInput` and `TextEdit`. `TextInput` is for a single line of editable plain text, while `TextEdit` handles multiline blocks of text and also supports rich text. `TextInput` is ideal for our **name**.

Importing the `QtQuick.Controls` module makes additional text-based components like `Label`, `TextField`, and `TextArea` available. Label inherits and extends Text, `TextField` inherits and extends `TextInput` and `TextArea` inherits and extends `TextEdit`. The basic controls are enough for us at this stage, but be aware that these alternatives exist. If you find yourself trying to do something with one of the basic controls which it doesn't seem to support, then import `QtQuick.Controls` and take a look at its more powerful cousin. It may well have the functionality you are looking for.

Let's build on what we've learned and create a new reusable component. As usual, we'll begin by preparing the Style properties we'll need:

```
readonly property real sizeScreenMargin: 20

readonly property color colourDataControlsBackground: "#ffffff"
readonly property color colourDataControlsFont: "#131313"
readonly property int pixelSizeDataControls: 18
readonly property real widthDataControls: 400
readonly property real heightDataControls: 40
```

Next, create `StringEditorSingleLine.qml` in `cm/cm-ui/components`. It's not the most beautiful of names, but at least it's descriptive!

 It's generally helpful to use a prefix with custom QML views and components to help distinguish them from the built-in Qt components and avoid naming conflicts. If we were using that approach with this project, we could have called this component `CMTextBox` or something equally short and simple. Use whatever approach and conventions work for you, it makes no functional difference.

Edit `components.qrc` and `qmldir` as we did previously to make the new component available in our components module.

What we're trying to achieve with this component is as follows:

- To be able to pass in any `StringDecorator` property from any data model and view/edit the value
- View a descriptive label for the control as defined in the `ui_label` property of the `StringDecorator`
- View/edit the `ui_value` property of the `StringDecorator` in a `TextBox`
- If the window is wide enough, then the label and textbox are laid out horizontally
- If the window is not wide enough, then the label and textbox are laid out vertically

With these goals in mind, implement `StringEditorSingleLine`, as follows:

```
import QtQuick 2.9
import CM 1.0
import assets 1.0

Item {
    property StringDecorator stringDecorator

    height: width > textLabel.width + textValue.width ?
    Style.heightDataControls : Style.heightDataControls * 2

    Flow {
        anchors.fill: parent

        Rectangle {
            width: Style.widthDataControls
            height: Style.heightDataControls
            color: Style.colourBackground
            Text {
```

```
                id: textLabel
                anchors {
                    fill: parent
                    margins: Style.heightDataControls / 4
                }
                text: stringDecorator.ui_label
                color: Style.colourDataControlsFont
                font.pixelSize: Style.pixelSizeDataControls
                verticalAlignment: Qt.AlignVCenter
            }
        }

    Rectangle {
        id: background
        width: Style.widthDataControls
        height: Style.heightDataControls
        color: Style.colourDataControlsBackground
        border {
            width: 1
            color: Style.colourDataControlsFont
        }
        TextInput {
            id: textValue
            anchors {
                fill: parent
                margins: Style.heightDataControls / 4
            }
            text: stringDecorator.ui_value
            color: Style.colourDataControlsFont
            font.pixelSize: Style.pixelSizeDataControls
            verticalAlignment: Qt.AlignVCenter
        }
    }

    Binding {
        target: stringDecorator
        property: "ui_value"
        value: textValue.text
    }
    }
}
```

We begin with a public StringDecorator property (public because it is in the root Item element), which we can set from outside of the component.

We introduce a new kind of element—Flow—to lay out our label and textbox for us. Rather than always laying out content in a single direction like row or column, the Flow item will lay out its child elements side by side until it runs out of available space and then wraps them like words on a page. We tell it how much available space it has to play with by anchoring it to the root Item.

Next comes our descriptive label in a Text control and the editable value in a TextInput control. We embed both controls in explicitly sized rectangles. The rectangles help us align the elements and give us the opportunity to draw backgrounds and borders.

The Binding component establishes a dependency between the properties of two different objects; in our case, the TextInput control called textValue and the StringDecorator instance called stringDecorator. The target property defines the object we want to update, the property is the Q_PROPERTY we want to set, and value is the value we want to set it to. This is a key element that gives us true two-way binding. Without this, we will be able to view the value from the StringDecorator, but any changes we make in the UI will not update the value.

Back in CreateClientView, replace the old Text element with our new component and pass in the ui_name property:

```
StringEditorSingleLine {
    stringDecorator: newClient.ui_name
}
```

Now build and run the app, navigate to the **Create Client view**, and try editing the name:

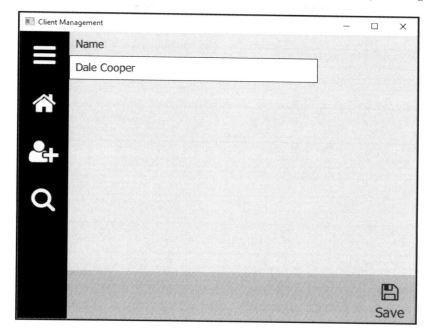

If you switch to the **Find Client view** and back again, you will see that the value is retained, demonstrating the updates are successfully being set in the string decorator.

Our newly bound view isn't exactly overflowing with data just yet, but over the coming chapters, we will add more and more to this view, so let's add a few finishing touches to prepare us.

Firstly, we only need to add another three or four properties to the view, and we'll run out of space as the default size we've set for the window is very small, so in MasterView bump the window size up to something comfortable for your display. I'll treat myself and go full HD at 1920 x 1080.

Even with a larger window to work with, we still need to prepare for the possibility of overflow, so we'll add our content to another new element called ScrollView. As its name suggests, it works in a similar way to flow and manages its content based on the space it has available to it. If the content exceeds the available space, it will present scrollbars for the user. It's also a very finger friendly control and on a touch screen, the user can just drag the content rather than having to fiddle around with a tiny scrollbar.

Although we only have one property currently, when we add more, we will need to lay them out so we'll add a column.

Finally, the controls are stuck to the bounds of the view, so we'll add a little gutter around the view and some spacing in the column.

The revised view should look as follows:

```
import QtQuick 2.9
import QtQuick.Controls 2.2
import CM 1.0
import assets 1.0
import components 1.0

Item {
    property Client newClient: masterController.ui_newClient

    Rectangle {
        anchors.fill: parent
        color: Style.colourBackground
    }

    ScrollView {
        id: scrollView
        anchors {
            left: parent.left
            right: parent.right
            top: parent.top
            bottom: commandBar. top
            margins: Style.sizeScreenMargin
        }
        clip: true
        Column {
            spacing: Style.sizeScreenMargin
            width: scrollView.width
            StringEditorSingleLine {
                stringDecorator: newClient.ui_name
                anchors {
                    left: parent.left
                    right: parent.right
                }
            }
        }
    }

    CommandBar {
        id: commandBar
```

```
        commandList:
masterController.ui_commandController.ui_createClientViewContextCommands
        }
    }
```

Build and run, and you should see the nice neat screen margin. You should also be able to resize the window from wide to narrow and see the string editor automatically adjust its layout accordingly.

Summary

This was a fairly hefty chapter, but we've covered arguably the most important element of any Line of Business application, and that is the data. We've implemented a framework of self-aware entities that can serialize themselves to and from JSON and started building data bound controls. We've designed and created our data models and are now entering the homeward stretch. In Chapter 6, *Unit Testing*, we'll show some love to our so far neglected unit test project and check that our entities are behaving as expected.

6
Unit Testing

In this chapter, we will take a look at a process that has really grown in popularity in the recent years—unit testing. We'll briefly talk about what it is and why we would want to do it before covering how to integrate it into our solution using Qt's very own unit testing tool, Qt Test. We will cover the following topics:

- Unit Testing principles
- The default Qt approach
- An alternative approach
- DataDecorator tests
- Entity tests
- Mocking

Unit testing

The essence of unit testing is to break an application down into its smallest functional blocks (units) and then test each unit with real-world scenarios within the scope of the initiative. For example, take a simple method that takes two signed integers and adds them together:

```
int add(intx, int y);
```

Some example scenarios can be as listed:

- Adding two positive numbers
- Adding two negative numbers
- Adding two zeroes
- Adding one positive and one negative number
- Adding zero and a positive number
- Adding zero and a negative number

We can write a test for each of these scenarios and then every time our code base changes (any code, not just our add() method), these tests can be executed to ensure that the code still behaves as expected. It is a really valuable tool to give you confidence that any code changes you make aren't having a detrimental effect on the existing functionality.

Historically, these tests would have been performed manually, but tooling exists that can enable us to write code to test code automatically, which sounds like a bit of a paradox, but it really works. Qt provides a tailored framework for unit testing Qt-based applications, called Qt Test, and that is what we will use.

 You can use other C++ testing frameworks such as Google test, which arguably offer more power and flexibility, particularly when used with Google mock, but can be a bit more fiddly to set up.

Test-driven development (TDD) takes unit testing to the next level and actually changes the way you write code in the first place. In essence, you write a test first. The test will initially fail (indeed, probably it won't even build) because you have no implementation. You then write the bare minimum of code it takes to make the test pass and then move on to writing the next test. You iteratively build out your implementation in this way until you have delivered the block of functionality required. Finally, you refactor the code to the required standard, using the completed unit tests to validate that the refactored code still behaves as expected. This is sometimes referred to as *Red-Green-Refactor*.

This isn't a book about unit testing, and it is certainly not about TDD, so we will be very loose with our approach, but it is a key part of modern application development, and it is important to know how it fits into your Qt projects.

We've demonstrated the mechanism for passing a simple piece of data (the welcome message) from our business logic project to our UI, so as always, starting as simply as possible, our first goal for this chapter is to write a rudimentary unit test for that behavior. Once done, we'll move on to test the data classes we implemented in the previous chapter.

The default Qt approach

When we created our `cm-tests` project, Qt Creator helpfully created a `ClientTests` class for us to use a starting point, containing a single test named `testCase1`. Let's dive straight in and execute this default test and see what happens. We'll then take a look at the code and discuss what's going on.

Switch the **Run** output to `cm-tests`, and compile and run:

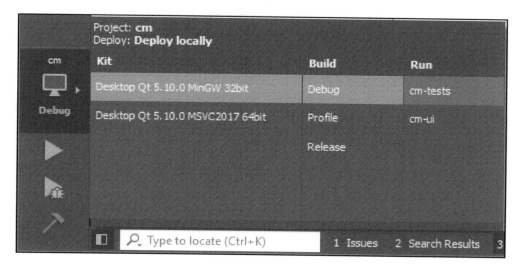

You won't see any fancy applications spring to life this time, but you will see some text in the **Application Output** pane in Qt Creator:

```
********* Start testing of ClientTests *********
Config: Using QtTest library 5.10.0, Qt 5.10.0 (i386-little_endian-ilp32
shared (dynamic) debug build; by GCC 5.3.0)
PASS   : ClientTests::initTestCase()
PASS   : ClientTests::testCase1()
PASS   : ClientTests::cleanupTestCase()
Totals: 3 passed, 0 failed, 0 skipped, 0 blacklisted, 0ms
********* Finished testing of ClientTests *********
```

We can see that three methods have been called, the second of which is our default unit test. The other two functions—initTestCase() and cleanupTestCase()—are special methods that execute before and after the suite of tests in the class, allowing you to set up any preconditions required to execute the tests and then perform any clean up afterward. All the three steps pass.

Now, in client-tests.cpp, add another method—testCase2()—which is the same as testCase1() but substitute the true condition for false. Note that the class declaration and method definitions are all in the same .cpp file, so you need to add the method in both places. Run the tests again:

```
********* Start testing of ClientTests *********
Config: Using QtTest library 5.10.0, Qt 5.10.0 (i386-little_endian-ilp32
shared (dynamic) debug build; by GCC 5.3.0)
PASS   : ClientTests::initTestCase()
PASS   : ClientTests::testCase1()
FAIL!  : ClientTests::testCase2() 'false' returned FALSE. (Failure)
..\..\cm\cm-tests\source\models\client-tests.cpp(37) : failure location
PASS   : ClientTests::cleanupTestCase()
Totals: 3 passed, 1 failed, 0 skipped, 0 blacklisted, 0ms
********* Finished testing of ClientTests *********
```

This time, you can see that testCase2() tried to verify that false was true, which of course it isn't, and our test fails, outputting our failure message in the process. initTestCase() and cleanupTestCase() are still executed at the beginning and end of the suite of tests.

Now we've seen what passing and failing tests look like, but what is actually going on?

We have a QObject derived class ClientTests, which implements an empty default constructor. We then have some methods declared as private Q_SLOTS. Much like Q_OBJECT, this is a macro that injects a bunch of clever boilerplate code for us, and much like Q_OBJECT, you don't need to worry about understanding its inner workings in order to use it. Each method in the class defined as one of these private slots is executed as a unit test.

The unit test methods then use the QVERIFY2 macro to verify a given boolean condition, namely that true is, well, true. If this fails, which we have engineered in testCase2, the helpful message failure will be output to the console.

If there is a QVERIFY2, then presumably there must be a QVERIFY1, right? Well, nearly, there is QVERIFY, which performs the same test but does not have the failure message parameter. Other commonly used macros are QCOMPARE, which verifies that two parameters of the same type are equivalent, and QVERIFY_EXCEPTION_THROWN, which verifies that an exception is thrown when a given expression is executed. This may sound odd, as we don't ideally want our code to throw exceptions. However, things aren't always ideal, and we should always write negative tests that verify how the code behaves when something does go wrong. A common example of this is where we have a method that accepts a pointer to an object as a parameter. We should write a negative test that verifies what happens if we pass in a nullptr (which is always a possibility, regardless of how careful you are). We may expect the code to happily ignore it and take no further action or we may want some sort of null argument exception to throw, which is where QVERIFY_EXCEPTION_THROWN comes in.

After the test case definitions, another macro QTEST_APPLESS_MAIN stubs out a main() hook to execute the tests and the final #include statement pulls in the .moc file produced by the build process. Every class that inherits from QObject will have a companion .moc file generated, containing all the magic metadata code created by Q_OBJECT and other associated macros.

Now, if you're thinking "why would you test if true is true and false is true?", then you absolutely wouldn't, this is a totally pointless pair of tests. The purpose of this exercise is just to look at how the default approach that Qt Creator has pulled together for us works, and it does work, but it has a few key failings that we will need to work to fix before we write a real test.

The first issue is that QTEST_APPLESS_MAIN creates a main() method in order to run our test cases in ClientTests. What happens when we write another test class? We'll have two main() methods and things won't go well. Another issue is that our test output is just piped to the **Application Output** pane. In a business environment, it is common to have build servers that pull application code, perform a build, run the unit test suite, and flag any test failures for investigation. In order for this to work, the build tool needs to be able to access the test output and can't read the **Application Output** pane in the IDE like a human can. Let's look at an alternative approach that solves these issues.

Custom approach

The custom approach we will take still applies the same basic concepts we've just discussed. At the heart of it, we will still have a test class that contains a suite of unit test methods to be executed. All we will do is supplement this with some additional boilerplate code to allow us to easily accommodate multiple test classes and pipe the output to files rather than the console.

Let's begin by adding a new class `TestSuite` to `cm-tests` in the source folder:

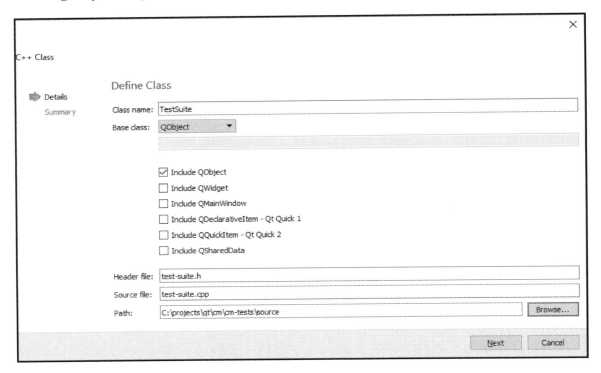

`test-suite.h:`

```
#ifndef TESTSUITE_H
#define TESTSUITE_H

#include <QObject>
#include <QString>
#include <QtTest/QtTest>

#include <vector>
```

```
    namespace cm {

    class TestSuite : public QObject
    {
        Q_OBJECT
    public:
        explicit TestSuite(const QString& _testName = "");
        virtual ~TestSuite();

        QString testName;
        static std::vector<TestSuite*>& testList();
    };

    }

    #endif
```

test-suite.cpp:

```
    #include "test-suite.h"

    #include <QDebug>

    namespace cm {

    TestSuite::TestSuite(const QString& _testName)
        : QObject()
        , testName(_testName)
    {
        qDebug() << "Creating test" << testName;
        testList().push_back(this);
        qDebug() << testList().size() << " tests recorded";
    }

    TestSuite::~TestSuite()
    {
        qDebug() << "Destroying test";
    }

    std::vector<TestSuite*>& TestSuite::testList()
    {
        static std::vector<TestSuite*> instance = std::vector<TestSuite*>();
        return instance;
    }

    }
```

Here, we are creating a base class that will be used for each of our test classes. There is generally a one-to-one relationship between a regular class and a test suite class, for example, the `Client` and `ClientTests` classes. Each derived instance of `TestSuite` adds itself to a shared vector. This can be a little confusing at first glance, so we are also writing some information out to the console using qDebug() so that you can follow what's going on. It will make more sense when we create our first class deriving from `TestSuite`.

Next, add a new C++ Source File `main.cpp`, again to the source folder:

`main.cpp`:

```cpp
#include <QtTest/QtTest>
#include <QDebug>

#include "test-suite.h"

using namespace cm;

int main(int argc, char *argv[])
{
    Q_UNUSED(argc);
    Q_UNUSED(argv);

    qDebug() << "Starting test suite...";
    qDebug() << "Accessing tests from " << &TestSuite::testList();
    qDebug() << TestSuite::testList().size() << " tests detected";

    int failedTestsCount = 0;

    for(TestSuite* i : TestSuite::testList()) {
        qDebug() << "Executing test " << i->testName;
        QString filename(i->testName + ".xml");
        int result = QTest::qExec(i, QStringList() << " " << "-o" <<
                                  filename << "-xunitxml");
        qDebug() << "Test result " << result;
        if(result != 0) {
            failedTestsCount++;
        }
    }

    qDebug() << "Test suite complete - " <<
        QString::number(failedTestsCount) << " failures detected.";

    return failedTestsCount;
}
```

This looks more complicated than it actually is because of the `qDebug()` statements added for information. We iterate through each of the registered test classes and use the static `QTest::qExec()` method to detect and run all tests discovered within them. A key addition, however, is that we create an XML file for each class and pipe out the results to it.

This mechanism solves our two problems. We now have a single `main()` method that will detect and run all of our tests, and we get a separate XML file containing output for each of our test suites. However, before you can build the project, you will need to revisit `client-tests.cpp` and either comment out or remove the `QTEST_APPLESS_MAIN` line, or we'll be back to the problem of multiple `main()` methods. Don't worry about the rest of `client-tests.cpp` for now; we'll revisit it later when we start testing our data classes.

Build and run now, and you'll get a different set of text in `Application Output`:

```
Starting test suite...
Accessing tests from 0x40b040
0 tests detected
Test suite complete - "0" failures detected.
```

Let's go ahead and implement our first `TestSuite`. We have a `MasterController` class that presents a message string to the UI, so let's write a simple test that verifies that the message is correct. We will need to reference code from `cm-lib` in the `cm-tests` project, so ensure that the relevant `INCLUDE` directives are added to `cm-tests.pro`:

```
INCLUDEPATH += source \
    ../cm-lib/source
```

Create a new companion test class called `MasterControllerTests` in `cm-tests/source/controllers`.

`master-controller-tests.h`:

```cpp
#ifndef MASTERCONTROLLERTESTS_H
#define MASTERCONTROLLERTESTS_H

#include <QtTest>

#include <controllers/master-controller.h>
#include <test-suite.h>

namespace cm {
namespace controllers {

class MasterControllerTests : public TestSuite
{
```

```
    Q_OBJECT

public:
    MasterControllerTests();

private slots:
    /// @brief Called before the first test function is executed
    void initTestCase();
    /// @brief Called after the last test function was executed.
    void cleanupTestCase();
    /// @brief Called before each test function is executed.
    void init();
    /// @brief Called after every test function.
    void cleanup();

private slots:
    void welcomeMessage_returnsCorrectMessage();

private:
    MasterController masterController;
};

}}

#endif
```

We've explicitly added the `initTestCase()` and `cleanupTestCase()` scaffolding methods so that there is no mystery as to where they come from. We've also added another couple of special scaffolding methods for completeness: `init()` and `cleanup()`. The difference is that these methods are executed before and after each individual test, as opposed to before and after the entire suite of tests.

 None of these methods are doing anything for us and are there just for future reference. They can safely be removed if you want to streamline things.

`master-controller-tests.cpp`:

```
#include "master-controller-tests.h"

namespace cm {
namespace controllers { // Instance

static MasterControllerTests instance;
```

```
MasterControllerTests::MasterControllerTests()
    : TestSuite( "MasterControllerTests" )
{
}
}


namespace controllers { // Scaffolding

void MasterControllerTests::initTestCase()
{
}

void MasterControllerTests::cleanupTestCase()
{
}

void MasterControllerTests::init()
{
}

void MasterControllerTests::cleanup()
{
}

}

namespace controllers { // Tests

void MasterControllerTests::welcomeMessage_returnsCorrectMessage()
{
    QCOMPARE( masterController.welcomeMessage(), QString("Welcome to the
Client Management system!") );
}

}}
```

We again have a single test, but this time, it actually serves some meaningful purpose. We want to test that when we instantiate a MasterController object and access its welcomeMessage method, it returns the message that we want, which will be **Welcome to the Client Management system!**.

Unlike the scaffolding methods, the naming of your tests is entirely down to preference. I tend to loosely follow the `methodIAmTesting_givenSomeScenario_doesTheCorrectThing` format, for example:

```
divideTwoNumbers_givenTwoValidNumbers_returnsCorrectResult()
divideTwoNumbers_givenZeroDivisor_throwsInvalidArgumentException()
```

We construct an instance of `MasterController` as a private member variable that we will use to test against. In the implementation, we specify the name of the test suite via the constructor, and we also create a static instance of the test class. This is the trigger that adds `MasterControllerTests` to the static vector we saw in the `TestSuite` class.

Finally, for the implementation of our test, we test the value of the `welcomeMessage` of our `masterController` instance with the message we want using the `QCOMPARE` macro. Note that because `QCOMPARE` is a macro, you won't get implicit typecasting, so you need to ensure that the types of the expected and actual results are the same. Here, we've achieved that by constructing a `QString` object from the literal text.

Run qmake, and build and run to see the results of our test in the **Application Output** pane:

```
Creating test "MasterControllerTests"
1 tests recorded
Starting test suite...
Accessing tests from 0x40b040
1 tests detected
Executing test "MasterControllerTests"
Test result 1
Test suite complete - "1" failures detected.
Destroying test
```

This begins with the registration of the `MasterControllerTests` class via the static instance. The `main()` method iterates the collection of registered test suites and finds one, then executes all the unit tests within that suite. The test suite contains one unit test that runs and promptly fails. This may seem to be less helpful than earlier as there is no indication as to which test failed or why. However, remember that this output is simply from the qDebug() statements we added for extra information; it is not the true output from the test execution. In `master-controller-tests.cpp` we instantiated the `TestSuite` with a `testName` parameter of `MasterControllerTests`, so the output will have been piped to a file named `MasterControllerTests.xml`.

Navigate to the `cm/binaries` folder and drill down through the folders to where we direct our project output for the selected configuration and in there, you will see `MasterControllerTests.xml`:

```
<testsuite name="cm::controllers::MasterControllerTests" tests="3"
failures="1" errors="0">
    <properties>
        <property name="QTestVersion" value="5.10.0"/>
        <property name="QtVersion" value="5.10.0"/>
        <property name="QtBuild" value="Qt 5.10.0 (i386-little_endian-
                ilp32 shared (dynamic) debug build; by GCC 5.3.0)"/>
    </properties>
    <testcase name="initTestCase" result="pass"/>
    <testcase name="welcomeMessage_returnsCorrectMessage"
                result="fail">
    <failure result="fail" message="Compared values are not the same Actual
(masterController.welcomeMessage) : "This is MasterController to Major Tom"
Expected (QString("Welcome to the Client Management system!")): "Welcome to
the Client Management system!""/>
    </testcase>
    <testcase name="cleanupTestCase" result="pass"/>
    <system-err/>
</testsuite>
```

Here, we have the full output from the tests, and you can see that the failure was because the welcome message we got from `masterController` was **This is MasterController to Major Tom**, and we expected **Welcome to the Client Management system!**.

`MasterController` is not behaving as expected, and we've found a bug, so head over to `master-controller.cpp` and fix the problem:

```
QString welcomeMessage = "Welcome to the Client Management system!";
```

Rebuild both projects, execute the tests again, and bask in the glory of a 100% pass rate:

```
Creating test "MasterControllerTests"
1 tests recorded
Starting test suite...
Accessing tests from 0x40b040
1 tests detected
Executing test "MasterControllerTests"
Test result 0
Test suite complete - "0" failures detected.
Destroying test
```

Now that we have the testing framework set up, let's test something a little more complex than a simple string message and validate the work we did in the last chapter.

DataDecorator tests

In `Chapter 5`, *Data*, we created various classes deriving from `DataDecorator`. Let's create companion test classes for each of those and test the following functionalities:

- Object construction
- Setting the value
- Getting the value as JSON
- Updating the value from JSON

In `cm-tests/source/data`, create the `DateTimeDecoratorTests`, `EnumeratorDecoratorTests`, `IntDecoratorTests`, and `StringDecoratorTests` classes.

Let's begin with the simplest suite, `IntDecoratorTests`. The tests will be broadly similar across the suites, so once we've written one suite, we will be able to copy most of it across to the other suites and then supplement as necessary.

`int-decorator-tests.h`:

```
#ifndef INTDECORATORTESTS_H
#define INTDECORATORTESTS_H

#include <QtTest>

#include <data/int-decorator.h>
#include <test-suite.h>

namespace cm {
namespace data {

class IntDecoratorTests : public TestSuite
{
    Q_OBJECT

public:
    IntDecoratorTests();

private slots:
    void constructor_givenNoParameters_setsDefaultProperties();
```

```cpp
        void constructor_givenParameters_setsProperties();
        void setValue_givenNewValue_updatesValueAndEmitsSignal();
        void setValue_givenSameValue_takesNoAction();
        void jsonValue_whenDefaultValue_returnsJson();
        void jsonValue_whenValueSet_returnsJson();
        void update_whenPresentInJson_updatesValue();
        void update_whenNotPresentInJson_updatesValueToDefault();
    };

}}

#endif
```

A common approach is to follow a "method as a unit" approach, where each method is the smallest testable unit in a class and then that unit is tested in multiple ways. So we begin by testing the constructor, both with and without parameters. The setValue() method should only do anything when we actually change the value, so we test both setting a different value and the same value. Next, we test that we can convert the decorator to a JSON value, both with a default value (0 in the case of an int) and with a set value. Finally, we perform a couple of tests against the update() method. If we pass in a JSON that contains the property, then we expect the value to be updated as per the JSON value. However, if the property is missing from the JSON, we expect the class to handle it gracefully and reset to a default value instead.

Note that we aren't explicitly testing the value() method. This is just a simple accessor method with no side effects, and we will be calling it in the other unit tests, so we will be indirectly testing it there. Feel free to create additional tests for it if you wish.

int-decorator-tests.cpp:

```cpp
    #include "int-decorator-tests.h"

    #include <QSignalSpy>

    #include <data/entity.h>

    namespace cm {
    namespace data { // Instance

    static IntDecoratorTests instance;

    IntDecoratorTests::IntDecoratorTests()
        : TestSuite( "IntDecoratorTests" )
    {
    }
```

```
}

namespace data { // Tests

void
IntDecoratorTests::constructor_givenNoParameters_setsDefaultProperties()
{
    IntDecorator decorator;
    QCOMPARE(decorator.parentEntity(), nullptr);
    QCOMPARE(decorator.key(), QString("SomeItemKey"));
    QCOMPARE(decorator.label(), QString(""));
    QCOMPARE(decorator.value(), 0);
}

void IntDecoratorTests::constructor_givenParameters_setsProperties()
{
    Entity parentEntity;
    IntDecorator decorator(&parentEntity, "Test Key", "Test Label",
                                                        99);
    QCOMPARE(decorator.parentEntity(), &parentEntity);
    QCOMPARE(decorator.key(), QString("Test Key"));
    QCOMPARE(decorator.label(), QString("Test Label"));
    QCOMPARE(decorator.value(), 99);
}

void IntDecoratorTests::setValue_givenNewValue_updatesValueAndEmitsSignal()
{
    IntDecorator decorator;
    QSignalSpy valueChangedSpy(&decorator,
                                &IntDecorator::valueChanged);
    QCOMPARE(decorator.value(), 0);
    decorator.setValue(99);
    QCOMPARE(decorator.value(), 99);
    QCOMPARE(valueChangedSpy.count(), 1);
}

void IntDecoratorTests::setValue_givenSameValue_takesNoAction()
{
    Entity parentEntity;
    IntDecorator decorator(&parentEntity, "Test Key", "Test Label",
                                                        99);
    QSignalSpy valueChangedSpy(&decorator,
                                &IntDecorator::valueChanged);
    QCOMPARE(decorator.value(), 99);
    decorator.setValue(99);
    QCOMPARE(decorator.value(), 99);
    QCOMPARE(valueChangedSpy.count(), 0);
}
```

```
void IntDecoratorTests::jsonValue_whenDefaultValue_returnsJson()
{
    IntDecorator decorator;
    QCOMPARE(decorator.jsonValue(), QJsonValue(0));
}
void IntDecoratorTests::jsonValue_whenValueSet_returnsJson()
{
    IntDecorator decorator;
    decorator.setValue(99);
    QCOMPARE(decorator.jsonValue(), QJsonValue(99));
}


void IntDecoratorTests::update_whenPresentInJson_updatesValue()
{
    Entity parentEntity;
    IntDecorator decorator(&parentEntity, "Test Key", "Test Label", 99);
    QSignalSpy valueChangedSpy(&decorator,
                               &IntDecorator::valueChanged);
    QCOMPARE(decorator.value(), 99);
    QJsonObject jsonObject;
    jsonObject.insert("Key 1", "Value 1");
    jsonObject.insert("Test Key", 123);
    jsonObject.insert("Key 3", 3);
    decorator.update(jsonObject);
    QCOMPARE(decorator.value(), 123);
    QCOMPARE(valueChangedSpy.count(), 1);
}


void IntDecoratorTests::update_whenNotPresentInJson_updatesValueToDefault()
{
    Entity parentEntity;
    IntDecorator decorator(&parentEntity, "Test Key", "Test Label",
                                                                 99);
    QSignalSpy valueChangedSpy(&decorator,
                               &IntDecorator::valueChanged);
    QCOMPARE(decorator.value(), 99);
    QJsonObject jsonObject;
    jsonObject.insert("Key 1", "Value 1");
    jsonObject.insert("Key 2", 123);
    jsonObject.insert("Key 3", 3);
    decorator.update(jsonObject);
    QCOMPARE(decorator.value(), 0);
    QCOMPARE(valueChangedSpy.count(), 1);
}

}}
```

Unit tests tend to follow an *Arrange > Act > Assert* pattern. Preconditions for the test are fulfilled first: variables are initialized, classes are configured, and so on. Then, an action is performed, generally calling the function being tested. Finally, the results of the action are checked. Sometimes one or more of these steps will not be necessary or may be merged with another, but that is the general pattern.

We begin testing the constructor by initializing a new `IntDecorator` without passing in any parameters and then test that the various properties of the object have been initialized to expected default values using QCOMPARE to match actual against expected values. We then repeat the test, but this time, we pass in values for each of the parameters and verify that they have been updated in the instance.

When testing the `setValue()` method, we need to check whether or not the `valueChanged()` signal is emitted. We can do this by connecting a lambda to the signal that sets a flag when called, as follows:

```
bool isCalled = false;
QObject::connect(&decorator, &IntDecorator::valueChanged, [&isCalled](){
    isCalled = true;
});

/*...Perform action...*/

QVERIFY(isCalled);
```

However, a much simpler solution we've used here is to use Qt's QSignalSpy class that keeps track of calls to a specified signal. We can then check how many times a signal has been called using the `count()` method.

The first `setValue()` test ensures that when we provide a new value that is different to the existing one, the value is updated and the `valueChanged()` signal is emitted once. The second test ensures that when we set the same value, no action is taken and the signal is not emitted. Note that we use an additional QCOMPARE call in both cases to assert that the value is what we expect it to be before the action is taken. Consider the following pseudo test:

1. Set up your class.
2. Perform an action.
3. Test that the value is 99.

If everything works as expected, step 1 sets the value to 0, step 2 takes the correct action and updates the value to 99, and step 3 passes because the value is 99. However, step 1 could be faulty and wrongly sets the value to 99, step 2 is not even implemented and takes no action, and yet step 3 (and the test) passes because the value is 99. With a QCOMPARE precondition after step 1, this is avoided.

The jsonValue() tests are simple equality checks, both with a default value and a set value.

Finally, with the update() tests, we construct a couple of JSON objects. In one object, we add an item that has the same key as our decorator object ("Test Key"), which we expect to be matched and the associated value (123) passed through to setValue(). In the second object, the key is not present. In both cases, we also add other extraneous items to ensure that the class can correctly ignore them. The post action checks are the same as for the setValue() tests.

The StringDecoratorTests class is essentially the same as IntDecoratorTests, just with a different value data type and default values of empty string " " rather than 0.

DateTimeDecorator also follows the same pattern, but with additional tests for the string formatting helper methods toIso8601String() and so on.

EnumeratorDecoratorTests performs the same tests but requires a little more setup because of the need for an enumerator and associated mapper. In the body of the tests, whenever we test value(), we also need to test valueDescription() to ensure that the two remain aligned. For example, whenever the value is eTestEnum::Value2, the valueDescription() must be Value 2. Note that we always use the enumerated values in conjunction with the value() checks and static_cast them to an int. Consider the following example:

```
QCOMPARE(decorator.value(), static_cast<int>(eTestEnum::Value2));
```

It may be tempting to make this much shorter by just using the raw int value:

```
QCOMPARE(decorator.value(), 2);
```

The problem with this approach, other than the number 2 having much less meaning to readers of the code than the enumerated `Value2`, is that the values of `eTestEnum` can change and render the test invalid. Consider this example:

```
enum eTestEnum {
    Unknown = 0,
    MyAmazingNewTestValue,
    Value1,
    Value2,
    Value3
};
```

Due to the insertion of `MyAmazingNewTestValue`, the numeric equivalent of `Value2` is actually now 3. Any tests that used the number 2 to represent `Value2` are now wrong, whereas those that use the more long-winded `static_cast<int>(eTestEnum::Value2)` are still correct.

Rebuild and run the new test suites, and they should all happily pass and give us renewed confidence in the code we wrote earlier. With the data decorators tested, let's move on to our data models next.

Entity Tests

Now that we have some confidence that our data decorators are working as expected, let's move up a level and test our data entities. The Client class is the root of our model hierarchy and by testing that, we can test our other models in the process.

We already have `client-tests.cpp` in `cm-tests/source/models` that Qt Creator added for us when we created the project, so go ahead and add a companion header file `client-tests.h`.

`client-tests.h`:

```
#ifndef CLIENTTESTS_H
#define CLIENTTESTS_H

#include <QtTest>
#include <QJsonObject>

#include <models/client.h>
#include <test-suite.h>

namespace cm {
```

```cpp
namespace models {

class ClientTests : public TestSuite
{
    Q_OBJECT

public:
    ClientTests();

private slots:
    void constructor_givenParent_setsParentAndDefaultProperties();
    void constructor_givenParentAndJsonObject_setsParentAndProperties();
    void toJson_withDefaultProperties_constructsJson();
    void toJson_withSetProperties_constructsJson();
    void update_givenJsonObject_updatesProperties();
    void update_givenEmptyJsonObject_updatesPropertiesToDefaults();

private:
    void verifyBillingAddress(const QJsonObject& jsonObject);
    void verifyDefaultBillingAddress(const QJsonObject& jsonObject);
    void verifyBillingAddress(Address* address);
    void verifyDefaultBillingAddress(Address* address);
    void verifySupplyAddress(const QJsonObject& jsonObject);
    void verifyDefaultSupplyAddress(const QJsonObject& jsonObject);
    void verifySupplyAddress(Address* address);
    void verifyDefaultSupplyAddress(Address* address);
    void verifyAppointments(const QJsonObject& jsonObject);
    void verifyDefaultAppointments(const QJsonObject& jsonObject);
    void verifyAppointments(const QList<Appointment*>& appointments);
    void verifyDefaultAppointments(const QList<Appointment*>&
appointments);
    void verifyContacts(const QJsonObject& jsonObject);
    void verifyDefaultContacts(const QJsonObject& jsonObject);
    void verifyContacts(const QList<Contact*>& contacts);
    void verifyDefaultContacts(const QList<Contact*>& contacts);

    QByteArray jsonByteArray = R"(
    {
        "reference": "CM0001",
        "name": "Mr Test Testerson",
        "billingAddress": {
            "building": "Billing Building",
            "city": "Billing City",
            "postcode": "Billing Postcode",
            "street": "Billing Street"
        },
        "appointments": [
          {"startAt": "2017-08-20T12:45:00", "endAt": "2017-08-
```

```
                    20T13:00:00", "notes": "Test appointment 1"},
            {"startAt": "2017-08-21T10:30:00", "endAt": "2017-08-
                    21T11:30:00", "notes": "Test appointment 2"}
        ],
        "contacts": [
            {"contactType": 2, "address":"email@test.com"},
            {"contactType": 1, "address":"012345678"}
        ],
        "supplyAddress": {
            "building": "Supply Building",
            "city": "Supply City",
            "postcode": "Supply Postcode",
            "street": "Supply Street"
        }
    })";
};


}}

#endif
```

There are three main areas we want to test here:

- Object construction
- Serialization to JSON
- Deserialization from JSON

As with previous suites, we have a couple of different flavors of test for each area—one with default data and one with specified data. In the private section, you will see numerous verify methods. They are to encapsulate the functionality required to test a particular subset of our data. The advantages of doing this are the same as with regular code: they make the unit tests much more concise and readable, and they allow easy reuse of the validation rules. Also, in the private section, we define a blob of JSON we can use to construct our Client instances. A `QByteArray`, as its name suggests, is simply an array of bytes that comes with numerous associated helpful functions:

```
void ClientTests::constructor_givenParent_setsParentAndDefaultProperties()
{
    Client testClient(this);
    QCOMPARE(testClient.parent(), this);
    QCOMPARE(testClient.reference->value(), QString(""));
    QCOMPARE(testClient.name->value(), QString(""));

    verifyDefaultBillingAddress(testClient.billingAddress);
    verifyDefaultSupplyAddress(testClient.supplyAddress);
```

```
    verifyDefaultAppointments(testClient.appointments-
                        >derivedEntities());
    verifyDefaultContacts(testClient.contacts->derivedEntities());
}

void
ClientTests::constructor_givenParentAndJsonObject_setsParentAndProperties()
{
    Client testClient(this,
QJsonDocument::fromJson(jsonByteArray).object());
    QCOMPARE(testClient.parent(), this);
    QCOMPARE(testClient.reference->value(), QString("CM0001"));
    QCOMPARE(testClient.name->value(), QString("Mr Test Testerson"));

    verifyBillingAddress(testClient.billingAddress);
    verifySupplyAddress(testClient.supplyAddress);
    verifyAppointments(testClient.appointments->derivedEntities());
    verifyContacts(testClient.contacts->derivedEntities());
}
```

Starting with the constructor tests, we instantiate a new Client, both with and without a JSON object. Note that in order to convert our JSON byte array to a `QJsonObject`, we need to pass it through a `QJsonDocument`. Once we have our initialized client, we check the name property and utilize the verify methods to test the state of the child objects for us. Regardless of whether or not we supply any initial data via a JSON object, we expect the `supplyAddress` and `billingAddress` objects to be created for us automatically as well as the appointments and contacts collections. By default, the collections should be empty:

```
void ClientTests::toJson_withDefaultProperties_constructsJson()
{
    Client testClient(this);
    QJsonDocument jsonDoc(testClient.toJson());
    QVERIFY(jsonDoc.isObject());
    QJsonObject jsonObject = jsonDoc.object();
    QVERIFY(jsonObject.contains("reference"));
    QCOMPARE(jsonObject.value("reference").toString(), QString(""));
    QVERIFY(jsonObject.contains("name"));
    QCOMPARE(jsonObject.value("name").toString(), QString(""));
    verifyDefaultBillingAddress(jsonObject);
    verifyDefaultSupplyAddress(jsonObject);
    verifyDefaultAppointments(jsonObject);
    verifyDefaultContacts(jsonObject);
}

void ClientTests::toJson_withSetProperties_constructsJson()
```

```
{
    Client testClient(this,
QJsonDocument::fromJson(jsonByteArray).object());
    QCOMPARE(testClient.reference->value(), QString("CM0001"));
    QCOMPARE(testClient.name->value(), QString("Mr Test Testerson"));

    verifyBillingAddress(testClient.billingAddress);
    verifySupplyAddress(testClient.supplyAddress);
    verifyAppointments(testClient.appointments->derivedEntities());
    verifyContacts(testClient.contacts->derivedEntities());
    QJsonDocument jsonDoc(testClient.toJson());
    QVERIFY(jsonDoc.isObject());
    QJsonObject jsonObject = jsonDoc.object();
    QVERIFY(jsonObject.contains("reference"));
    QCOMPARE(jsonObject.value("reference").toString(), QString("CM0001"));
    QVERIFY(jsonObject.contains("name"));
    QCOMPARE(jsonObject.value("name").toString(), QString("Mr Test
                                                Testerson"));
    verifyBillingAddress(jsonObject);
    verifySupplyAddress(jsonObject);
    verifyAppointments(jsonObject);
    verifyContacts(jsonObject);
}
```

The toJson() tests follow much the same pattern. We construct an object without a JSON object so that we get default values for all the properties and child objects. We then immediately construct a QJsonDocument using a call to toJson() in the constructor to get the serialized JSON object for us. The name property is tested, and then we utilize the verify methods once more. When constructing a **Client** using JSON, we add precondition checks to ensure that our properties have been set correctly before we again call toJson() and test the results:

```
void ClientTests::update_givenJsonObject_updatesProperties()
{
    Client testClient(this);
    testClient.update(QJsonDocument::fromJson(jsonByteArray).object());
    QCOMPARE(testClient.reference->value(), QString("CM0001"));
    QCOMPARE(testClient.name->value(), QString("Mr Test Testerson"));

    verifyBillingAddress(testClient.billingAddress);
    verifySupplyAddress(testClient.supplyAddress);
    verifyAppointments(testClient.appointments->derivedEntities());
    verifyContacts(testClient.contacts->derivedEntities());
}

void ClientTests::update_givenEmptyJsonObject_updatesPropertiesToDefaults()
```

```
{
    Client testClient(this,
QJsonDocument::fromJson(jsonByteArray).object());
    QCOMPARE(testClient.reference->value(), QString("CM0001"));
    QCOMPARE(testClient.name->value(), QString("Mr Test Testerson"));
    verifyBillingAddress(testClient.billingAddress);
    verifySupplyAddress(testClient.supplyAddress);
    verifyAppointments(testClient.appointments->derivedEntities());
    verifyContacts(testClient.contacts->derivedEntities());
    testClient.update(QJsonObject());
    QCOMPARE(testClient.reference->value(), QString(""));
    QCOMPARE(testClient.name->value(), QString(""));

    verifyDefaultBillingAddress(testClient.billingAddress);
    verifyDefaultSupplyAddress(testClient.supplyAddress);
    verifyDefaultAppointments(testClient.appointments-
                            >derivedEntities());
    verifyDefaultContacts(testClient.contacts->derivedEntities());
}
```

The update() tests are the same as toJson(), but the other way around. This time, we construct a JSON object using our byte array and pass it in to update(), checking the state of the model afterward.

The various private verification methods are all simply sets of checks that save us having to repeat the same code over and over. Consider the given example:

```
void ClientTests::verifyDefaultSupplyAddress(Address* address)
{
    QVERIFY(address != nullptr);
    QCOMPARE(address->building->value(), QString(""));
    QCOMPARE(address->street->value(), QString(""));
    QCOMPARE(address->city->value(), QString(""));
    QCOMPARE(address->postcode->value(), QString(""));
}
```

Build and run the unit tests again and the new **Client** tests should all happily pass.

Mocking

The unit tests we've written so far have all been pretty straightforward. While our **Client** class isn't totally independent, its dependencies are all other data models and decorators that it can own and change at will. However, looking forward, we will want to persist client data in a database. Let's look at a few examples of how this can work and discuss how the design decisions we make impact the testability of the Client class.

Open up the `scratchpad` project and create a new header `mocking.h` file, where we'll implement a dummy Client class to play around with.

`mocking.h`:

```cpp
#ifndef MOCKING_H
#define MOCKING_H

#include <QDebug>

class Client
{
public:
    void save()
    {
        qDebug() << "Saving Client";
    }
};

#endif
```

In `main.cpp`, `#include <mocking.h>`, update the `engine.load()` line to load the default `main.qml` if it doesn't already and add a few lines to spin up and save a dummy Client object:

```cpp
engine.load(QUrl(QStringLiteral("qrc:/main.qml")));

Client client;
client.save();
```

Build and run the app, ignore the window, and take a look at the **Application Output** console:

```
Saving Client
```

We have a way to ask a client to save itself, but it needs a database to save itself too. Let's encapsulate our database management functionality into a `DatabaseController` class. In mocking.h, add the following implementation before the Client class. Note that you need to forward declare Client:

```
class Client;

class DatabaseController
{
public:
    DatabaseController()
    {
        qDebug() << "Creating a new database connection";
    }

    void save(Client* client)
    {
        qDebug() << "Saving a Client to the production database";
    }
};
```

Now, edit the Client class:

```
class Client
{
    DatabaseController databaseController;

public:
    void save()
    {
        qDebug() << "Saving Client";
        databaseController.save(this);
    }
};
```

Back in `main.cpp`, replace the Client lines with the following:

```
qDebug() << "Running the production code...";

Client client1;
client1.save();
Client client2;
client2.save();
```

Now we create and save two clients rather than just one. Build, run, and check the console again:

```
Running the production code...
Creating a new database connection
Saving Client
Saving a Client to the production database
Creating a new database connection
Saving Client
Saving a Client to the production database
```

Okay, now we're saving our clients to the production database, but we're creating a new database connection for every client, which seems a bit wasteful. The Client class needs an instance of a `DatabaseController` to function, and this is known as a dependency. However, we do not need the Client to be responsible for creating that instance; we can instead pass—or *inject*—the instance in via the constructor and manage the lifetime of the `DatabaseController` elsewhere. This technique of Dependency Injection is a form of a broader design pattern known as **Inversion of Control**. Let's pass a reference to a shared `DatabaseController` into our Client class instead:

```cpp
class Client
{
    DatabaseController& databaseController;

public:
    Client(DatabaseController& _databaseController)
        : databaseController(_databaseController)
    {
    }

    void save()
    {
        qDebug() << "Saving Client";
        databaseController.save(this);
    }
};
```

Over in `main.cpp`:

```
qDebug() << "Running the production code...";

DatabaseController databaseController;

Client client1(databaseController);
client1.save();
Client client2(databaseController);
client2.save();
```

Build and run the following:

```
Running the production code...
Creating a new database connection
Saving Client
Saving a Client to the production database
Saving Client
Saving a Client to the production database
```

Great, we've got a highly-efficient decoupled system architecture in place; let's test it.

In `mocking.h`, add a pretend test suite after the Client class:

```
class ClientTestSuite
{
public:
    void saveTests()
    {
        DatabaseController databaseController;
        Client client1(databaseController);
        client1.save();
        Client client2(databaseController);
        client2.save();

        qDebug() << "Test passed!";
    }
};
```

In `main.cpp`, after saving `client2`, add the following to run our tests:

```
qDebug() << "Running the test code...";

ClientTestSuite testSuite;
testSuite.saveTests();
```

Build and run this:

```
Running the production code...
Creating a new database connection
Saving Client
Saving a Client to the production database
Saving Client
Saving a Client to the production database
Running the test code...
Creating a new database connection
Saving Client
Saving a Client to the production database
Saving Client
Saving a Client to the production database
Test passed!
```

Our test passed, fantastic! What's not to love about that? Well, the fact that we've just saved some test data to our production database.

If you don't already implement interfaces for the majority of your classes, you soon will after you start unit testing for this precise reason. It's not used solely to avoid nasty side effects like writing test data to a production database; it allows you to simulate all kinds of behaviors that make unit testing so much easier.

So, let's move our `DatabaseController` behind an interface. Replace the plain `DatabaseController` in `mocking.h` with a supercharged interface-driven version:

```cpp
class IDatabaseController
{
public:
    virtual ~IDatabaseController(){}
    virtual void save(Client* client) = 0;
};

class DatabaseController : public IDatabaseController
{
public:
    DatabaseController()
    {
        qDebug() << "Creating a new database connection";
    }

    void save(Client* client) override
    {
        qDebug() << "Saving a Client to the production database";
    }
```

```
};
```

With the interface in place, we can now create a fake or mock implementation:

```
class MockDatabaseController : public IDatabaseController
{
public:
    MockDatabaseController()
    {
        qDebug() << "Absolutely not creating any database connections
                                                    at all";
    }

    void save(Client* client) override
    {
        qDebug() << "Just testing - not saving any Clients to any
                                            databases";
    }
};
```

Next, tweak our Client to hold a reference to the interface rather than the concrete implementation:

```
class Client
{
    IDatabaseController& databaseController;

public:
    Client(IDatabaseController& _databaseController)
        : databaseController(_databaseController)
    {
    }

    void save()
    {
        qDebug() << "Saving Client";
        databaseController.save(this);
    }
};
```

Finally, change our test suite to create a mock controller to pass into the clients:

```
void saveTests()
{
    MockDatabaseController databaseController;
    ...
}
```

Build and run this:

```
Running the production code...
Creating a new database connection
Saving Client
Saving a Client to the production database
Saving Client
Saving a Client to the production database
Running the test code...
Absolutely not creating any database connections at all
Saving Client
Just testing - not saving any Clients to any databases
Saving Client
Just testing - not saving any Clients to any databases
Test passed!
```

Perfect. By programming to interfaces and injecting dependencies, we can safely test in isolation. We can create as many mock implementations as we need and use them to simulate whatever behavior we want, enabling us to test multiple different scenarios. Once you get more involved in mocking, it really pays to use a dedicated framework like **google mock**, as they save you the hassle of having to write a bunch of boilerplate mock classes. You can easily mock the interface once using helper macros and then specify behaviors for individual methods on the fly.

Summary

In this chapter, we've taken our first proper look at the unit testing project, and you've seen how to implement unit testing using the Qt Test framework. We've also discussed the importance of programming to interfaces to enable mocking. Now we have unit tests in place for our main data classes, so if we ever accidentally change the behavior, the unit tests will fail and highlight a potential problem for us.

As we discussed, this is not a book about test driven development, and we will sometimes cut corners and go against the advice in this chapter to keep the explanation of other concepts as simple as possible, but I do urge you to implement unit testing of some kind in your projects if you can, as it is a very valuable practice that is always worth the additional time investment. Some developers like the rigor of full-blown TDD, whereas others prefer to write unit test after the fact to verify the work they have done. Find an approach that works for you and your coding style.

We will return to the test project occasionally to demonstrate certain behaviors. but we'll certainly not be achieving 100% code coverage. Now that you have the test project and scaffolding in place, it's just a case of adding further test classes for each class you want to test. As long as you inherit from `TestSuite` in the same way as we have in this chapter, they will be automatically detected and executed when you run the test project.

In `Chapter 7`, *Persistence*, we'll go ahead and implement the functionality we just discussed—persisting our data to a database.

7
Persistence

In Chapter 5, *Data*, we created a framework for capturing and holding data in memory. However, this is only half of the story, as without persisting the data to some external destination, it will be lost as soon as we close the application. In this chapter, we will build on our earlier work and save our data to disk in a SQLite database so that it can live on beyond the lifetime of the application. Once saved, we will also build methods for finding, editing, and deleting our data. To get all these operations for free in our various data models, we will extend our data entities so that they can load and save to our database automatically, without us having to write boilerplate code in each class. We will cover the following topics:

- SQLite
- Primary keys
- Creating clients
- Finding clients
- Editing clients
- Deleting clients

SQLite

General purpose database technology has fragmented in the recent years with the explosion of NoSQL and Graph databases. However, SQL databases are still fighting fit and absolutely an appropriate choice in a lot of applications. Qt comes with built-in support for several SQL database driver types, and can be extended with custom drivers. MySQL and PostgreSQL are very popular open source SQL database engines and are both supported by default, but are intended for use on servers and require administration, which makes them a bit unnecessarily complicated for our purposes. Instead, we will use the much more lightweight SQLite, which is commonly used as a client-side database and is very popular in mobile applications due to its small footprint.

According to the official website at `https://www.sqlite.org`, "SQLite is a self-contained, high-reliability, embedded, full-featured, public-domain, SQL database engine. SQLite is the most used database engine in the world". Paired with Qt's SQL related classes, it's a snap to create a database and store your data.

The first thing we need to do is add the SQL module to our library project to get access to all of Qt's SQL goodness. In `cm-lib.pro`, add the following:

```
QT += sql
```

Next, we'll take onboard what we discussed in the previous chapter and implement our database-related functionality behind an interface. Create a new `i-database-controller.h` header file in `cm-lib/source/controllers`:

```
#ifndef IDATABASECONTROLLER_H
#define IDATABASECONTROLLER_H

#include <QJsonArray>
#include <QJsonObject>
#include <QList>
#include <QObject>
#include <QString>

#include <cm-lib_global.h>

namespace cm {
namespace controllers {

class CMLIBSHARED_EXPORT IDatabaseController : public QObject
{
    Q_OBJECT

public:
```

```
        IDatabaseController(QObject* parent)  : QObject(parent){}
        virtual ~IDatabaseController(){}

        virtual bool createRow(const QString& tableName, const QString& id,
                           const QJsonObject& jsonObject) const = 0;
        virtual bool deleteRow(const QString& tableName, const QString& id)
                                                    const = 0;
        virtual QJsonArray find(const QString& tableName, const QString&
                                             searchText) const = 0;
        virtual QJsonObject readRow(const QString& tableName, const
                                        QString& id) const = 0;
        virtual bool updateRow(const QString& tableName, const QString& id,
                           const QJsonObject& jsonObject) const = 0;
    };

    }}

    #endif
```

Here, we are implementing the four basic functions of (**Create**, **Read**, **Update**, and **Delete**) **CRUD**, which are relevant to persistent storage in general, not just SQL databases. We supplement these functions with an additional find() method that we will use to find an array of matching clients based on supplied search text.

Now, let's create a concrete implementation of the interface. Create a new DatabaseController class in cm-lib/source/controllers.

database-controller.h:

```
    #ifndef DATABASECONTROLLER_H
    #define DATABASECONTROLLER_H

    #include <QObject>
    #include <QScopedPointer>

    #include <controllers/i-database-controller.h>

    #include <cm-lib_global.h>

    namespace cm {
    namespace controllers {

    class CMLIBSHARED_EXPORT DatabaseController : public IDatabaseController
    {
        Q_OBJECT

    public:
```

```
    explicit DatabaseController(QObject* parent = nullptr);
    ~DatabaseController();

    bool createRow(const QString& tableName, const QString& id, const
                    QJsonObject& jsonObject) const override;
    bool deleteRow(const QString& tableName, const QString& id) const
                                                            override;
    QJsonArray find(const QString& tableName, const QString&
                                searchText) const override;
    QJsonObject readRow(const QString& tableName, const QString& id)
                                        const override;
    bool updateRow(const QString& tableName, const QString& id, const
                    QJsonObject& jsonObject) const override;

private:
    class Implementation;
    QScopedPointer<Implementation> implementation;
};

}}

#endif
```

Now, let's walk through each of the key implementation details in `database-controller.cpp`:

```
class DatabaseController::Implementation
{
public:
    Implementation(DatabaseController* _databaseController)
        : databaseController(_databaseController)
    {
        if (initialise()) {
            qDebug() << "Database created using Sqlite version: " +
                                            sqliteVersion();
            if (createTables()) {
                qDebug() << "Database tables created";
            } else {
                qDebug() << "ERROR: Unable to create database tables";
            }
        } else {
            qDebug() << "ERROR: Unable to open database";
        }
    }

    DatabaseController* databaseController{nullptr};
    QSqlDatabase database;
```

```
private:
    bool initialise()
    {
        database = QSqlDatabase::addDatabase("QSQLITE", "cm");
        database.setDatabaseName( "cm.sqlite" );
        return database.open();
    }

    bool createTables()
    {
        return createJsonTable( "client" );
    }

    bool createJsonTable(const QString& tableName) const
    {
        QSqlQuery query(database);
        QString sqlStatement = "CREATE TABLE IF NOT EXISTS " +
          tableName + " (id text primary key, json text not null)";

        if (!query.prepare(sqlStatement)) return false;

        return query.exec();
    }

    QString sqliteVersion() const
    {
        QSqlQuery query(database);

        query.exec("SELECT sqlite_version()");

        if (query.next()) return query.value(0).toString();

        return QString::number(-1);
    }
};
```

Starting with the private implementation, we've broken the initialization into two operations: initialise() instantiates a connection to a SQLite database with a file named cm.sqlite, and this operation will first create the database file for us if it doesn't already exist. The file will be created in the same folder as the application executable, createTables(), then creates any tables that we need which don't already exist in the database. Initially, we only need a single table named client, but this can be easily extended later. We delegate the actual work of creating the named table to the createJsonTable() method so that we can reuse it for multiple tables.

A conventional normalized relational database approach would be to persist each of our data models in their own table, with fields that match the properties of the class. Recall the model diagram back in Chapter 5, *Data*, which is as follows:

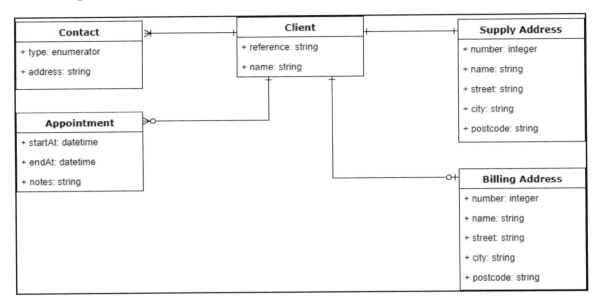

We could create a Client table with the "reference" and "name" fields, a contact table with the "type", "address", and other fields. However, we will instead leverage the JSON serialization code we've already implemented and implement a pseudo document-style database. We will utilize a single client table that will store a unique ID for the client along with the whole client object hierarchy serialized to JSON.

Finally, we've also added a sqliteVersion() utility method to identify which version of SQLite the database is using:

```
bool DatabaseController::createRow(const QString& tableName, const QString&
id, const QJsonObject& jsonObject) const
{
    if (tableName.isEmpty()) return false;
    if (id.isEmpty()) return false;
    if (jsonObject.isEmpty()) return false;

    QSqlQuery query(implementation->database);

    QString sqlStatement = "INSERT OR REPLACE INTO " + tableName + "
                          (id, json) VALUES (:id, :json)";
```

```
    if (!query.prepare(sqlStatement)) return false;

    query.bindValue(":id", QVariant(id));
    query.bindValue(":json",
  QVariant(QJsonDocument(jsonObject).toJson(QJsonDocument::Compact)));

    if(!query.exec()) return false;

    return query.numRowsAffected() > 0;
}

bool DatabaseController::deleteRow(const QString& tableName, const QString&
id) const
{
    if (tableName.isEmpty()) return false;
    if (id.isEmpty()) return false;

    QSqlQuery query(implementation->database);

    QString sqlStatement = "DELETE FROM " + tableName + " WHERE
                            id=:id";

    if (!query.prepare(sqlStatement)) return false;

    query.bindValue(":id", QVariant(id));

    if(!query.exec()) return false;

    return query.numRowsAffected() > 0;
}

QJsonObject DatabaseController::readRow(const QString& tableName, const
QString& id) const
{
    if (tableName.isEmpty()) return {};
    if (id.isEmpty()) return {};

    QSqlQuery query(implementation->database);

    QString sqlStatement = "SELECT json FROM " + tableName + " WHERE
                            id=:id";

    if (!query.prepare(sqlStatement)) return {};

    query.bindValue(":id", QVariant(id));

    if (!query.exec()) return {};
```

```
    if (!query.first()) return {};

    auto json = query.value(0).toByteArray();
    auto jsonDocument = QJsonDocument::fromJson(json);

    if (!jsonDocument.isObject()) return {};

    return jsonDocument.object();
}

bool DatabaseController::updateRow(const QString& tableName, const QString&
id, const QJsonObject& jsonObject) const
{
    if (tableName.isEmpty()) return false;
    if (id.isEmpty()) return false;
    if (jsonObject.isEmpty()) return false;

    QSqlQuery query(implementation->database);

    QString sqlStatement = "UPDATE " + tableName + " SET json=:json
                           WHERE id=:id";

    if (!query.prepare(sqlStatement)) return false;

    query.bindValue(":id", QVariant(id));
    query.bindValue(":json",
  QVariant(QJsonDocument(jsonObject).toJson(QJsonDocument::Compact)));

    if(!query.exec()) return false;

    return query.numRowsAffected() > 0;
}
```

The CRUD operations are all based around the `QSqlQuery` class and prepared `sqlStatements`. In all cases, we first perform some perfunctory checks on the parameters to ensure that we're not trying to do something silly. We then concatenate the table name into a SQL string, representing parameters with the `:myParameter` syntax. After preparing the statement, parameters are subsequently substituted in using the `bindValue()` method on the query object.

When creating, deleting, or updating rows, we simply return a `true`/`false` success indicator on query execution. Assuming that the query prepares and executes without error, we check that the number of rows affected by the operation is greater than 0. The read operation returns a JSON object parsed from the JSON text stored in the matching record. If no record is found or if the JSON cannot be parsed, then we return a default JSON object:

```
QJsonArray DatabaseController::find(const QString& tableName, const
QString& searchText) const
{
    if (tableName.isEmpty()) return {};
    if (searchText.isEmpty()) return {};

    QSqlQuery query(implementation->database);

    QString sqlStatement = "SELECT json FROM " + tableName + " where
                        lower(json) like :searchText";

    if (!query.prepare(sqlStatement)) return {};

    query.bindValue(":searchText", QVariant("%" + searchText.toLower()
                                            + "%"));

    if (!query.exec()) return {};

    QJsonArray returnValue;

    while ( query.next() ) {
        auto json = query.value(0).toByteArray();
        auto jsonDocument = QJsonDocument::fromJson(json);
        if (jsonDocument.isObject()) {
            returnValue.append(jsonDocument.object());
        }
    }

    return returnValue;
}
```

Finally, the `find()` method does essentially the same thing as the CRUD operations but compiles an array of JSON objects as there may be more than one match. Note that we use the `like` keyword in the SQL statement, combined with the `%` wildcard character, to find any JSON that contains the search text. We also convert both sides of the comparison to lowercase to make the search effectively case-insensitive.

Primary keys

Integral to most of these operations is an ID parameter used as the primary key in our table. To support the persistence of our entities using this new database controller, we need to add a property to our `Entity` class that uniquely identifies an instance of that entity.

In `entity.cpp`, add a member variable to `Entity::Implementation`:

```
QString id;
```

Then, initialize it in the constructor:

```
Implementation(Entity* _entity, IDatabaseController* _databaseController,
const QString& _key)
    : entity(_entity)
    , databaseController(_databaseController)
    , key(_key)
    , id(QUuid::createUuid().toString())
{
}
```

When we instantiate a new `Entity`, we need to generate a new unique ID, and we use the **QUuid** class to this for us with the `createUuid()` method. A **Universally Unique Identifier (UUID)** is essentially a randomly generated number that we then convert to a string in the "{xxxxxxxx-xxxx-xxxx-xxxx-xxxxxxxxxxxx}" format, where "x" is a hex digit. You will need to `#include <QUuid>`.

Next, provide a public accessor method for it:

```
const QString& Entity::id() const
{
    return implementation->id;
}
```

The challenge now is that if we are creating an `Entity` that already has an ID (for example, loading a client from the database), we need some mechanism for overwriting the generated ID value with the known value. We'll do this in the `update()` method:

```
void Entity::update(const QJsonObject& jsonObject)
{
    if (jsonObject.contains("id")) {
        implementation->id = jsonObject.value("id").toString();
    }

    ...


}
```

Similarly, when we serialize the object to JSON, we need to include the ID too:

```
QJsonObject Entity::toJson() const
{
    QJsonObject returnValue;
    returnValue.insert("id", implementation->id);
    ...
}
```

Great! This gives us automatically generated unique IDs for all of our data models, which we can use as the primary key in our database table. However, a common usecase with database tables is that there is actually an existing field that is a great candidate for use as a primary key, for example, a National Insurance or Social Security number, an account reference, or site ID. Let's add a mechanism for specifying a data decorator to use as the ID that will override the default UUID, if set.

In our `Entity` class, add a new private member in `Implementation`:

```
class Entity::Implementation
{
    ...
    StringDecorator* primaryKey{nullptr};
    ...
}
```

You will need to `#include` the `StringDecorator` header. Add a protected mutator method to set it:

```
void Entity::setPrimaryKey(StringDecorator* primaryKey)
{
    implementation->primaryKey = primaryKey;
}
```

We can then tweak our `id()` method to return us the primary key value if appropriate, otherwise default to the generated UUID value:

```
const QString& Entity::id() const
{
    if(implementation->primaryKey != nullptr &&
!implementation->primaryKey->value().isEmpty()) {
        return implementation->primaryKey->value();
    }
    return implementation->id;
}
```

Then, in the `client.cpp` constructor, after we have instantiated all the data decorators, we can specify that we want to use the reference field as our primary key:

```
Client::Client(QObject* parent)
    : Entity(parent, "client")
{
    ...

    setPrimaryKey(reference);
}
```

Let's add a couple of tests to verify this behavior. We'll verify that if a reference value is set, the `id()` method returns that value, otherwise it returns a generated UUID loosely of the "{xxxxxxxx-xxxx-xxxx-xxxx-xxxxxxxxxxxx}" format.

In `client-tests.h` of the `cm-tests` project, add two new tests in the private slots scope:

```
void id_givenPrimaryKeyWithNoValue_returnsUuid();
void id_givenPrimaryKeyWithValue_returnsPrimaryKey();
```

Then, implement the tests in `client-tests.cpp`:

```
void ClientTests::id_givenPrimaryKeyWithNoValue_returnsUuid()
{
    Client testClient(this);

    // Using individual character checks
```

```
    QCOMPARE(testClient.id().left(1), QString("{"));
    QCOMPARE(testClient.id().mid(9, 1), QString("-"));
    QCOMPARE(testClient.id().mid(14, 1), QString("-"));
    QCOMPARE(testClient.id().mid(19, 1), QString("-"));
    QCOMPARE(testClient.id().mid(24, 1), QString("-"));
    QCOMPARE(testClient.id().right(1), QString("}"));

    // Using regular expression pattern matching
    QVERIFY(QRegularExpression("\\{.{8}-(.{4})-(.{4})-(.
                        {12})\\}").match(testClient.id()).hasMatch());
}

void ClientTests::id_givenPrimaryKeyWithValue_returnsPrimaryKey()
{
    Client testClient(this,
QJsonDocument::fromJson(jsonByteArray).object());
    QCOMPARE(testClient.reference->value(), QString("CM0001"));
    QCOMPARE(testClient.id(), testClient.reference->value());
}
```

Note that the checks are effectively performed twice in the first test just to demonstrate a couple of different approaches you can take. First, we check using individual character matches ('{', '-', and '}'), which is quite long-winded but easy for other developers to read and understand. Then, we perform the check again using Qt's regular expression helper class. This is much shorter but more difficult to parse for normal humans who don't speak regular expression syntax.

Build and run the tests, and they should validate the changes we have just implemented.

Creating clients

Let's put our new infrastructure to use and wire up the CreateClientView. If you remember, we present a save command that when clicked on, calls onCreateClientSaveExecuted() on CommandController. In order to be able to perform anything useful, CommandController needs visibility of the client instance to be serialized and saved, and an implementation of the IDatabaseController interface to perform the create operation for us.

Inject them into the constructor in `command-controller.h`, including any necessary headers:

```
explicit CommandController(QObject* _parent = nullptr, IDatabaseController*
databaseController = nullptr, models::Client* newClient = nullptr);
```

As we've seen a few times now, add the member variables to `Implementation`:

```
IDatabaseController* databaseController{nullptr};
Client* newClient{nullptr};
```

Pass them through the `CommandController` constructor to the Implementation constructor:

```
Implementation(CommandController* _commandController, IDatabaseController*
_databaseController, Client* _newClient)
    : commandController(_commandController)
    , databaseController(_databaseController)
    , newClient(_newClient)
{
    ...
}

CommandController::CommandController(QObject* parent, IDatabaseController*
databaseController, Client* newClient)
    : QObject(parent)
{
    implementation.reset(new Implementation(this, databaseController,
newClient));
}
```

Now we can update the `onCreateClientSaveExecuted()` method to create our new client:

```
void CommandController::onCreateClientSaveExecuted()
{
    qDebug() << "You executed the Save command!";

implementation->databaseController->createRow(implementation->newClient->ke
y(), implementation->newClient->id(), implementation->newClient->toJson());

    qDebug() << "New client saved.";
}
```

Our client instance provides us with all the information we need to be able to save it to the database, and the database controller performs the database interactions.

Our CommandController is now ready, but we're not actually injecting the database controller or new client in yet, so head over to master-controller.cpp and add an instance of a DatabaseController as we did with CommandController and NavigationController. Add a private member, accessor method, and Q_PROPERTY.

In the Implementation constructor, we need to ensure that we initialize the new client and DatabaseController before we initialize the CommandController, and then pass the pointers through:

```
Implementation(MasterController* _masterController)
    : masterController(_masterController)
{
    databaseController = new DatabaseController(masterController);
    navigationController = new NavigationController(masterController);
    newClient = new Client(masterController);
    commandController = new CommandController(masterController,
databaseController, newClient);
}
```

Build and run cm-ui, and you should see messages in the **Application Output** from the newly instantiated DatabaseController, telling you that it has created the database and table:

```
Database created using Sqlite version: 3.20.1
Database tables created
```

Take a look at the output folder where your binaries are, and you will see a new cm.sqlite file.

If you navigate to **Create Client View**, enter a name, and click on the **Save** button, you will see further output, confirming that the new client has been saved successfully:

```
You executed the Save command!
New client saved
```

Let's take a look inside our database and see what work has been done for us. There are several SQLite browsing applications and web browser plugins available, but the one I tend to use is found at `http://sqlitebrowser.org/`. Download and install this, or any other client of your choice for your operating system, and open the `cm.sqlite` file:

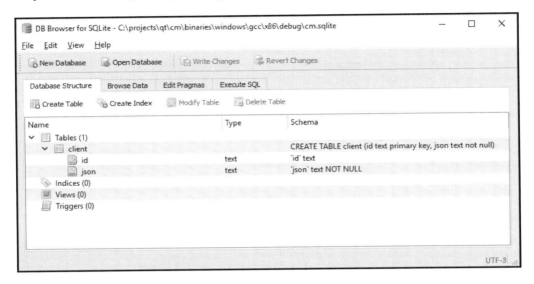

You will see that we have a **client** table, just as we asked for, with two fields: **id** and **json**. **Browse Data** for the **client** table, and you will see our newly created record with the **name** property we entered on the UI:

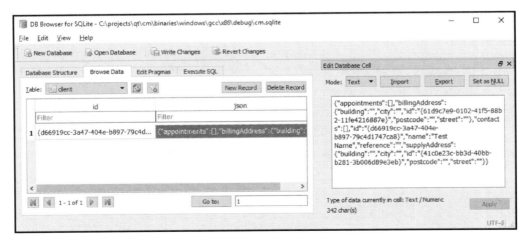

Fantastic, we have created our first client in the database. Note that the `DatabaseController` initialization methods are idempotent, so you can launch the application again and the existing database will not be affected. Similarly, if you manually delete the `cm.sqlite` file, then launching the application will create a new version for you (without the old data), which is a simple way of deleting test data.

Let's make a quick tweak to add the `reference` property of the client. In `CreateClientView`, duplicate the `StringEditorSingleLine` component bound to `ui_name`, and bind the new control to `ui_reference`. Build, run, and create a new client:

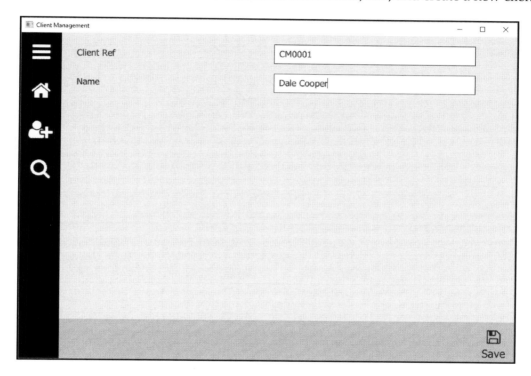

Our new client happily uses the specified client reference as the unique primary key:

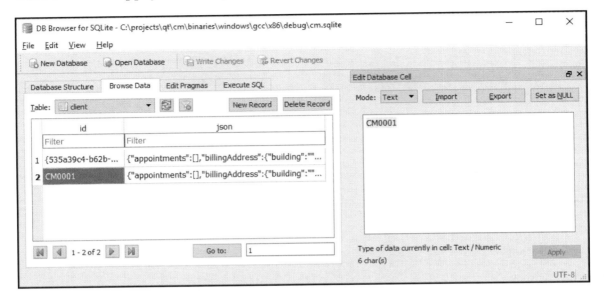

Panels

Now, let's flesh out our `CreateClientView` a little so that we can actually save some meaningful data rather than just a bunch of empty strings. We still have lots of fields to add in, so we'll break things up a little, and also visually separate the data from the different models, by encapsulating them in discreet panels with descriptive titles and a drop shadow to give our UI a bit of pizzazz:

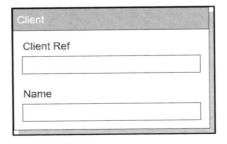

We'll begin by creating a generic panel component. Create a new QML file in `cm-ui/components` named `Panel.qml`. Update `components.qrc` and `qmldir`, as we have done for all the other components:

```
import QtQuick 2.9
import assets 1.0

Item {
    implicitWidth: parent.width
    implicitHeight: headerBackground.height +
    contentLoader.implicitHeight + (Style.sizeControlSpacing * 2)
    property alias headerText: title.text
    property alias contentComponent: contentLoader.sourceComponent

    Rectangle {
        id: shadow
        width: parent.width
        height: parent.height
        x: Style.sizeShadowOffset
        y: Style.sizeShadowOffset
        color: Style.colourShadow
    }

    Rectangle {
        id: headerBackground
        anchors {
            top: parent.top
            left: parent.left
            right: parent.right
        }
        height: Style.heightPanelHeader
        color: Style.colourPanelHeaderBackground

        Text {
            id: title
            text: "Set Me!"
            anchors {
                fill: parent
                margins: Style.heightDataControls / 4
            }
            color: Style.colourPanelHeaderFont
            font.pixelSize: Style.pixelSizePanelHeader
            verticalAlignment: Qt.AlignVCenter
        }
    }

    Rectangle {
```

```
                id: contentBackground
                anchors {
                    top: headerBackground.bottom
                    left: parent.left
                    right: parent.right
                    bottom: parent.bottom
                }
                color: Style.colourPanelBackground

                Loader {
                    id: contentLoader
                    anchors {
                        left: parent.left
                        right: parent.right
                        top: parent.top
                        margins: Style.sizeControlSpacing
                    }
                }
            }
        }
    }
```

This is an extremely dynamic component. Unlike our other components, where we pass in a string or maybe even a custom class, here we are passing in the entire contents of the panel. We achieve this using a `Loader` component, which loads a QML subtree on demand. We alias the `sourceComponent` property so that calling elements can inject their desired content at runtime.

Due to the dynamic nature of the content, we can't set the component to be a fixed size, so we leverage the `implicitWidth` and `implicitHeight` properties to tell parent elements how large the component wants to be based on the size of the title bar plus the size of the dynamic content.

To render the shadow, we draw a simple `Rectangle`, ensuring that it is rendered first by placing it near the top of the file. We then use the x and y properties to offset it from the rest of the elements, moving it slightly across and down. The remaining `Rectangle` elements for the header strip and panel background are then drawn over the top of the shadow.

To support the styling here, we need to add a collection of new `Style` properties:

```
readonly property real sizeControlSpacing: 10

readonly property color colourPanelBackground: "#ffffff"
readonly property color colourPanelBackgroundHover: "#ececec"
readonly property color colourPanelHeaderBackground: "#131313"
readonly property color colourPanelHeaderFont: "#ffffff"
readonly property color colourPanelFont: "#131313"
readonly property int pixelSizePanelHeader: 18
readonly property real heightPanelHeader: 40
readonly property real sizeShadowOffset: 5
readonly property color colourShadow: "#dedede"
```

Next, let's add a component for address editing so that we can reuse it for both the supply and billing addresses. Create a new QML file in `cm-ui/components` named `AddressEditor.qml`. Update `components.qrc` and `qmldir` as earlier.

We'll use our new `Panel` component as the root element and add an `Address` property, so that we can pass in an arbitrary data model to bind to:

```
import QtQuick 2.9
import CM 1.0
import assets 1.0

Panel {
    property Address address

    contentComponent:
        Column {
            id: column
            spacing: Style.sizeControlSpacing
            StringEditorSingleLine {
                stringDecorator: address.ui_building
                anchors {
                    left: parent.left
                    right: parent.right
                }
            }
            StringEditorSingleLine {
                stringDecorator: address.ui_street
                anchors {
                    left: parent.left
                    right: parent.right
                }
            }
            StringEditorSingleLine {
```

```
                    stringDecorator: address.ui_city
                    anchors {
                        left: parent.left
                        right: parent.right
                    }
                }
                StringEditorSingleLine {
                    stringDecorator: address.ui_postcode
                    anchors {
                        left: parent.left
                        right: parent.right
                    }
                }
            }
        }
    }
}
```

Here, you can see the flexibility of our new `Panel` component in action, thanks to the embedded `Loader` element. We can pass in whatever QML content we want, and it will be presented in the panel.

Finally, we can update our `CreateClientView` to add our new refactored address components. We'll also move the client controls onto their own panel:

```
import QtQuick 2.9
import QtQuick.Controls 2.2
import CM 1.0
import assets 1.0
import components 1.0

Item {
    property Client newClient: masterController.ui_newClient

    Column {
        spacing: Style.sizeScreenMargin
        anchors {
            left: parent.left
            right: parent.right
            top: parent.top
            margins: Style.sizeScreenMargin
        }
        Panel {
            headerText: "Client Details"
            contentComponent:
                Column {
                    spacing: Style.sizeControlSpacing
                    StringEditorSingleLine {
                        stringDecorator: newClient.ui_reference
```

```
                    anchors {
                        left: parent.left
                        right: parent.right
                    }
                }
                StringEditorSingleLine {
                    stringDecorator: newClient.ui_name
                    anchors {
                        left: parent.left
                        right: parent.right
                    }
                }
            }
        }
        AddressEditor {
            address: newClient.ui_supplyAddress
            headerText: "Supply Address"
        }
        AddressEditor {
            address: newClient.ui_billingAddress
            headerText: "Billing Address"
        }
    }
    CommandBar {
        commandList:
masterController.ui_commandController.ui_createClientViewContextCommands
    }
}
```

Before we build and run, we just need to tweak the background color of our
`StringEditorSingleLine textLabel` so that it matches the panels they are now
displayed on:

```
Rectangle {
    width: Style.widthDataControls
    height: Style.heightDataControls
    color: Style.colourPanelBackground
    Text {
        id: textLabel
        ...
    }
}
```

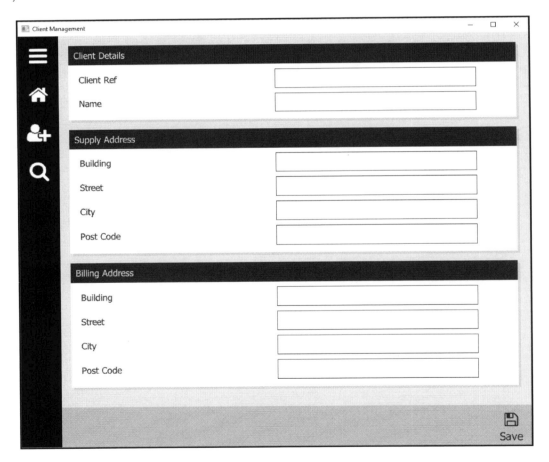

Go ahead and create a new client and check the database. You should now see the supply and billing address details successfully saved. We've now got the C in our CRUD operational, so let's move on to the 'R'.

Finding clients

We've just successfully saved our first clients to the database, so let's now look at how we can find and view that data. We'll encapsulate our searching functionality in a dedicated class in cm-lib, so go ahead and create a new class named ClientSearch in cm-lib/source/models.

client-search.h:

```
#ifndef CLIENTSEARCH_H
#define CLIENTSEARCH_H

#include <QScopedPointer>

#include <cm-lib_global.h>
#include <controllers/i-database-controller.h>
#include <data/string-decorator.h>
#include <data/entity.h>
#include <data/entity-collection.h>
#include <models/client.h>

namespace cm {
namespace models {

class CMLIBSHARED_EXPORT ClientSearch : public data::Entity
{
    Q_OBJECT
    Q_PROPERTY( cm::data::StringDecorator* ui_searchText READ
                                          searchText CONSTANT )
    Q_PROPERTY( QQmlListProperty<cm::models::Client> ui_searchResults
                READ ui_searchResults NOTIFY searchResultsChanged )

public:
    ClientSearch(QObject* parent = nullptr,
    controllers::IDatabaseController* databaseController = nullptr);
    ~ClientSearch();

    data::StringDecorator* searchText();
    QQmlListProperty<Client> ui_searchResults();
    void search();
```

```
    signals:
        void searchResultsChanged();

    private:
        class Implementation;
        QScopedPointer<Implementation> implementation;
    };

    }}

    #endif
```

client-search.cpp:

```
    #include "client-search.h"
    #include <QDebug>

    using namespace cm::controllers;
    using namespace cm::data;

    namespace cm {
    namespace models {

    class ClientSearch::Implementation
    {
    public:
        Implementation(ClientSearch* _clientSearch, IDatabaseController*
                                                    _databaseController)
            : clientSearch(_clientSearch)
            , databaseController(_databaseController)
        {
        }

        ClientSearch* clientSearch{nullptr};
        IDatabaseController* databaseController{nullptr};
        data::StringDecorator* searchText{nullptr};
        data::EntityCollection<Client>* searchResults{nullptr};
    };

    ClientSearch::ClientSearch(QObject* parent, IDatabaseController*
    databaseController)
        : Entity(parent, "ClientSearch")
    {
        implementation.reset(new Implementation(this, databaseController));
        implementation->searchText =
    static_cast<StringDecorator*>(addDataItem(new StringDecorator(this,
    "searchText", "Search Text")));
        implementation->searchResults =
```

```
static_cast<EntityCollection<Client>*>(addChildCollection(new
EntityCollection<Client>(this, "searchResults")));

    connect(implementation->searchResults,
&EntityCollection<Client>::collectionChanged, this,
&ClientSearch::searchResultsChanged);
}

ClientSearch::~ClientSearch()
{
}

StringDecorator* ClientSearch::searchText()
{
    return implementation->searchText;
}

QQmlListProperty<Client> ClientSearch::ui_searchResults()
{
    return QQmlListProperty<Client>(this,
implementation->searchResults->derivedEntities());
}

void ClientSearch::search()
{
    qDebug() << "Searching for " << implementation->searchText->value() <<
"...";
}

}}
```

We need to capture some text from the user, search the database using that text, and display the results as a list of matching clients. We accommodate the text using a `StringDecorator`, implement a `search()` method to perform the search for us, and finally, add an `EntityCollection<Client>` to store the results. One additional point of interest here is that we need to signal to the UI when the search results have changed so that it knows that it needs to rebind the list. To do this, we notify using the signal `searchResultsChanged()`, and we connect this signal directly to the `collectionChanged()` signal built into `EntityCollection`. Now, whenever the list that is hidden away in `EntityCollection` is updated, the UI will be automatically notified of the change and will redraw itself as needed.

Next, add an instance of `ClientSearch` to `MasterController`, just as we did for the new client model. Add a private member variable of the `ClientSearch*` type named `clientSearch`, and initialize it in the `Implementation` constructor. Remember to pass the `databaseController` dependency to the constructor. Now that we are passing more and more dependencies, we need to be careful about the initialization order. `ClientSearch` has a dependency on `DatabaseController`, and when we come to implement our search commands in `CommandController`, that will have a dependency on `ClientSearch`. So ensure that you initialize `DatabaseController` before `ClientSearch` and that `CommandController` comes after both of them. To finish off the changes to `MasterController`, add a `clientSearch()` accessor method and a `Q_PROPERTY` named `ui_clientSearch`.

As usual, we need to register the new class in the QML subsystem before we can use it in the UI. In `main.cpp`, `#include <models/client-search.h>` and register the new type:

```
qmlRegisterType<cm::models::ClientSearch>("CM", 1, 0, "ClientSearch");
```

With all that in place, we can wire up our `FindClientView`:

```
import QtQuick 2.9
import assets 1.0
import CM 1.0
import components 1.0

Item {
    property ClientSearch clientSearch: masterController.ui_clientSearch

    Rectangle {
        anchors.fill: parent
        color: Style.colourBackground

        Panel {
            id: searchPanel
            anchors {
                left: parent.left
                right: parent.right
                top: parent.top
                margins: Style.sizeScreenMargin
            }
            headerText: "Find Clients"
            contentComponent:
                StringEditorSingleLine {
                    stringDecorator: clientSearch.ui_searchText
                    anchors {
                        left: parent.left
```

```
                                    right: parent.right
                        }
                    }
                }
            }
        }
```

We access the `ClientSearch` instance via `MasterController` and create a shortcut to it with a property. We also utilize our new `Panel` component again, which gives us a nice consistent look and feel across views with very little work:

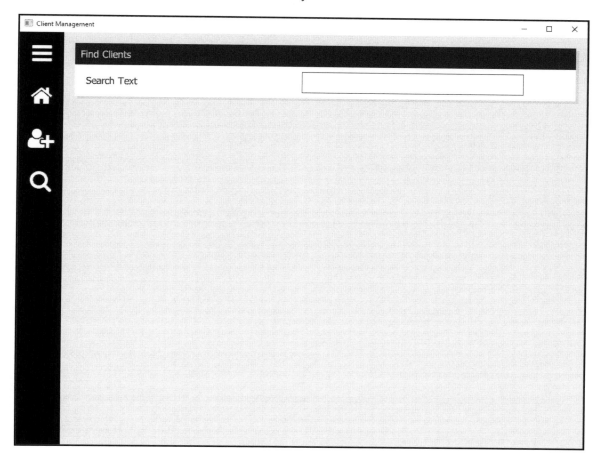

The next step is to add a command button for us to be able to instigate a search. We do this back over in `CommandController`. Before we get into the commands, we have an additional dependency on the `ClientSearch` instance, so add a parameter to the constructor:

```
CommandController::CommandController(QObject* parent, IDatabaseController*
databaseController, Client* newClient, ClientSearch* clientSearch)
    : QObject(parent)
{
    implementation.reset(new Implementation(this, databaseController,
newClient, clientSearch));
}
```

Pass the parameter through to the `Implementation` class and store it in a private member variable, just as we did with `newClient`. Hop back to `MasterController` briefly and add the `clientSearch` instance into the `CommandController` initialization:

```
commandController = new CommandController(masterController,
databaseController, newClient, clientSearch);
```

Next, in `CommandController`, duplicate and rename the private member variable, accessor, and `Q_PROPERTY` that we added for the create client view so that you end up with a `ui_findClientViewContextCommands` property for the UI to use.

Create an additional public slot, `onFindClientSearchExecuted()`, which will be called when we hit the search button:

```
void CommandController::onFindClientSearchExecuted()
{
    qDebug() << "You executed the Search command!";

    implementation->clientSearch->search();
}
```

Now we have an empty command list for our find view and a delegate to be called when we click on the button; all we need to do now is add a search button to the `Implementation` constructor:

```
Command* findClientSearchCommand = new Command( commandController, QChar(
0xf002 ), "Search" );
QObject::connect( findClientSearchCommand, &Command::executed,
commandController, &CommandController::onFindClientSearchExecuted );
findClientViewContextCommands.append( findClientSearchCommand );
```

That's it for the command plumbing; we can now easily add a command bar to
FindClientView. Insert the following as the last element within the root item:

```
CommandBar {
    commandList:
masterController.ui_commandController.ui_findClientViewContextCommands
}
```

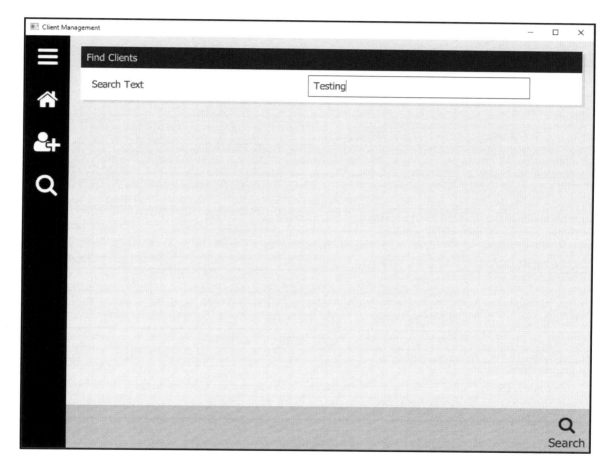

Enter some search text and click on the button, and you will see in the **Application Output**
console that everything triggers as expected:

```
You executed the Search command!
Searching for "Testing"...
```

Great, now what we need to do is take the search text, query the SQLite database for a list of results, and display those results on screen. Fortunately, we've already done the groundwork for querying the database, so we can easily implement that:

```
void ClientSearch::search()
{
    qDebug() << "Searching for " << implementation->searchText->value()
                << "...";

    auto resultsArray = implementation->databaseController-
        >find("client", implementation->searchText->value());
    implementation->searchResults->update(resultsArray);

    qDebug() << "Found " << implementation->searchResults-
            >baseEntities().size() << " matches";
}
```

There is a bit more work to do on the UI side to display the results. We need to bind to the ui_searchResults property and dynamically display some sort of QML subtree for each of the clients in the list. We will use a new QML component, ListView, to do the heavy lifting for us. Let's start simple to demonstrate the principle and then build out from there. In FindClientView, immediately after the Panel element, add the following:

```
ListView {
    id: itemsView
    anchors {
        top: searchPanel.bottom
        left: parent.left
        right: parent.right
        bottom: parent.bottom
        margins: Style.sizeScreenMargin
    }
    clip: true
    model: clientSearch.ui_searchResults
    delegate:
        Text {
            text: modelData.ui_reference.ui_label + ": " +
                    modelData.ui_reference.ui_value
            font.pixelSize: Style.pixelSizeDataControls
            color: Style.colourPanelFont
        }
}
```

The two key properties of a `ListView` are as listed:

- The `model`, which is the list of items that you want to display
- The `delegate`, which is how you want to visually represent each item

In our case, we bind the model to our `ui_searchResults` and represent each item with a simple `Text` element displaying the client reference number. Of particular importance here is the `modelData` property, which is magically injected into the delegate for us and exposes the underlying item (which is a client object, in this case).

Build, run, and perform a search for a piece of text you know exists in the JSON for one of the test clients you have created so far, and you will see that the reference number is displayed for each of the results. If you get more than one result and they lay out incorrectly, don't worry, as we will replace the delegate anyway:

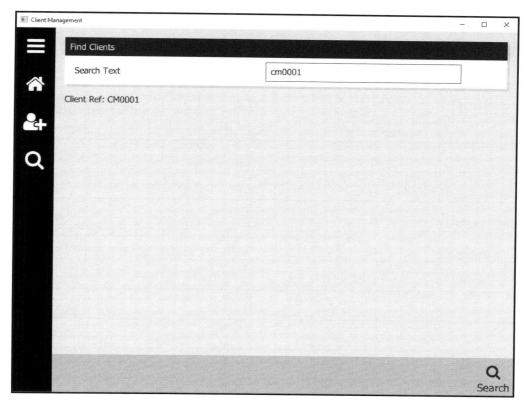

To keep things neat and tidy, we'll write a new custom component to use as the delegate. Create `SearchResultDelegate` in `cm-ui/components`, and update `components.qrc` and `qmldir` as usual:

```
import QtQuick 2.9
import assets 1.0
import CM 1.0

Item {
    property Client client

    implicitWidth: parent.width
    implicitHeight: Math.max(clientColumn.implicitHeight,
        textAddress.implicitHeight) + (Style.heightDataControls / 2)

    Rectangle {
        id: background
        width: parent.width
        height: parent.height
        color: Style.colourPanelBackground

        Column {
            id: clientColumn
            width: parent / 2
            anchors {
                left: parent.left
                top: parent.top
                margins: Style.heightDataControls / 4
            }
            spacing: Style.heightDataControls / 2

            Text {
                id: textReference
                anchors.left: parent.left
                text: client.ui_reference.ui_label + ": " +
                    client.ui_reference.ui_value
                font.pixelSize: Style.pixelSizeDataControls
                color: Style.colourPanelFont
            }
            Text {
                id: textName
                anchors.left: parent.left
                text: client.ui_name.ui_label + ": " +
                    client.ui_name.ui_value
                font.pixelSize: Style.pixelSizeDataControls
                color: Style.colourPanelFont
            }
```

```
    }

    Text {
        id: textAddress
        anchors {
            top: parent.top
            right: parent.right
            margins: Style.heightDataControls / 4
        }
        text: client.ui_supplyAddress.ui_fullAddress
        font.pixelSize: Style.pixelSizeDataControls
        color: Style.colourPanelFont
        horizontalAlignment: Text.AlignRight
    }

    Rectangle {
        id: borderBottom
        anchors {
            bottom: parent.bottom
            left: parent.left
            right: parent.right
        }
        height: 1
        color: Style.colourPanelFont
    }

    MouseArea {
        anchors.fill: parent
        cursorShape: Qt.PointingHandCursor
        hoverEnabled: true
        onEntered: background.state = "hover"
        onExited: background.state = ""
        onClicked: masterController.selectClient(client)
    }

    states: [
        State {
            name: "hover"
            PropertyChanges {
                target: background
                color: Style.colourPanelBackgroundHover
            }
        }
    ]
}
}
```

There isn't really anything new here, we've just combined techniques covered in other components. Note that the `MouseArea` element will trigger a method on `masterController` that we haven't implemented yet, so don't worry if you run this and get an error when you click on one of the clients.

Replace the old `Text` delegate in `FindClientView` with our new component using the `modelData` property to set the `client`:

```
ListView {
    id: itemsView
    ...
    delegate:
        SearchResultDelegate {
            client: modelData
        }
}
```

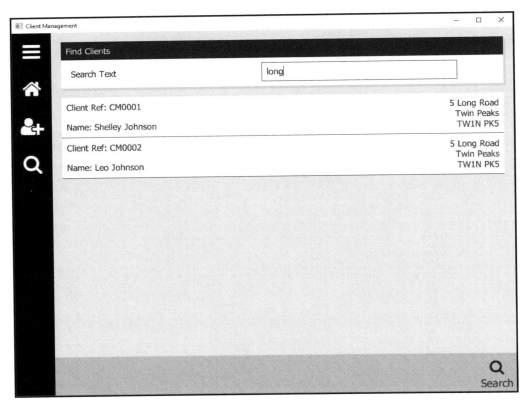

Now, let's implement the `selectClient()` method on `MasterController`:

 We can just emit the `goEditClientView()` signal directly from the `SearchResultDelegate` and bypass `MasterController` entirely. This is a perfectly valid approach and is indeed simpler; however, I prefer to route all the interactions through the business logic layer, even if all the business logic does is to emit the navigation signal. This means that if you need to add any further logic later on, everything is already wired up and you don't need to change any of the plumbing. It's also much easier to debug C++ than QML.

In `master-controller.h`, we need to add our new method as a public slot as it will be called directly from the UI, which won't have visibility of a regular public method:

```
public slots:
    void selectClient(cm::models::Client* client);
```

Provide the implementation in `master-controller.cpp`, simply calling the relevant signal on the navigation coordinator and passing through the client:

```
void MasterController::selectClient(Client* client)
{
    implementation->navigationController->goEditClientView(client);
}
```

With the searching and selection in place, we can now turn our attention to editing clients.

Editing clients

With an existing client now located and loaded from the database, we need a mechanism to be able to view and edit the data. Let's prepare by first creating the context commands we will use in the edit view. Repeat the steps we took for the Find Client View and in `CommandController`, add a new list of commands named `editClientViewContextCommands`, along with an accessor method and `Q_PROPERTY`.

Create a new slot to be called when the user saves their changes on the edit view:

```
void CommandController::onEditClientSaveExecuted()
{
    qDebug() << "You executed the Save command!";
}
```

Add a new save command to the list that calls the slot when executed:

```
Command* editClientSaveCommand = new Command( commandController, QChar(
0xf0c7 ), "Save" );
QObject::connect( editClientSaveCommand, &Command::executed,
commandController, &CommandController::onEditClientSaveExecuted );
editClientViewContextCommands.append( editClientSaveCommand );
```

We now have a list of commands we can present to the Edit Client View; however, a challenge that we now need to overcome is that when we execute this command, the `CommandController` has no idea which client instance it needs to work with. We can't pass in the selected client as a dependency to the constructor like we do with the new client, because we have no idea which client the user will select. One option would be to move the list of edit commands out of the `CommandController` and into the client model. Then, each client instance can present its own commands to the UI. However, this means that command functionality is fractured, and we lose the nice encapsulation that the command controller gives us. It also bloats the **client** model with functionality it shouldn't care about. Instead, we will add the currently selected client as a member within `CommandController` and set it whenever the user navigates to the `editClientView`. In `CommandController::Implementation`, add the following:

```
Client* selectedClient{nullptr};
```

Add a new public slot:

```
void CommandController::setSelectedClient(cm::models::Client* client)
{
    implementation->selectedClient = client;
}
```

Now that we have the selected client available, we can go ahead and complete the implementation of the save slot. Again, we've already done the hard work in the `DatabaseController` and client classes, so this method is really straightforward:

```
void CommandController::onEditClientSaveExecuted()
{
    qDebug() << "You executed the Save command!";

implementation->databaseController->updateRow(implementation->selectedClien
t->key(), implementation->selectedClient->id(),
implementation->selectedClient->toJson());

    qDebug() << "Updated client saved.";
}
```

From the UI point of view, editing an existing client will essentially be the same as creating a new client. So much so, in fact, that we can even probably use the same view and just pass in a different client object in each case. However, we'll keep the two functions separate and just copy and tweak the QML we've already written for creating a client. Update `EditClientView`:

```
import QtQuick 2.9
import QtQuick.Controls 2.2
import CM 1.0
import assets 1.0
import components 1.0

Item {
    property Client selectedClient
    Component.onCompleted:
masterController.ui_commandController.setSelectedClient(selectedClient)

    Rectangle {
        anchors.fill: parent
        color: Style.colourBackground
    }

    ScrollView {
        id: scrollView
        anchors {
            left: parent.left
            right: parent.right
            top: parent.top
            bottom: commandBar. top
            margins: Style.sizeScreenMargin
        }
        clip: true

        Column {
            spacing: Style.sizeScreenMargin
            width: scrollView.width

            Panel {
                headerText: "Client Details"
                contentComponent:
                    Column {
                        spacing: Style.sizeControlSpacing
                        StringEditorSingleLine {
                            stringDecorator:
                            selectedClient.ui_reference
                            anchors {
                                left: parent.left
```

```
                            right: parent.right
                        }
                    }
                    StringEditorSingleLine {
                        stringDecorator: selectedClient.ui_name
                        anchors {
                            left: parent.left
                            right: parent.right
                        }
                    }
                }
            }
        }

        AddressEditor {
            address: selectedClient.ui_supplyAddress
            headerText: "Supply Address"
        }

        AddressEditor {
            address: selectedClient.ui_billingAddress
            headerText: "Billing Address"
        }
        }
    }

    CommandBar {
        id: commandBar
        commandList:
  masterController.ui_commandController.ui_editClientViewContextCommands
    }
}
```

We change the client property to match the `selectedClient` property `MasterView` sets in the `Connections` element. We use the `Component.onCompleted` slot to call through to `CommandController` and set the currently selected client. Finally, we update `CommandBar` to reference the new context command list we just added.

Build and run, and you should now be able to make changes to a selected client and use the **Save** button to update the database.

Deleting clients

The final part of our CRUD operations is deleting an existing client. Let's trigger this via a new button on `EditClientView`. We'll begin by adding the slot that will be called when the button is pressed to `CommandController`:

```
void CommandController::onEditClientDeleteExecuted()
{
    qDebug() << "You executed the Delete command!";

implementation->databaseController->deleteRow(implementation->selectedClien
t->key(), implementation->selectedClient->id());
    implementation->selectedClient = nullptr;

    qDebug() << "Client deleted.";

    implementation->clientSearch->search();
}
```

This follows the same pattern as the other slots, except this time we also clear the `selectedClient` property as although the client instance still exists in application memory, it has been semantically deleted by the user. We also refresh the search so that the deleted client is removed from the search results. As this method stands, we've performed the correct database interaction but the user will be left on `editClientView` for a client that they have just asked to be deleted. What we want is for the user to be navigated back to the dashboard. In order to do this, we need to add `NavigationController` as an additional dependency to our `CommandController` class. Replicate what we did for the `DatabaseController` dependency so that we can inject it into the constructor. Remember to update `MasterController` and pass in the navigation controller instance.

With an instance of a database controller available, we can then send the user to the
Dashboard View:

```
void CommandController::onEditClientDeleteExecuted()
{
    . . .

    implementation->navigationController->goDashboardView();
}
```

Now that we have the navigation controller available, we can also improve the experience
when creating new clients. Rather than leaving the user on the new client view, let's
perform a search for the newly created client ID and navigate them to the results. They can
then easily select the new client if they wish to view or edit:

```
void CommandController::onCreateClientSaveExecuted()
{
    . . .

    implementation->clientSearch->searchText()-
                    >setValue(implementation->newClient->id());
    implementation->clientSearch->search();
    implementation->navigationController->goFindClientView();
}
```

With the deletion slot complete, we can now add a new delete command to the
`editClientContextCommands` list in `CommandController`:

```
Command* editClientDeleteCommand = new Command( commandController, QChar(
0xf235 ), "Delete" );
QObject::connect( editClientDeleteCommand, &Command::executed,
commandController, &CommandController::onEditClientDeleteExecuted );
editClientViewContextCommands.append( editClientDeleteCommand );
```

We are now presented with the option to delete an existing client:

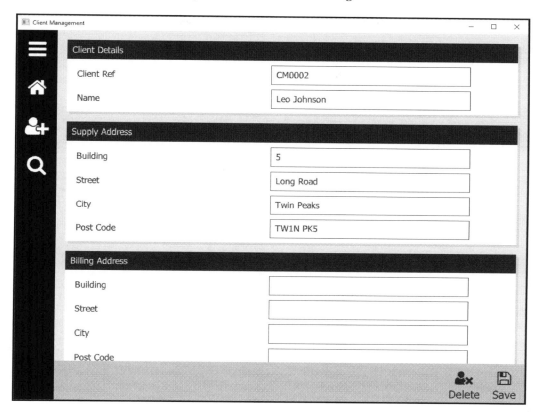

If you delete a client, you will see that the row is removed from the database and the user is successfully navigated back to the dashboard. However, you will also see that the **Application Output** window is full of QML warnings along the lines of `qrc:/views/EditClientView:62: TypeError: Cannot read property 'ui_billingAddress' of null.`

The reason for this is that the edit view is bound to a client instance that is part of the search results. When we refresh the search, we delete the old search results, which means that the edit view is now bound to `nullptr` and can no longer access the data. This continues to happen even if you navigate to the dashboard before refreshing the search, because of the asynchronous nature of the signals/slots used to perform the navigation. One way of fixing these warnings is to add null checks on all the bindings in the view and bind to local temporary objects if the main object is null. Consider the following example:

```
StringEditorSingleLine {
    property StringDecorator temporaryObject
    stringDecorator: selectedClient ? selectedClient.ui_reference :
    temporaryObject
    anchors {
        left: parent.left
        right: parent.right
    }
}
```

So, if `selectedClient` is not null, bind to the `ui_reference` property of that, otherwise bind to `temporaryObject`. You can even add a level of indirection to the root Client property and substitute the entire client object:

```
property Client selectedClient
property Client localTemporaryClient
property Client clientToBindTo: selectedClient ? selectedClient :
localTemporaryClient
```

Here, `selectedClient` will be set by the parent as normal; `localTemporaryClient` will not be set, so a default instance will be created locally. `clientToBindTo` will then pick the appropriate object to use and all the child controls can bind to that. As these bindings are dynamic, if `selectedClient` was deleted after loading the view (as in our case), then `clientToBindTo` will automatically switch over.

As this is just a demonstration project, it is safe for us to ignore the warnings, so we will take no action here to keep things simple.

Summary

In this chapter, we added database persistence for our client models. We made it generic and flexible so that we can easily persist other model hierarchies by simply adding a new table to our `DatabaseController` class. We covered all the core CRUD operations, including a free text search capability that matches against the entire JSON object.

In `Chapter 8`, *Web Requests*, we will continue the theme of reaching outside of our application for data and look at another extremely common Line of Business application requirement making HTTP requests to web services.

8
Web Requests

This chapter takes us worldwide as we venture even further out from our application to the internet. Beginning with writing some helper classes to manage web requests for us, we will pull data from a live RSS feed and interpret it via some XML processing. With the parsed data at hand, we can then put our QML skills to use and display the items on a new view. Clicking on one of the RSS items will launch a web browser window in order to view the related article in more detail. We will cover the following topics:

- Network access
- Web Requests
- RSS View
- RSS

Network access

The low-level networking protocol negotiation is all handled internally by Qt, and we can easily get connected to the outside world via the `QNetworkAccessManager` class. To be able to access this functionality, we need to add the `network` module to `cm-lib.pro`:

```
QT += sql network
```

One of Qt's weaknesses is the lack of interfaces, making unit testing difficult in some cases. If we just use `QNetworkAccessManager` directly, we won't be able to test our code without making real calls to the network, which is undesirable. However, a quick and easy solution to this problem is to hide the Qt implementation behind an interface of our own, and we will do that here.

For the purposes of this chapter, all we need to be able to do with the network is check that we have connectivity and send a HTTP GET request. With this in mind, create a header file `i-network-access-manager.h` in a new folder `cm-lib/source/networking` and implement the interface:

```
#ifndef INETWORKACCESSMANAGER_H
#define INETWORKACCESSMANAGER_H

#include <QNetworkReply>
#include <QNetworkRequest>

namespace cm {
namespace networking {

class INetworkAccessManager
{
public:
    INetworkAccessManager(){}
    virtual ~INetworkAccessManager(){}

    virtual QNetworkReply* get(const QNetworkRequest& request) = 0;
    virtual bool isNetworkAccessible() const = 0;
};

}}

#endif
```

`QNetworkRequest` is another Qt class that represents a request to be sent over the network, and `QNetworkReply` represents a response received over the network. We will ideally hide these implementations behind interfaces too, but let's make do with the network access interface for now. With that in place, go ahead and create a concrete implementation class `NetworkAccessManager` in the same folder:

`network-access-manager.h`:

```
#ifndef NETWORKACCESSMANAGER_H
#define NETWORKACCESSMANAGER_H

#include <QObject>
#include <QScopedPointer>
#include <networking/i-network-access-manager.h>

namespace cm {
namespace networking {
```

```cpp
    class NetworkAccessManager : public QObject, public INetworkAccessManager
    {
        Q_OBJECT

    public:
        explicit NetworkAccessManager(QObject* parent = nullptr);
        ~NetworkAccessManager();

        QNetworkReply* get(const QNetworkRequest& request) override;
        bool isNetworkAccessible() const override;

    private:
        class Implementation;
        QScopedPointer<Implementation> implementation;
    };

    }}

    #endif
```

network-access-manager.cpp:

```cpp
    #include "network-access-manager.h"
    #include <QNetworkAccessManager>

    namespace cm {
    namespace networking {

    class NetworkAccessManager::Implementation
    {
    public:
        Implementation()
        {}
        QNetworkAccessManager networkAccessManager;
    };

    NetworkAccessManager::NetworkAccessManager(QObject *parent)
        : QObject(parent)
        , INetworkAccessManager()
    {
        implementation.reset(new Implementation());
    }

    NetworkAccessManager::~NetworkAccessManager()
    {
    }

    QNetworkReply* NetworkAccessManager::get(const QNetworkRequest& request)
```

```
{
    return implementation->networkAccessManager.get(request);
}

bool NetworkAccessManager::isNetworkAccessible() const
{
    return implementation->networkAccessManager.networkAccessible() ==
QNetworkAccessManager::Accessible;
}

}}
```

All we are doing is holding a private instance of QNetworkAccessManager and passing calls to our interface through to it. The interface can easily be extended to include additional functionality like HTTP POST requests with the same approach.

Web Requests

If you haven't worked with the HTTP protocol before, it boils down to a conversation between a client and a server consisting of requests and responses. For example, we can make a request to www.bbc.co.uk in our favorite web browser, and we will receive a response containing various news items and articles. In the get() method of our NetworkAccessManager wrapper, we reference a QNetworkRequest (our request to a server) and a QNetworkReply (the server's response back to us). While we won't directly hide QNetworkRequest and QNetworkReply behind their own independent interfaces, we will take the concept of a web request and corresponding response and create an interface and implementation for that interaction. Still in cm-lib/source/networking, create an interface header file i-web-request.h:

```
#ifndef IWEBREQUEST_H
#define IWEBREQUEST_H

#include <QUrl>

namespace cm {
namespace networking {

class IWebRequest
{
public:
    IWebRequest(){}
    virtual ~IWebRequest(){}
```

```
    virtual void execute() = 0;
    virtual bool isBusy() const = 0;
    virtual void setUrl(const QUrl& url) = 0;
    virtual QUrl url() const = 0;
};

}}

#endif
```

The key piece of information for an HTTP request is the URL the request is to be sent to, represented by the QUrl Qt class. We provide an url() accessor and setUrl() mutator for the property. The other two methods are to check whether the isBusy() web request object is making a request or receiving a response and also to execute() or send the request to the network. Again, with the interface in place, let's move on straight to the implementation with a new WebRequest class in the same folder.

web-request.h:

```
#ifndef WEBREQUEST_H
#define WEBREQUEST_H

#include <QList>
#include <QObject>
#include <QSslError>
#include <networking/i-network-access-manager.h>
#include <networking/i-web-request.h>

namespace cm {
namespace networking {

class WebRequest : public QObject, public IWebRequest
{
    Q_OBJECT

public:
    WebRequest(QObject* parent, INetworkAccessManager*
networkAccessManager, const QUrl& url);
    WebRequest(QObject* parent = nullptr) = delete;
    ~WebRequest();

public:
    void execute() override;
    bool isBusy() const override;
    void setUrl(const QUrl& url) override;
    QUrl url() const override;
```

```
    signals:
        void error(QString message);
        void isBusyChanged();
        void requestComplete(int statusCode, QByteArray body);
        void urlChanged();

    private slots:
        void replyDelegate();
        void sslErrorsDelegate( const QList<QSslError>& _errors );

    private:
        class Implementation;
        QScopedPointer<Implementation> implementation;
    };

    }}

    #endif
```

web-request.cpp:

```
    #include "web-request.h"

    #include <QMap>
    #include <QNetworkReply>
    #include <QNetworkRequest>

    namespace cm {
    namespace networking { // Private Implementation

    static const QMap<QNetworkReply::NetworkError, QString> networkErrorMapper
    = {
        {QNetworkReply::ConnectionRefusedError, "The remote server refused the
    connection (the server is not accepting requests)."},
        /* ...section shortened in print for brevity...*/
        {QNetworkReply::UnknownServerError, "An unknown error related to the
    server response was detected."}
    };

    class WebRequest::Implementation
    {
    public:
        Implementation(WebRequest* _webRequest, INetworkAccessManager*
    _networkAccessManager, const QUrl& _url)
            : webRequest(_webRequest)
            , networkAccessManager(_networkAccessManager)
            , url(_url)
        {
```

```
        }

        WebRequest* webRequest{nullptr};
        INetworkAccessManager* networkAccessManager{nullptr};
        QUrl url {};
        QNetworkReply* reply {nullptr};

    public:
        bool isBusy() const
        {
            return isBusy_;
        }

        void setIsBusy(bool value)
        {
            if (value != isBusy_) {
                isBusy_ = value;
                emit webRequest->isBusyChanged();
            }
        }

    private:
        bool isBusy_{false};
    };
}

namespace networking {  // Structors
WebRequest::WebRequest(QObject* parent, INetworkAccessManager*
networkAccessManager, const QUrl& url)
    : QObject(parent)
    , IWebRequest()
{
    implementation.reset(new WebRequest::Implementation(this,
networkAccessManager, url));
}

WebRequest::~WebRequest()
{
}
}

namespace networking { // Methods
void WebRequest::execute()
{
    if(implementation->isBusy()) {
        return;
    }
```

```
    if(!implementation->networkAccessManager->isNetworkAccessible()) {
        emit error("Network not accessible");
        return;
    }

    implementation->setIsBusy(true);
    QNetworkRequest request;
    request.setUrl(implementation->url);
    implementation->reply =
implementation->networkAccessManager->get(request);

    if(implementation->reply != nullptr) {
        connect(implementation->reply, &QNetworkReply::finished, this,
&WebRequest::replyDelegate);
        connect(implementation->reply, &QNetworkReply::sslErrors, this,
&WebRequest::sslErrorsDelegate);
    }
}

bool WebRequest::isBusy() const
{
    return implementation->isBusy();
}

void WebRequest::setUrl(const QUrl& url)
{
    if(url != implementation->url) {
        implementation->url = url;
        emit urlChanged();
    }
}

QUrl WebRequest::url() const
{
    return implementation->url;
}
}

namespace networking { // Private Slots
void WebRequest::replyDelegate()
{
    implementation->setIsBusy(false);

    if (implementation->reply == nullptr) {
        emit error("Unexpected error - reply object is null");
        return;
    }
```

```
    disconnect(implementation->reply, &QNetworkReply::finished, this,
&WebRequest::replyDelegate);
    disconnect(implementation->reply, &QNetworkReply::sslErrors, this,
&WebRequest::sslErrorsDelegate);

    auto statusCode =
implementation->reply->attribute(QNetworkRequest::HttpStatusCodeAttribute).
toInt();
    auto responseBody = implementation->reply->readAll();
    auto replyStatus = implementation->reply->error();
    implementation->reply->deleteLater();

    if (replyStatus != QNetworkReply::NoError) {
        emit error(networkErrorMapper[implementation->reply->error()]);
    }

    emit requestComplete(statusCode, responseBody);
}

void WebRequest::sslErrorsDelegate(const QList<QSslError>& errors)
{
    QString sslError;
    for (const auto& error : errors) {
        sslError += error.errorString() + "\n";
    }
    emit error(sslError);
}

}}
```

The implementation looks more complicated than it is purely because of the lengthy error code map. In the event of some sort of problem, Qt will report the error using an enumerator. The purpose of the map is simply to match the enumerator to a human readable error description that we can present to the user or write to the console or a log file.

In addition to the interface methods, we also have a handful of signals that we can use to tell any interested observers about events that have happened:

- error() will be emitted in the event of a problem and will pass the error description as a parameter
- isBusyChanged() is fired when a request starts or finishes and the request becomes either busy or idle

- `requestComplete()` is emitted when the response has been received and processed and will contain the HTTP status code and an array of bytes representing the response body
- `urlChanged()` will be fired when the URL is updated

We also have a couple of private slots that will be the delegates for processing a reply and handling any SSL errors. They are connected to signals on the `QNetworkReply` object when we execute a new request and disconnected again when we receive the reply.

The meat of the implementation is really two methods—`execute()` to send the request and `replyDelegate()` to process the response.

When executing, we first ensure that we are not already busy executing another request and then check with the network access manager that we have an available connection. Assuming that we do, we then set the busy flag and construct a `QNetworkRequest` using the currently set URL. We then pass the request onto our network access manager (injected as an interface, so we can change its behavior) and finally, we connect our delegate slots and wait for a response.

When we receive the reply, we unset the busy flag and disconnect our slots before reading the response details we are interested in, principally the HTTP status code and response body. We check that the reply completed successfully (note that a "negative" HTTP response code in the ranges 4xx or 5xx still count as successfully complete requests in this context) and emit the details for any interested parties to capture and process.

RSS View

Let's add a new view to our app where we can display some information from a web service using our new classes.

There is nothing new or complicated here, so I won't show all the code, but there are a few steps to remember:

1. Create a new `RssView.qml` view in `cm-ui/views` and copy the QML from `SplashView` for now, replacing the "Splash View" text with "Rss View"
2. Add the view to `views.qrc` in the `/views` prefix block and with an alias `RssView.qml`
3. Add the `goRssView()` signal to `NavigationController`

4. In `MasterView`, add the `onGoRssView` slot to the Connections element and use it to navigate to `RssView`

5. In `NavigationBar`, add a new `NavigationButton` with `iconCharacter` `\uf09e`, description `RSS Feed`, and `hoverColour` as `#8acece`, and use the `onNavigationButtonClicked` slot to call `goRssView()` on the `NavigationController`

With just a few simple steps, we've now got a brand new view wired up that we can access using the navigation bar:

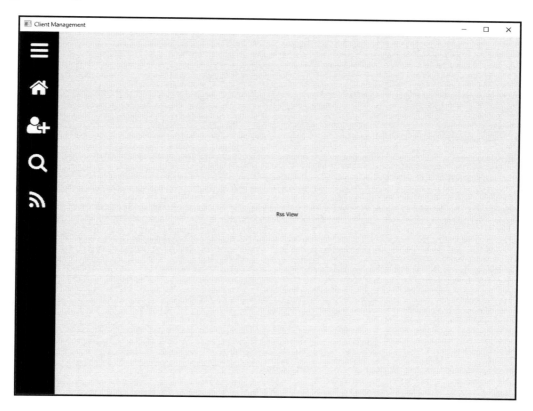

Next, we'll add a context command bar to the view with the following steps:

1. In `CommandController`, add a new private member list `rssViewContextCommands`

2. Add an accessor method `ui_rssViewContextCommands()`

3. Add a `Q_PROPERTY` named `ui_rssViewContextCommands`
4. Add a new slot `onRssRefreshExecuted()` that simply writes a debug message to the console; for now to indicate it has been called
5. Append a new command called `rssRefreshCommand` to `rssViewContextCommands` with the `0xf021` icon character and "Refresh" label and connect it to the `onRssRefreshExecuted()` slot
6. In `RssView`, add a `CommandBar` component with the `commandList` wired up to `ui_rssViewContextCommands` on the command controller

All the hard work from earlier chapters is really paying dividends now; our new view has got its own command bar and a fully functional refresh button. When you click on it, it should write out the debug message you added to the console:

Next, we need to create instances of our `NetworkAccessManager` and `WebRequest` classes. As usual, we will add these to `MasterController` and inject a dependency to `CommandController`.

In `MasterController`, add two new private members:

```
NetworkAccessManager* networkAccessManager{nullptr};
WebRequest* rssWebRequest{nullptr};
```

Remember to include the relevant headers. Instantiate these new members in the `Implementation` constructor, ensuring that they are created before `commandController`:

```
networkAccessManager = new NetworkAccessManager(masterController);
rssWebRequest = new WebRequest(masterController, networkAccessManager,
QUrl("http://feeds.bbci.co.uk/news/rss.xml?edition=uk"));
```

Here we are using the URL for a BBC RSS feed relevant to the UK; feel free to swap this for another feed of your choice simply by replacing the hyperlink text.

Next, pass `rssWebRequest` as a new parameter to the `commandController` constructor:

```
commandController = new CommandController(masterController,
databaseController, navigationController, newClient, clientSearch,
rssWebRequest);
```

Next, edit `CommandController` to take this new parameter as a pointer to the interface:

```
explicit CommandController(QObject* _parent = nullptr, IDatabaseController*
databaseController = nullptr, NavigationController* navigationController =
nullptr, models::Client* newClient = nullptr, models::ClientSearch*
clientSearch = nullptr, networking::IWebRequest* rssWebRequest = nullptr);
```

Pass this pointer through the `Implementation` constructor and store it in a private member variable as we do for all the other dependencies:

```
IWebRequest* rssWebRequest{nullptr};
```

We can now update the `onRssRefreshExecuted()` slot to execute the web request:

```
void CommandController::onRssRefreshExecuted()
{
    qDebug() << "You executed the Rss Refresh command!";

    implementation->rssWebRequest->execute();
}
```

The command controller now reacts to the user pressing the refresh button and executes the web request. However, we don't currently do anything when we receive the response. Let's add a delegate to `MasterController` in the public slots section:

```
void MasterController::onRssReplyReceived(int statusCode, QByteArray body)
{
    qDebug() << "Received RSS request response code " << statusCode << ":";
    qDebug() << body;
}
```

Now, after we instantiate `rssWebRequest` in `Implementation`, we can wire up the `requestComplete` signal to our new delegate:

```
QObject::connect(rssWebRequest, &WebRequest::requestComplete,
masterController, &MasterController::onRssReplyReceived);
```

Now build and run the application, navigate to the RSS View, and click on **Refresh**. After a brief delay, while the request is executed, you will see all sorts of nonsense printed to the Application Output console:

```
Received RSS request response code 200 :
"<?xml version=\"1.0\" encoding=\"UTF-8\"?>\n<?xml-stylesheet title=..."
```

Congratulations! You've got an RSS feed! Now, what is it?

RSS

Rich Site Summary (RSS) is a format for delivering regularly changing web content and is essentially an entire website, news broadcast, blog, or similar condensed down to bullet points. Each item consists of bare-bones information like the date and a descriptive title and is supplied with a hyperlink to the website page that contains the full article.

The data is extended from XML and must adhere to defined standards as described at `http://www.rssboard.org/rss-specification`.

Boiling it down to the basics for the purposes of this example, the XML looks as follows:

```
<rss>
    <channel>
        <title></title>
        <description></description>
        <link></link>
        <image>
            <url></url>
```

```
        <title></title>
        <link></link>
        <width></width>
        <height></height>
    </image>
    <item>
        <title></title>
        <description></description>
        <link></link>
        <pubDate></pubDate>
    </item>
    <item>
            ...
        </item>
    </channel>
</rss>
```

Inside the root `<rss>` node, we have a `<channel>` node, which in turn contains an `<image>` node and a collection of one or more `<item>` nodes.

We'll model these nodes as classes, but first we need to pull in the XML module and write a small helper class to do some parsing for us. In `cm-lib.pro` and `cm-ui.pro`, add the `xml` module to the modules in the `QT` variable; consider this example:

```
QT += sql network xml
```

Next, create a new `XmlHelper` class in a new folder `cm-lib/source/utilities`.

`xml-helper.h`:

```
#ifndef XMLHELPER_H
#define XMLHELPER_H

#include <QDomNode>
#include <QString>

namespace cm {
namespace utilities {

class XmlHelper
{
public:
    static QString toString(const QDomNode& domNode);

private:
    XmlHelper(){}
    static void appendNode(const QDomNode& domNode, QString& output);
```

```
        };

        }}

        #endif

xml-helper.cpp:

        #include "xml-helper.h"

        namespace cm {
        namespace utilities {

        QString XmlHelper::toString(const QDomNode& domNode)
        {
            QString returnValue;
            for(auto i = 0; i < domNode.childNodes().size(); ++i) {
                QDomNode subNode = domNode.childNodes().at(i);
                appendNode(subNode, returnValue);
            }
            return returnValue;
        }

        void XmlHelper::appendNode(const QDomNode& domNode, QString& output)
        {
            if(domNode.nodeType() == QDomNode::TextNode) {
                output.append(domNode.nodeValue());
                return;
            }

            if(domNode.nodeType() == QDomNode::AttributeNode) {
                output.append(" ");
                output.append(domNode.nodeName());
                output.append("=\"");
                output.append(domNode.nodeValue());
                output.append("\"");
                return;
            }

            if(domNode.nodeType() == QDomNode::ElementNode) {
                output.append("<");
                output.append(domNode.nodeName());
                // Add attributes
                for(auto i = 0; i < domNode.attributes().size(); ++i) {
                    QDomNode subNode = domNode.attributes().item(i);
                    appendNode(subNode, output);
                }
                output.append(">");
```

```
        for(auto i = 0; i < domNode.childNodes().size(); ++i) {
            QDomNode subNode = domNode.childNodes().at(i);
            appendNode(subNode, output);
        }
        output.append("</" + domNode.nodeName() + ">");
    }
}

}}
```

I won't go into too much detail about what this class does as it isn't the focus of the chapter, but essentially, if we receive an XML node that contains HTML markup (which is quite common in RSS), the XML parser gets a bit confused and breaks up the HTML into XML nodes too, which isn't what we want. Consider this example:

```
<xmlNode>
    Here is something from a website that has a <a href="http://www.bbc.co.uk">hyperlink</a> in it.
</xmlNode>
```

In this case, the XML parser will see <a> as XML and break up the content into three child nodes similar to this:

```
<xmlNode>
    <textNode1>Here is something from a website that has a </textNode1>
    <a href="http://www.bbc.co.uk">hyperlink</a>
    <textNode2>in it.</textNode2>
</xmlNode>
```

This makes it difficult to display the contents of xmlNode to the user on the UI. Instead, we use XmlHelper to parse the contents manually and construct a single string, which is much easier to work with.

Now, let's move on to the RSS classes. In a new `cm-lib/source/rss` folder, create new `RssChannel`, `RssImage`, and `RssItem` classes.

`rss-image.h`:

```
#ifndef RSSIMAGE_H
#define RSSIMAGE_H

#include <QObject>
#include <QScopedPointer>
#include <QtXml/QDomNode>
#include <cm-lib_global.h>
```

```
namespace cm {
namespace rss {

class CMLIBSHARED_EXPORT RssImage : public QObject
{
    Q_OBJECT
    Q_PROPERTY(quint16 ui_height READ height CONSTANT)
    Q_PROPERTY(QString ui_link READ link CONSTANT)
    Q_PROPERTY(QString ui_title READ title CONSTANT)
    Q_PROPERTY(QString ui_url READ url CONSTANT)
    Q_PROPERTY(quint16 ui_width READ width CONSTANT)

public:
    explicit RssImage(QObject* parent = nullptr, const QDomNode& domNode =
QDomNode());
    ~RssImage();

    quint16 height() const;
    const QString& link() const;
    const QString& title() const;
    const QString& url() const;
    quint16 width() const;

private:
    class Implementation;
    QScopedPointer<Implementation> implementation;
};

}}

#endif
```

rss-image.cpp:

```
#include "rss-image.h"

namespace cm {
namespace rss {

class RssImage::Implementation
{
public:
    QString url;      // Mandatory. URL of GIF, JPEG or PNG that represents
the channel.
    QString title;    // Mandatory.  Describes the image.
    QString link;     // Mandatory.  URL of the site.
    quint16 width;    // Optional.  Width in pixels.  Max 144, default
                                                                88.
```

```
    quint16 height; // Optional.  Height in pixels.  Max 400, default
                                                                    31

    void update(const QDomNode& domNode)
    {
        QDomElement imageUrl = domNode.firstChildElement("url");
        if(!imageUrl.isNull()) {
            url = imageUrl.text();
        }
        QDomElement imageTitle = domNode.firstChildElement("title");
        if(!imageTitle.isNull()) {
            title = imageTitle.text();
        }
        QDomElement imageLink = domNode.firstChildElement("link");
        if(!imageLink.isNull()) {
            link = imageLink.text();
        }
        QDomElement imageWidth = domNode.firstChildElement("width");
        if(!imageWidth.isNull()) {
            width = static_cast<quint16>(imageWidth.text().toShort());
        } else {
            width = 88;
        }
        QDomElement imageHeight = domNode.firstChildElement("height");
        if(!imageHeight.isNull()) {
            height = static_cast<quint16>
                                (imageHeight.text().toShort());
        } else {
            height = 31;
        }
    }
};

RssImage::RssImage(QObject* parent, const QDomNode& domNode)
    : QObject(parent)
{
    implementation.reset(new Implementation());
    implementation->update(domNode);
}

RssImage::~RssImage()
{
}

quint16 RssImage::height() const
{
    return implementation->height;
}
```

```
const QString& RssImage::link() const
{
    return implementation->link;
}

const QString& RssImage::title() const
{
    return implementation->title;
}

const QString& RssImage::url() const
{
    return implementation->url;
}

quint16 RssImage::width() const
{
    return implementation->width;
}

}}
```

This class is just a regular plain data model with the exception that it will be constructed from an XML `<image>` node represented by Qt's `QDomNode` class. We use the `firstChildElement()` method to locate the `<url>`, `<title>`, and `<link>` mandatory child nodes and then access the value of each node via the **text()** method. The `<width>` and `<height>` nodes are optional and if they are not present, we use the default image size of 88 x 31 pixels.

rss-item.h:

```
#ifndef RSSITEM_H
#define RSSITEM_H

#include <QDateTime>
#include <QObject>
#include <QscopedPointer>
#include <QtXml/QDomNode>
#include <cm-lib_global.h>

namespace cm {
namespace rss {

class CMLIBSHARED_EXPORT RssItem : public QObject
{
    Q_OBJECT
    Q_PROPERTY(QString ui_description READ description CONSTANT)
```

```
    Q_PROPERTY(QString ui_link READ link CONSTANT)
    Q_PROPERTY(QDateTime ui_pubDate READ pubDate CONSTANT)
    Q_PROPERTY(QString ui_title READ title CONSTANT)

public:
    RssItem(QObject* parent = nullptr, const QDomNode& domNode =
QDomNode());
    ~RssItem();

    const QString& description() const;
    const QString& link() const;
    const QDateTime& pubDate() const;
    const QString& title() const;

private:
    class Implementation;
    QScopedPointer<Implementation> implementation;
};

}}

#endif
```

rss-item.cpp:

```
#include "rss-item.h"
#include <QTextStream>
#include <utilities/xml-helper.h>

using namespace cm::utilities;

namespace cm {
namespace rss {
class RssItem::Implementation
{
public:
    Implementation(RssItem* _rssItem)
        : rssItem(_rssItem)
    {
    }

    RssItem* rssItem{nullptr};
    QString description;    // This or Title mandatory.  Either the
                            synopsis or full story.  HTML is allowed.
    QString link;           // Optional. Link to full story.  Populated
                                    if Description is only the synopsis.
    QDateTime pubDate;      // Optional. When the item was published.
                        RFC 822 format e.g. Sun, 19 May 2002 15:21:36 GMT.
```

```
    QString title;              // This or Description mandatory.

    void update(const QDomNode& domNode)
    {
        for(auto i = 0; i < domNode.childNodes().size(); ++i) {
            QDomNode childNode = domNode.childNodes().at(i);
            if(childNode.nodeName() == "description") {
                description = XmlHelper::toString(childNode);
            }
        }
        QDomElement itemLink = domNode.firstChildElement("link");
        if(!itemLink.isNull()) {
            link = itemLink.text();
        }
        QDomElement itemPubDate = domNode.firstChildElement("pubDate");
        if(!itemPubDate.isNull()) {
            pubDate = QDateTime::fromString(itemPubDate.text(),
                                            Qt::RFC2822Date);
        }
        QDomElement itemTitle = domNode.firstChildElement("title");
        if(!itemTitle.isNull()) {
            title = itemTitle.text();
        }
    }
};

RssItem::RssItem(QObject* parent, const QDomNode& domNode)
{
    implementation.reset(new Implementation(this));
    implementation->update(domNode);
}

RssItem::~RssItem()
{
}

const QString& RssItem::description() const
{
    return implementation->description;
}

const QString& RssItem::link() const
{
    return implementation->link;
}

const QDateTime& RssItem::pubDate() const
{
```

```
        return implementation->pubDate;
    }

    const QString& RssItem::title() const
    {
        return implementation->title;
    }

}}
```

This class is much the same as the last. This time we put our XMLHelper class to use when parsing the <description> node as that has a good chance of containing HTML tags. Also note that Qt also helpfully contains the Qt::RFC2822Date format specifier when converting a string to a QDateTime object using the static QDateTime::fromString() method. This is the format used in the RSS specification and saves us from having to manually parse the dates ourselves.

rss-channel.h:

```
#ifndef RSSCHANNEL_H
#define RSSCHANNEL_H

#include <QDateTime>
#include <QtXml/QDomElement>
#include <QtXml/QDomNode>
#include <QList>
#include <QObject>
#include <QtQml/QQmlListProperty>
#include <QString>

#include <cm-lib_global.h>
#include <rss/rss-image.h>
#include <rss/rss-item.h>

namespace cm {
namespace rss {

class CMLIBSHARED_EXPORT RssChannel : public QObject
{
    Q_OBJECT
    Q_PROPERTY(QString ui_description READ description CONSTANT)
    Q_PROPERTY(cm::rss::RssImage* ui_image READ image CONSTANT)
    Q_PROPERTY(QQmlListProperty<cm::rss::RssItem> ui_items READ
                                            ui_items CONSTANT)
    Q_PROPERTY(QString ui_link READ link CONSTANT)
    Q_PROPERTY(QString ui_title READ title CONSTANT)
```

```
public:
    RssChannel(QObject* parent = nullptr, const QDomNode& domNode =
QDomNode());
    ~RssChannel();

    void addItem(RssItem* item);
    const QString& description() const;
    RssImage* image() const;
    const QList<RssItem*>& items() const;
    const QString& link() const;
    void setImage(RssImage* image);
    const QString& title() const;
    QQmlListProperty<RssItem> ui_items();

    static RssChannel* fromXml(const QByteArray& xmlData, QObject*
                                           parent = nullptr);

private:
    class Implementation;
    QScopedPointer<Implementation> implementation;
};

}}

#endif
```

rss-channel.cpp:

```
#include "rss-channel.h"
#include <QtXml/QDomDocument>

namespace cm {
namespace rss {

class RssChannel::Implementation
{
public:
    QString description;                // Mandatory.  Phrase or sentence
describing the channel.
    RssImage* image{nullptr};           // Optional.  Image representing the
channel.
    QList<RssItem*> items;              // Optional.  Collection representing
stories.
    QString link;                      // Mandatory.  URL to the corresponding
HTML website.
    QString title;                      // Mandatory.  THe name of the Channel.

    void update(const QDomNode& domNode)
```

```
        {
            QDomElement channelDescription =
    domNode.firstChildElement("description");
            if(!channelDescription.isNull()) {
                description = channelDescription.text();
            }
            QDomElement channelLink = domNode.firstChildElement("link");
            if(!channelLink.isNull()) {
                link = channelLink.text();
            }
            QDomElement channelTitle = domNode.firstChildElement("title");
            if(!channelTitle.isNull()) {
                title = channelTitle.text();
            }
        }
};

RssChannel::RssChannel(QObject* parent, const QDomNode& domNode)
    : QObject(parent)
{
    implementation.reset(new Implementation());
    implementation->update(domNode);
}

RssChannel::~RssChannel()
{
}

void RssChannel::addItem(RssItem* item)
{
    if(!implementation->items.contains(item)) {
        item->setParent(this);
        implementation->items.push_back(item);
    }
}

const QString&  RssChannel::description() const
{
    return implementation->description;
}

RssImage* RssChannel::image() const
{
    return implementation->image;
}

const QList<RssItem*>&  RssChannel::items() const
{
```

```
        return implementation->items;
}

const QString&  RssChannel::link() const
{
        return implementation->link;
}

void RssChannel::setImage(RssImage* image)
{
        if(implementation->image) {
            implementation->image->deleteLater();
            implementation->image = nullptr;
        }
        image->setParent(this);
        implementation->image = image;
}

const QString& RssChannel::title() const
{
        return implementation->title;
}
QQmlListProperty<RssItem> RssChannel::ui_items()
{
        return QQmlListProperty<RssItem>(this, implementation->items);
}

RssChannel* RssChannel::fromXml(const QByteArray& xmlData, QObject* parent)
{
        QDomDocument doc;
        doc.setContent(xmlData);
        auto channelNodes = doc.elementsByTagName("channel");
        // Rss must have 1 channel
        if(channelNodes.size() != 1) return nullptr;
        RssChannel* channel = new RssChannel(parent, channelNodes.at(0));
        auto imageNodes = doc.elementsByTagName("image");
        if(imageNodes.size() > 0) {
            channel->setImage(new RssImage(channel, imageNodes.at(0)));
        }
        auto itemNodes = doc.elementsByTagName("item");
        for (auto i = 0; i < itemNodes.size(); ++i) {
            channel->addItem(new RssItem(channel, itemNodes.item(i)));
        }
        return channel;
}

}}
```

This class is broadly the same as the previous classes, but because this is the root object of our XML tree, we also have a static fromXml() method. The goal here is to take the byte array from the RSS web request response containing the RSS feed XML and have the method create an RSS Channel, Image, and Items hierarchy for us.

We pass the XML byte array into the Qt QDomDocument class, much like we have done previously with JSON and the QJsonDocument class. We find the <channel> tag using the elementsByTagName() method and then construct a new RssChannel object using that tag as the QDomNode parameter of the constructor. The RssChannel populates its own properties, thanks to the update() method. We then locate the <image> and <item> child nodes and create new RssImage and RssItem instances that are added to the root RssChannel object. Again, the classes are capable of populating their own properties from the supplied QDomNode.

Before we forget, let's also register the classes in main():

```
qmlRegisterType<cm::rss::RssChannel>("CM", 1, 0, "RssChannel");
qmlRegisterType<cm::rss::RssImage>("CM", 1, 0, "RssImage");
qmlRegisterType<cm::rss::RssItem>("CM", 1, 0, "RssItem");
```

We can now add an RssChannel to our MasterController for the UI to bind to:

1. In MasterController, add a new rssChannel private member variable of the RssChannel* type
2. Add an rssChannel() accessor method
3. Add a rssChannelChanged() signal
4. Add a Q_PROPERTY named ui_rssChannel using the accessor for READ and signal for NOTIFY

Rather than creating one construction when we don't have any RSS data to feed it, we'll do it in the RSS reply delegate:

```
void MasterController::onRssReplyReceived(int statusCode, QByteArray body)
{
    qDebug() << "Received RSS request response code " << statusCode << ":";
    qDebug() << body;

    if(implementation->rssChannel) {
        implementation->rssChannel->deleteLater();
        implementation->rssChannel = nullptr;
        emit rssChannelChanged();
    }
```

```
implementation->rssChannel = RssChannel::fromXml(body, this);
emit rssChannelChanged();
}
```

We perform some housekeeping that checks whether we already have an old channel object in memory and if we do, it safely deletes it using the `deleteLater()` method of `QObject`. We then go ahead and construct a new channel using the XML data from the web request.

 Always use `deleteLater()` on `QObject` derived classes rather than the standard C++ `delete` keyword as the destruction will be synchronized with the event loop and you will minimize the risk of unexpected exceptions.

We will display the RSS items in the response in a similar way to how we managed the search results, with a `ListView` and associated delegate. Add `RssItemDelegate.qml` to `cm-ui/components` and perform the usual steps of editing the `components.qrc` and `qmldir` files:

```qml
import QtQuick 2.9
import assets 1.0
import CM 1.0

Item {
    property RssItem rssItem
    implicitWidth: parent.width
    implicitHeight: background.height

    Rectangle {
        id: background
        width: parent.width
        height: textPubDate.implicitHeight + textTitle.implicitHeight +
                    borderBottom.height + (Style.sizeItemMargin * 3)
        color: Style.colourPanelBackground

        Text {
            id: textPubDate
            anchors {
                top: parent.top
                left: parent.left
                right: parent.right
                margins: Style.sizeItemMargin
            }
            text: Qt.formatDateTime(rssItem.ui_pubDate, "ddd, d MMM
                                                yyyy @ h:mm ap")
            font {
                pixelSize: Style.pixelSizeDataControls
```

```
            italic: true
            weight: Font.Light
        }
        color: Style.colorItemDateFont
}

Text {
    id: textTitle
    anchors {
        top: textPubDate.bottom
        left: parent.left
        right: parent.right
        margins: Style.sizeItemMargin
    }
    text: rssItem.ui_title
    font {
        pixelSize: Style.pixelSizeDataControls
    }
    color: Style.colorItemTitleFont
    wrapMode: Text.Wrap
}

Rectangle {
    id: borderBottom
    anchors {
        top: textTitle.bottom
        left: parent.left
        right: parent.right
        topMargin: Style.sizeItemMargin
    }
    height: 1
    color: Style.colorItemBorder
}

MouseArea {
    anchors.fill: parent
    cursorShape: Qt.PointingHandCursor
    hoverEnabled: true
    onEntered: background.state = "hover"
    onExited: background.state = ""
    onClicked: if(rssItem.ui_link !== "") {
                Qt.openUrlExternally(rssItem.ui_link);
            }
}

states: [
    State {
        name: "hover"
```

```
                    PropertyChanges {
                        target: background
                        color: Style.colourPanelBackgroundHover
                    }
                }
            ]
        }
    }
}
```

To support this component, we will need to add a few more Style properties:

```
readonly property color colourItemBackground: "#fefefe"
readonly property color colourItemBackgroundHover: "#efefef"
readonly property color colorItemBorder: "#efefef"
readonly property color colorItemDateFont: "#636363"
readonly property color colorItemTitleFont: "#131313"
readonly property real sizeItemMargin: 5
```

We can now utilize this delegate in `RssView`:

```
import QtQuick 2.9
import assets 1.0
import components 1.0

Item {
    Rectangle {
        anchors.fill: parent
        color: Style.colourBackground
    }

    ListView {
        id: itemsView
        anchors {
            top: parent.top
            left: parent.left
            right: parent.right
            bottom: commandBar.top
            margins: Style.sizeHeaderMargin
        }
        clip: true
        model: masterController.ui_rssChannel ?
masterController.ui_rssChannel.ui_items : 0
        delegate: RssItemDelegate {
            rssItem: modelData
        }
    }

    CommandBar {
```

```
        id: commandBar
        commandList:
masterController.ui_commandController.ui_rssViewContextCommands
    }
}
```

Build and run, navigate to the RSS View, and click on the **Refresh** button to make the web request and display the response:

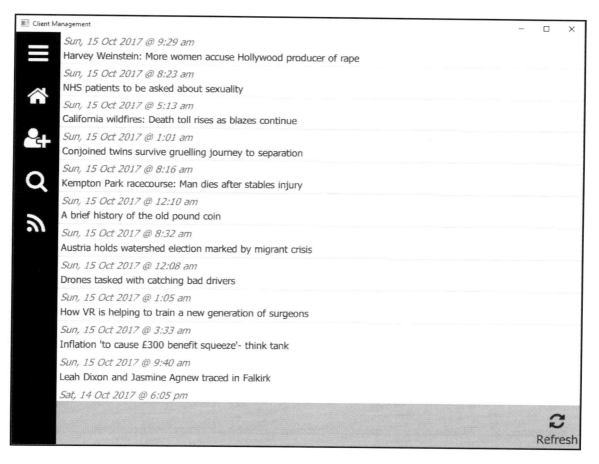

Hover over the items to see the cursor effects and click on an item to open it in your default web browser. Qt handles this action for us in the `Qt.openUrlExternally()` method, to which we pass the RSS Item `link` property.

Summary

In this chapter, we extended our reach outside of our application and began interacting with external APIs using HTTP requests over the internet. We abstracted the Qt functionality using our own interfaces to improve decoupling and make our components more test friendly. We took a quick look at RSS and its structure and how to process XML node trees using Qt's XML module. Finally, we reinforced the great UI work we've been doing and added an interactive view to display an RSS feed and launch the default web browser for a given URL.

In Chapter 9, *Wrapping Up*, we will take a look at the steps required to package our application for deployment to other computers.

9
Wrapping Up

In this chapter, we will mop up a couple of subjects that didn't quite make it into the earlier chapters. We'll make our application more testable by moving object creation into an object factory. We'll make our UI even more dynamic by adding scaling capabilities. `EnumeratorDecorator` properties get their own UI components, and we'll put them to use when we add contact management. Finally, we'll wrap everything up by packaging and deploying our application. We will cover the following topics:

- Object factories
- Dynamic UI scaling
- Adding an image to the Dashboard
- Enumerator selectors
- Managing Contacts
- Deployment and installation of our application

Object factory

In a larger system with more comprehensive `MasterController` tests in place, having all of that object creation hard-coded inside the private implementation will cause problems because of the tight coupling between the `MasterController` and its dependencies. One option will be to create all the other objects in `main()` instead and inject them into the `MasterController` constructor as we have done with the other controllers. This will mean injecting a lot of constructor parameters, and it is handy to be able to keep the `MasterController` instance as the parent of all the other objects, so we will inject a single object factory that the controller can use for all of its object creation needs instead.

The critical part of this factory pattern is to hide everything behind interfaces, so when testing `MasterController`, you can pass in a mock factory and control all the object creation. In `cm-lib`, create a new `i-object-factory.h` header file in `source/framework`:

```
#ifndef IOBJECTFACTORY_H
#define IOBJECTFACTORY_H

#include <controllers/i-command-controller.h>
#include <controllers/i-database-controller.h>
#include <controllers/i-navigation-controller.h>
#include <models/client.h>
#include <models/client-search.h>
#include <networking/i-network-access-manager.h>
#include <networking/i-web-request.h>

namespace cm {
namespace framework {

class IObjectFactory
{
public:
    virtual ~IObjectFactory(){}

    virtual models::Client* createClient(QObject* parent) const = 0;
    virtual models::ClientSearch* createClientSearch(QObject* parent,
controllers::IDatabaseController* databaseController) const = 0;
    virtual controllers::ICommandController*
createCommandController(QObject* parent, controllers::IDatabaseController*
databaseController, controllers::INavigationController*
navigationController, models::Client* newClient, models::ClientSearch*
clientSearch, networking::IWebRequest* rssWebRequest) const = 0;
    virtual controllers::IDatabaseController*
createDatabaseController(QObject* parent) const = 0;
    virtual controllers::INavigationController*
createNavigationController(QObject* parent) const = 0;
    virtual networking::INetworkAccessManager*
createNetworkAccessManager(QObject* parent) const = 0;
    virtual networking::IWebRequest* createWebRequest(QObject* parent,
networking::INetworkAccessManager* networkAccessManager, const QUrl& url)
const = 0;
};

}}

#endif
```

All the objects we will create will be moved behind interfaces apart from the models. This is because they are essentially just data containers, and we can easily create real instances in a test scenario with no side effects.

 We will skip that exercise here for brevity and leave it as an exercise for the reader. Use `IDatabaseController` as an example or refer to the code samples.

With the factory interface available, change the `MasterController` constructor to take an instance as a dependency:

```
MasterController::MasterController(QObject* parent, IObjectFactory*
objectFactory)
    : QObject(parent)
{
    implementation.reset(new Implementation(this, objectFactory));
}
```

We pass the object through to `Implementation` and store it in a private member variable as we have done numerous times before. With the factory available, we can now move all the `new` based object creation statements into a concrete implementation of the `IObjectFactory` interface (the `ObjectFactory` class) and replace those statements in `MasterController` with something more abstract and testable:

```
Implementation(MasterController* _masterController, IObjectFactory*
_objectFactory)
    : masterController(_masterController)
    , objectFactory(_objectFactory)
{
    databaseController =
objectFactory->createDatabaseController(masterController);
    clientSearch = objectFactory->createClientSearch(masterController,
databaseController);
    navigationController =
objectFactory->createNavigationController(masterController);
    networkAccessManager =
objectFactory->createNetworkAccessManager(masterController);
    rssWebRequest = objectFactory->createWebRequest(masterController,
networkAccessManager,
QUrl("http://feeds.bbci.co.uk/news/rss.xml?edition=uk"));
    QObject::connect(rssWebRequest, &IWebRequest::requestComplete,
masterController, &MasterController::onRssReplyReceived);
    newClient = objectFactory->createClient(masterController);
    commandController =
objectFactory->createCommandController(masterController,
```

```
databaseController, navigationController, newClient, clientSearch,
rssWebRequest);
}
```

Now, when testing `MasterController`, we can pass in a mock implementation of the `IObjectFactory` interface and control the creation of objects. In addition to implementing `ObjectFactory` and passing it to `MasterController` when we instantiate it, one further change is that in `main.cpp`, we now need to register the interfaces to `NavigationController` and `CommandController`, rather than the concrete implementations. We do this by simply swapping out the `qmlRegisterType` statements with the `qmlRegisterUncreatableType` companion:

```
qmlRegisterUncreatableType<cm::controllers::INavigationController>("CM", 1,
0, "INavigationController", "Interface");
qmlRegisterUncreatableType<cm::controllers::ICommandController>("CM", 1, 0,
"ICommandController", "Interface");
```

UI scaling

We've focused a lot on responsive UI in this book, using anchors and relative positioning where possible so that when the user resizes the window, the contents scale and adjust themselves appropriately. We've also pulled all the "hard-coded" properties like sizes and colors into a centralized Style object.

If we pick a property concerned with sizing, for example, `sizeScreenMargin`, it currently has a fixed value of 20. If we decide to increase the starting size of our **Window** element in `MasterView`, this screen margin size will remain the same. Now, it's really easy to increase the screen margin too, thanks to the Style object, but it would be nice if all the hard-coded properties could scale up and down dynamically along with our **Window** element. That way, we can try out different window sizes without having to update Style each time.

As we've already seen, the flexibility of QML is extended even further with the built-in JavaScript support, and we can do just that.

First, let's create new width and height properties for the window in Style:

```
readonly property real widthWindow: 1920
readonly property real heightWindow: 1080
```

Use these new properties in `MasterView`:

```
Window {
    width: Style.widthWindow
    height: Style.heightWindow
    ....
}
```

All the size properties in Style that we've created so far are relevant to this window size of 1920 x 1080, so let's record that as new properties in Style:

```
readonly property real widthWindowReference: 1920
readonly property real heightWindowReference: 1080
```

We can then use the reference sizes and the actual sizes to calculate scaling factors in the horizontal and vertical axes. So in simple terms, if we design everything with a window width of 1,000 in mind and then we set the window to be 2,000 wide, we want everything to scale horizontally by a factor of 2. Add the following functions to Style:

```
function hscale(size) {
    return Math.round(size * (widthWindow / widthWindowReference))
}
function vscale(size) {
    return Math.round(size * (heightWindow / heightWindowReference))
}
function tscale(size) {
    return Math.round((hscale(size) + vscale(size)) / 2)
}
```

The `hscale` and `vscale` functions calculate the horizontal and vertical scaling factors respectively. For certain size properties like pixel size for fonts, there is no independent width and height, so we can calculate an average of the horizontal and vertical scales using the `tscale` function.

We can then wrap any properties we want to scale in the appropriate function. For example, our screen margin can use the `tscale` function:

```
readonly property real sizeScreenMargin: tscale(20)
```

Now, not only can you increase the initial size of the window in Style, but your selected properties will automatically scale to the new size.

A really useful module you can add to help with sizing is
`QtQuick.Window`. We already added this to `MasterView` in order to
access the Window element. There is another object in that module,
Screen, which makes available information regarding the user's display. It
contains properties for things like the width and height of the screen, and
orientation and pixel density, which can be useful if you're working with
high DPI displays such as the Microsoft Surface or Macbook. You can use
these values in conjunction with your Style properties to do things such as
making your window fullscreen, or make it 50% of the screen size and
positioning it in the center of the display.

Dashboard

A Dashboard or "home page" is a great place to welcome users and present the current state
of play. Daily messages, facts and figures, performance charts, or simply some company
branding can all help orient and focus the user. Let's jazz up our Dashboard view a little
and demonstrate how to display images to boot.

Grab an image of your choice that has a 1:1 aspect ratio, which means that the width is the
same as the height. It's not necessary to be square, it's just simpler to manage the scaling for
the purposes of this example. I have picked the **Packt** logo, which is 500 x 500 pixels, and
which I have saved as `packt-logo-500x500.jpg`. Save it to `cm/cm-ui/assets` and add it
to our `assets.qrc` resources:

```
<file alias="packt-logo-500x500">assets/packt-logo-500x500.jpg</file>
```

Add some new Style properties, leveraging our new scaling capabilities:

```
readonly property color colourDashboardBackground: "#f36f24"
readonly property color colourDashboardFont: "#ffffff"
readonly property int pixelSizeDashboard: tscale(36)
readonly property real sizeDashboardLogo: tscale(500)
```

Then, we can add our image to `DashboardView`:

```
Item {
    Rectangle {
        anchors.fill: parent
        color: Style.colourDashboardBackground

        Image {
            id: logo
            source: "qrc:/assets/packt-logo-500x500"
```

```
            anchors.centerIn: parent
            width: Style.sizeDashboardLogo
            height: Style.sizeDashboardLogo
        }

        Text {
            anchors {
                top: logo.bottom
                horizontalCenter: logo.horizontalCenter
            }
            text: "Client Management System"
            color: Style.colourDashboardFont
            font.pixelSize: Style.pixelSizeDashboard
        }
    }
}
```

Now, when we go to the Dashboard, we can see something a bit more stimulating:

Enumerator selectors

Back in `Chapter 5`, *Data*, we created a Contact model where we implemented a `ContactType` property with an `EnumeratorDecorator`. For the other string-based properties we've worked with in the book, a simple textbox is a fine solution for capturing data, but how can we capture an enumerated value? The user can't be expected to know the underlying integer values of the enumerator, and asking them to type in a string representation of the option they want is asking for trouble. What we really want is a drop-down list that somehow utilizes the `contactTypeMapper` container we added to the class. We'd like to present the string descriptions to the user to pick from but then store the integer value in the `EnumeratorDecorator` object.

Desktop applications generally present drop-down lists in a particular way, with some kind of selector you press that then pops out (or more accurately, drops down!) a scrollable list of options to choose from. However, QML is geared toward not only cross-platform, but cross-device applications, too. Many laptops have touch capable screens, and more and more hybrid devices are appearing in the market that act as both laptops and tablets. As such, it's important to consider how "finger friendly" our application is, even if we're not planning on building the next big thing for the mobile stores, and the classic drop-down list can be difficult to work with on a touch screen. Let's instead use a button-based approach as used on mobile devices.

Unfortunately, we can't really work directly with our existing `std::map` in QML, so we will need to add a few new classes to bridge the gap for us. We'll represent each key/value pair as a `DropDownValue` and hold a collection of these objects in a `DropDown` object. A `DropDown` object should take a `std::map<int, QString>` in its constructor and create the `DropDownValue` collection for us.

Create the `DropDownValue` class first in `cm-lib/source/data`.

`dropdown-value.h`:

```
#ifndef DROPDOWNVALUE_H
#define DROPDOWNVALUE_H

#include <QObject>
#include <cm-lib_global.h>

namespace cm {
namespace data {

class CMLIBSHARED_EXPORT DropDownValue : public QObject
{
```

```
    Q_OBJECT
    Q_PROPERTY(int ui_key MEMBER key CONSTANT )
    Q_PROPERTY(QString ui_description MEMBER description CONSTANT)

public:
    DropDownValue(QObject* parent = nullptr, int key = 0, const QString&
description = "");
    ~DropDownValue();

public:
    int key{0};
    QString description{""};
};

}}

#endif
```

dropdown-value.cpp:

```
#include "dropdown-value.h"

namespace cm {
namespace data {

DropDownValue::DropDownValue(QObject* parent, int _key, const QString&
_description)
        : QObject(parent)
{
    key = _key;
    description = _description;
}

DropDownValue::~DropDownValue()
{
}

}}
```

There's nothing complicated here, it's just a QML friendly wrapper for an integer value and associated string description.

Next, create the `DropDown` class, again in `cm-lib/source/data`.

`dropdown.h`:

```
#ifndef DROPDOWN_H
#define DROPDOWN_H

#include <QObject>
#include <QtQml/QQmlListProperty>

#include <cm-lib_global.h>
#include <data/dropdown-value.h>

namespace cm {
namespace data {

class CMLIBSHARED_EXPORT DropDown : public QObject
{
    Q_OBJECT
    Q_PROPERTY(QQmlListProperty<cm::data::DropDownValue> ui_values READ
ui_values CONSTANT)

public:
    explicit DropDown(QObject* _parent = nullptr, const std::map<int,
QString>& values = std::map<int, QString>());
    ~DropDown();

public:
    QQmlListProperty<DropDownValue> ui_values();

public slots:
    QString findDescriptionForDropdownValue(int valueKey) const;

private:
    class Implementation;
    QScopedPointer<Implementation> implementation;
};

}}

#endif
```

`dropdown.cpp`:

```
#include "dropdown.h"

namespace cm {
namespace data {
```

```
class DropDown::Implementation
{
public:
    Implementation(DropDown* _dropdown, const std::map<int, QString>&
_values)
        : dropdown(_dropdown)
    {
        for(auto pair : _values) {
            values.append(new DropDownValue(_dropdown, pair.first,
pair.second));
        }
    }
    DropDown* dropdown{nullptr};
    QList<DropDownValue*> values;
};

DropDown::DropDown(QObject* parent, const std::map<int, QString>& values)
    : QObject(parent)
{
    implementation.reset(new DropDown::Implementation(this, values));
}

DropDown::~DropDown()
{
}

QString DropDown::findDescriptionForDropdownValue(int valueKey) const
{
    for (auto value : implementation->values) {
        if (value->key == valueKey) {
            if(!value->description.isEmpty()) {
                return value->description;
            }
            break;
        }
    }

    return "Select >";
}

QQmlListProperty<DropDownValue> DropDown::ui_values()
{
    return QQmlListProperty<DropDownValue>(this, implementation->values);
}

}}
```

As discussed, we implement a constructor that takes the same kind of `std::map` that we use in our `EnumeratorDecorator` class and create a collection of `DropDownValue` objects based on it. The UI can then access that collection via the `ui_values` property. The other capability we provide for the UI is via the `findDescriptionForDropdownValue` public slot, and this allows the UI to take a selected integer value from an `EnumeratorDecorator` and get the corresponding text description. If there is no current selection (that is, the description is an empty string), then we will return `Select >` to denote to the user that they need to make a selection.

As we will use these new types in QML, we need to register them in `main.cpp`:

```
qmlRegisterType<cm::data::DropDown>("CM", 1, 0, "DropDown");
qmlRegisterType<cm::data::DropDownValue>("CM", 1, 0, "DropDownValue");
```

Add a new `DropDown` property to the Contact named `ui_contactTypeDropDown` and in the constructor, instantiate the member variable with the `contactTypeMapper`. Now, whenever a Contact is presented in the UI, the associated `DropDown` will be available. This can quite easily go into a dedicated component like a drop-down manager instead, if you wanted to reuse drop-downs throughout the application, but for this example, let's avoid the additional complexity.

We will also need to be able to add a new contact object from the UI, so add a new public slot to `Client`:

```
void Client::addContact()
{
    contacts->addEntity(new Contact(this));
    emit contactsChanged();
}
```

With the C++ done, we can move on to the UI implementation.

We will need a couple of components for the dropdown selection. When presenting an `EnumeratorDecorator` property, we want to display the currently selected value, just as we do with our string editor. Visually, it will resemble a button with the associated string description as its label and when pressed, the user will be transitioned to the second component that is essentially a view. This subview will take up the whole of the content frame and present a list of all the available enumerated options, again represented as buttons. When the user makes their selection by pressing one of the buttons, they will be transitioned back to the original view, and their selection will be updated in the original component.

First, we'll create the view the user will transition to, which will list all the available options. To support this, we need a few additional properties in Style:

```
readonly property color colourDataSelectorBackground: "#131313"
readonly property color colourDataControlsBackgroundSelected: "#f36f24"
readonly property color colourDataSelectorFont: "#ffffff"
readonly property int sizeDataControlsRadius: tscale(5)
```

Create `EnumeratorSelectorView.qml` in `cm-ui/components`:

```
import QtQuick 2.9
import QtQuick.Controls 2.2
import CM 1.0
import assets 1.0

Item {
    id: stringSelectorView
    property DropDown dropDown
    property EnumeratorDecorator enumeratorDecorator
    property int selectedValue

    ScrollView {
        id: scrollView
        visible: true
        anchors.fill: parent
        anchors {
            top: parent.bottom
             left: parent.left
             right: parent.right
             bottom: parent.top
             margins: Style.sizeScreenMargin
        }

        Flow {
            flow: Grid.TopToBottom
            spacing: Style.sizeControlSpacing
            height: scrollView.height

            Repeater {
                id: repeaterAnswers
                model: dropDown.ui_values
                delegate:
                    Rectangle {
                        property bool isSelected: modelData.ui_key.ui_value
=== enumeratorDecorator.ui_value
                        width: Style.widthDataControls
                        height: Style.heightDataControls
```

```
                    radius: Style.sizeDataControlsRadius
                    color: isSelected ?
Style.colourDataControlsBackgroundSelected :
Style.colourDataSelectorBackground

                Text {
                    anchors {
                        fill: parent
                        margins: Style.heightDataControls / 4
                    }
                    text: modelData.ui_description
                    color: Style.colourDataSelectorFont
                    font.pixelSize: Style.pixelSizeDataControls
                    verticalAlignment: Qt.AlignVCenter
                }

                MouseArea {
                    anchors.fill: parent
                    onClicked: {
                        selectedValue = modelData.ui_key;
                        contentFrame.pop();
                    }
                }
            }
        }
    }
}

    Binding {
        target: enumeratorDecorator
        property: "ui_value"
        value: selectedValue
    }
}
```

Here, we use a **Repeater** element for the first time. A Repeater instantiates the QML element defined in its delegate property for each item it finds in its model property. We pass it the collection of `DropDownValue` objects as its model and create a delegate inline. The delegate is essentially another button with some selection code. We can create a new custom component and use that for the delegate instead to keep the code cleaner, but we'll skip that here for brevity. The key parts of this component are the `Binding` element that gives us the two-way binding to the supplied `EnumeratorDecorator`, and the `onClicked` event delegate in the `MouseArea`, which performs the update and pops this component off the stack, returning us to whichever view we came from.

Create a new `EnumeratorSelector.qml` in `cm-ui/components`:

```qml
import QtQuick 2.9
import QtQuick.Controls 2.2
import CM 1.0
import assets 1.0

Item {
    property DropDown dropDown
    property EnumeratorDecorator enumeratorDecorator
    id: enumeratorSelectorRoot
    height: width > textLabel.width + textAnswer.width ?
    Style.heightDataControls : Style.heightDataControls * 2

    Flow {
        anchors.fill: parent

        Rectangle {
            width: Style.widthDataControls
            height: Style.heightDataControls
            Text {
                id: textLabel
                anchors {
                    fill: parent
                    margins: Style.heightDataControls / 4
                }
                text: enumeratorDecorator.ui_label
                color: Style.colourDataControlsFont
                font.pixelSize: Style.pixelSizeDataControls
                verticalAlignment: Qt.AlignVCenter
            }
        }

        Rectangle {
            id: buttonAnswer
            width: Style.widthDataControls
            height: Style.heightDataControls
            radius: Style.sizeDataControlsRadius
            enabled: dropDown ? dropDown.ui_values.length > 0 : false
            color: Style.colourDataSelectorBackground

            Text {
                id: textAnswer
                anchors {
                    fill: parent
                    margins: Style.heightDataControls / 4
                }
```

```
                        text:
dropDown.findDescriptionForDropdownValue(enumeratorDecorator.ui_value)
                        color: Style.colourDataSelectorFont
                        font.pixelSize: Style.pixelSizeDataControls
                        verticalAlignment: Qt.AlignVCenter
                }

                MouseArea {
                    anchors.fill: parent
                    onClicked:
contentFrame.push("qrc:/components/EnumeratorSelectorView.qml",
 {dropDown: enumeratorSelectorRoot.dropDown,
  enumeratorDecorator: enumeratorSelectorRoot.enumeratorDecorator})
                }
            }
        }
    }
```

This component has a lot of similarities to `StringEditorSingleLine` in its layout, but it replaces the Text element with a button representation. We grab the value from the bound `EnumeratorDecorator` and pass that to the slot we created on the `DropDown` class to get the string description for the currently selected value. When the user presses the button, the `onClicked` event of the `MouseArea` performs the same kind of view transition we've seen in `MasterView`, taking the user to the new `EnumeratorSelectorView`.

We're cheating a bit here in that we are directly referencing the `StackView` in `MasterView` by its `contentFrame` ID. At design time, Qt Creator can't know what `contentFrame` is as it is in a totally different file, so it may flag it as an error, and you certainly won't get auto-completion. At runtime, however, this component will be part of the same QML hierarchy as `MasterView`, so it will be able to find it. This is a risky approach, because if another element in the hierarchy is also called `contentFrame`, then bad things may happen. A safer way to do this is to pass `contentFrame` all the way down through the QML hierarchy from `MasterView` as a `QtObject` property.

When we add or edit a Client, we currently ignore contacts and always have an empty collection. Let's take a look at how we can add objects to a collection and put our shiny new `EnumeratorSelector` to use while we're at it.

Contacts

We will need a handful of new UI components to manage our contacts. We've previously worked with an `AddressEditor` to look after our address details, so we'll continue in that mold and create a `ContactEditor` component. This component will display our collection of contacts, each of which will be represented by a `ContactDelegate`. Upon initially creating a new Client object, there won't be any contacts, so we also need some way for the user to add a new one. We'll enable that with a button press, and we'll create a new component for buttons we can add to a content view. Let's do that first.

To support this new component, as usual, we'll go ahead and add some properties to Style:

```
readonly property real widthFormButton: 240
readonly property real heightFormButton: 60
readonly property color colourFormButtonBackground: "#f36f24"
readonly property color colourFormButtonFont: "#ffffff"
readonly property int pixelSizeFormButtonIcon: 32
readonly property int pixelSizeFormButtonText: 22
readonly property int sizeFormButtonRadius: 5
```

Create `FormButton.qml` in `cm-ui/components`:

```
import QtQuick 2.9
import CM 1.0
import assets 1.0

Item {
    property alias iconCharacter: textIcon.text
    property alias description: textDescription.text
    signal formButtonClicked()
    width: Style.widthFormButton
    height: Style.heightFormButton

    Rectangle {
        id: background
        anchors.fill: parent
        color: Style.colourFormButtonBackground
        radius: Style.sizeFormButtonRadius

        Text {
            id: textIcon
            anchors {
                verticalCenter: parent.verticalCenter
                left: parent.left
                margins: Style.heightFormButton / 4
            }
        }
```

```
        font {
            family: Style.fontAwesome
            pixelSize: Style.pixelSizeFormButtonIcon
        }
        color: Style.colourFormButtonFont
        text: "\uf11a"
        horizontalAlignment: Text.AlignHCenter
        verticalAlignment: Text.AlignVCenter
    }

    Text {
        id: textDescription
        anchors {
            left: textIcon.left
            bottom: parent.bottom
            top: parent.top
            right: parent.right
        }
        font.pixelSize: Style.pixelSizeFormButtonText
        color: Style.colourFormButtonFont
        text: "SET ME!!"
        horizontalAlignment: Text.AlignHCenter
        verticalAlignment: Text.AlignVCenter
    }

    MouseArea {
        anchors.fill: parent
        cursorShape: Qt.PointingHandCursor
        hoverEnabled: true
        onEntered: background.state = "hover"
        onExited: background.state = ""
        onClicked: formButtonClicked()
    }

    states: [
        State {
            name: "hover"
            PropertyChanges {
                target: background
                color: Qt.darker(Style.colourFormButtonBackground)
            }
        }
    ]
    }
}
```

Here, we combine aspects of the `NavigationButton` and `CommandButton` controls we wrote earlier in the book. The only real difference is that it is intended for more free-form use in the main content frame rather than being constrained to one of the toolbars.

Next, let's add the component we'll use to display/edit a single Contact object. Create `ContactDelegate.qml` in `cm-ui/components`:

```
import QtQuick 2.9
import CM 1.0
import assets 1.0

Item {
    property Contact contact
    implicitWidth: flow.implicitWidth
    implicitHeight: flow.implicitHeight + borderBottom.implicitHeight +
Style.sizeItemMargin
    height: width > selectorType.width + textAddress.width +
Style.sizeScreenMargin
            ? selectorType.height + borderBottom.height +
Style.sizeItemMargin
            : selectorType.height + textAddress.height +
Style.sizeScreenMargin + borderBottom.height + Style.sizeItemMargin

    Flow {
        id: flow
        width: parent.width
        spacing: Style.sizeScreenMargin

        EnumeratorSelector {
            id: selectorType
            width: Style.widthDataControls
            dropDown: contact.ui_contactTypeDropDown
            enumeratorDecorator: contact.ui_contactType
        }

        StringEditorSingleLine {
            id: textAddress
            width: Style.widthDataControls
            stringDecorator: contact.ui_address
        }
    }

    Rectangle {
        id: borderBottom
        anchors {
            top: flow.bottom
            left: parent.left
```

```
                right: parent.right
                topMargin: Style.sizeItemMargin
            }
            height: 1
            color: Style.colorItemBorder
        }
    }
```

This is much the same as the `RssItemDelegate` we added in Chapter 8, *Web Requests*. We add our new `EnumeratorSelector` and bind it to the `ui_contactType` property, using `ui_contactTypeDropDown` to provide the control with the drop-down information it needs.

Create `ContactsEditor.qml` in `cm-ui/components`:

```
import QtQuick 2.9
import CM 1.0
import assets 1.0

Panel {
    property Client client
    id: contactsEditorRoot
    contentComponent:
        Column {
            id: column
            spacing: Style.sizeControlSpacing

            Repeater {
                id: contactsView
                model: client.ui_contacts
                delegate:
                    ContactDelegate {
                        width: contactsEditorRoot.width
                        contact: modelData
                    }
            }

            FormButton {
                iconCharacter: "\uf067"
                description: "Add Contact"
                onFormButtonClicked: {
                    client.addContact();
                }
            }
        }
    }
```

We've already done all the hard work in our ContactDelegate and FormButton controls, so this is really short and sweet. We add everything to a Panel so that the look and feel will be consistent with the rest of the views. We use another Repeater so that we can spin up a ContactDelegate for every contact in the collection and immediately after the contacts, we display a button to add a new contact to the list. In order to do this, we call the addContact() method we added earlier in this chapter.

Now, we just need to add instances of our ContactsEditor to the CreateClientView:

```
ContactsEditor {
    width: scrollView.width
    client: newClient
    headerText: "Contact Details"
}
```

We can also use the same component in EditClientView:

```
ContactsEditor {
    width: scrollView.width
    client: selectedClient
    headerText: "Contact Details"
}
```

That's it. **Build** and **Run**, and you can add and edit contacts to your heart's content:

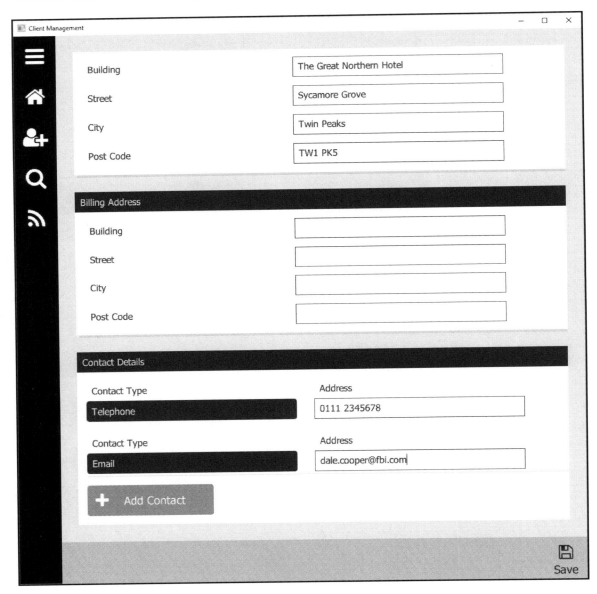

Once you save a new client, if you take a look at the database, you will see that the **contacts** array has been updated accordingly, as highlighted in the following screenshot:

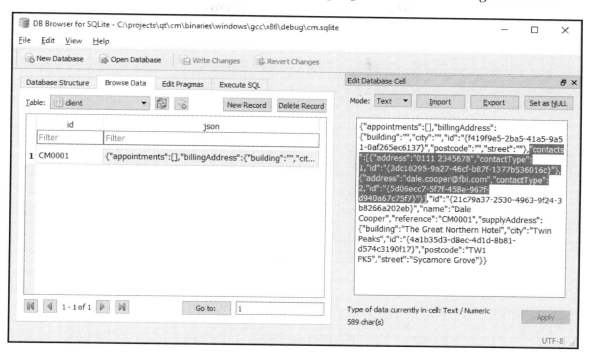

All that's left now is the appointments collection, and we've already covered all the skills you need to tackle that, so we'll leave that as an exercise for the reader and move on to the final topic—deploying our application to our end users.

Deployment preparation

The center piece of our application is the `cm-ui` executable. This is the file that gets launched by the end user and that opens graphical windows and orchestrates all the fancy stuff we've written. When we run the `cm-ui` project in Qt Creator, it opens the executable file for us and everything works perfectly. However, distributing our application to another user is unfortunately more complicated than simply plonking a copy of the executable on their machine and launching it.

Our executable has a variety of dependencies that need to be in place in order for it to run. A prime example of a dependency is our very own `cm-lib` library. Pretty much all of our business logic is hidden away in there, and without that functionality, our UI can't do much. The implementation details for dependency resolution across the various operating systems are complex and well beyond the scope of this book. However, the fundamental requirements of our application are the same, irrespective of the platform.

There are four categories of dependency that we need to consider and ensure that they are in place on our target user's machine in order for our application to function:

- Item 1: Custom libraries we've written or added to our solution manually. In this case, it is only the `cm-lib` library that we need to worry about.
- Item 2: The parts of the Qt framework that our application links to, both directly and indirectly. We already know some of these through the modules we've added to our `.pro` files, for example, the `qml` and quick modules require the `QtQml` and `QtQuick` components.
- Item 3: Any internal dependencies of the Qt framework itself. This includes platform-specific files, resources for the QML subsystem, and third-party libraries such as `sqlite` or `openssl`.
- Item 4: Any libraries required by the C++ compiler we have built the application with.

We've already worked extensively with item 1, back in `Chapter 2`, *Project Structure*, we put a lot of work into controlling exactly where that output goes. We haven't really needed to worry about items 2 and 3, because we have a full installation of the Qt Framework in our development machine and that takes care of everything for us. Similarly, item 4 is dictated by the kit we use, and if we have a compiler available on our machine, it follows that we have the libraries it needs too.

Identifying exactly what we need to copy for our end users (who more than likely don't have Qt or other development tools installed) can be an excruciating exercise. Even once we've done that, packaging everything up into a neat package or installer that is simple for the user to run can be a project in itself. Fortunately, Qt offers us some help in the form of bundled tools.

Linux and macOS X have a concept of application packages, whereby the application executable and all dependencies can be rolled up together into a single file that can then be easily distributed and launched at the click of a button. Windows is a bit more freestyle and if we want to bundle all of our files into a single installable file, we need to do a bit more work, but again, Qt comes to the rescue and comes with the fantastic Qt Installer Framework that simplifies it for us.

Let's take a look at each operating system in turn and produce an application package or installer for each.

OS X

First, build the solution using the kit of your choice in the **Release** mode. You already know that if we press the **Run** button in Qt Creator, our app launches and all is well. However, navigate to the `cm-ui.app` file in Finder and try and launch it directly; with this, things aren't quite so rosy:

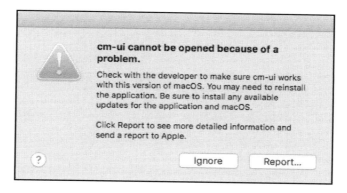

The problem here is missing dependencies. We can use **otool** to take a look at what those dependencies are. First, copy the `cm-ui.app` package to a new directory—`cm/installer/osx`.

This isn't strictly necessary, but I like to keep build and deployment files separate. This way, if we make a code change and rebuild the solution, we will only update the app in the binaries folder, and our deployment files remain untouched.

Next, have a poke around inside the app package and see what we're working with. In Finder, *Ctrl* and click on the `cm-ui.app` we just copied to the installer folder and select **Show Package Contents**. The bit we're interested in is the `Contents/MacOS` folder. In there, you will find our `cm-ui` application executable.

With that identified, open up a command terminal, navigate to `cm/installer/osx`, and run `otool` on the executable:

```
$ otool -L cm-ui.app/Contents/MacOS/cm-ui
```

You will see an output the same as (or similar to) the following:

```
cm-ui:
libcm-lib.1.dylib (compatibility version 1.0.0, current version 1.0.0)
@rpath/QtQuick.framework/Versions/5/QtQuick (compatibility version 5.9.0,
current version 5.9.1)
@rpath/QtQml.framework/Versions/5/QtQml (compatibility version 5.9.0,
current version 5.9.1)
@rpath/QtNetwork.framework/Versions/5/QtNetwork (compatibility version
5.9.0, current version 5.9.1)
@rpath/QtCore.framework/Versions/5/QtCore (compatibility version 5.9.0,
current version 5.9.1)
/System/Library/Frameworks/DiskArbitration.framework/Versions/A/DiskArbitra
tion (compatibility version 1.0.0, current version 1.0.0)
/System/Library/Frameworks/IOKit.framework/Versions/A/IOKit (compatibility
version 1.0.0, current version 275.0.0)
@rpath/QtGui.framework/Versions/5/QtGui (compatibility version 5.9.0,
current version 5.9.1)
@rpath/QtXml.framework/Versions/5/QtXml (compatibility version 5.9.0,
current version 5.9.1)
/System/Library/Frameworks/OpenGL.framework/Versions/A/OpenGL
(compatibility version 1.0.0, current version 1.0.0)
/System/Library/Frameworks/AGL.framework/Versions/A/AGL (compatibility
version 1.0.0, current version 1.0.0)
/usr/lib/libc++.1.dylib (compatibility version 1.0.0, current version
307.5.0)
/usr/lib/libSystem.B.dylib (compatibility version 1.0.0, current version
1238.50.2)
```

Let's remind ourselves of the dependencies we need to consider and look at how they relate to the output we've just seen:

- Custom libraries we've written or added to our solution manually (cm-lib). This is the libcm-lib.1.dylib reference. The fact that there is no path component suggests that the tool isn't quite sure where this file is located. Should it be in the same folder as the executable itself? Should it be in the standard /usr/lib/ folder? Fortunately, we can specify the location of this file when we package our app.
- The parts of the Qt framework that our application links to. QtQuick, QtQml, and such are all the framework modules we directly reference in our cm-ui code. Some of them are explicitly brought in via the QT variable in our cm-ui.pro file and others are implicitly included using things like QML.

- Any internal dependencies of the Qt framework itself. We don't see those listed earlier, but if we were to run otool against the QtQuick module, you would see that it is dependent on QtQml, QtNetwork, QtGui, and QtCore. There are also several system level libraries required, such as OpenGL, which we haven't explicitly coded against but are used by Qt.
- Any libraries required by the C++ compiler we have built the application with; libc++.1.dylib stands out here.

To bundle all of our dependencies manually, we can copy them all inside the app package and then perform some reconfiguration steps to update the location metadata we saw from otool.

Let's pick one of the framework dependencies—QtQuick—and quickly work through what we will have to do to achieve this, and then we'll move on to the really handy tool that does all of this very unpleasant grunt work for us.

First, we will create a Frameworks directory where the system will search for the bundled dependencies:

```
$ mkdir cm-ui.app/Contents/Frameworks
```

Next, we will physically copy the referenced file to that new directory. We know where to look for the existing file on our development machine, thanks to the preceding LC_RPATH entry, in this case /Users/<Your Username>/Qt5.9.1/5.9.1/clang_64/lib:

```
$ cp -R /Users/<Your Username>  /Qt5.9.1 /5.9.1/clang_64 /lib/
QtQuick.framework cm-ui.app/Contents/Frameworks
```

We then need to change the shared library identification name for the copied library file using install_name_tool:

```
$ install_name_tool -id @executable_path /../Frameworks /
QtQuick.framework/Versions/5/QtQuick cm-ui.app /Contents /Frameworks /
QtQuick.framework/Versions/5/QtQuick
```

The syntax here is `install_name_tool -id [New name] [Shared library file]`. To get to the library file (not the framework package, which is what we copied), we drill down to `Versions/5/QtQuick`. We set the ID of that binary to where the executable will look to find it, which, in this case, is in the `Frameworks` folder a level up (`../`) from the executable file itself.

Next, we also need to update the executable's list of dependencies to look in the correct place for this new file:

```
$ install_name_tool -change @rpath/QtQuick.framework/Versions/5/QtQuick
@executable_path/../Frameworks/QtQuick.framework/Versions/5/QtQuick cm-
ui.app/Contents/MacOs/cm-ui
```

The syntax here is `install_name_tool -change [old value] [new value] [executable file]`. We want to change the old `@rpath` entry for `QtQuick` to be the new `Frameworks` path we've just added. Again, we use the `@executable_path` variable so that the dependencies are always located in the same place relative to the executable. Now, the metadata in the executable and the shared library both match each other and relate to the `Frameworks` folder, which we have now added to our app package.

Remember, that's not all, because `QtQuick` itself has dependencies, so we will need to copy and reconfigure all of those files too and then check their dependencies. Once we've exhausted the whole dependency tree for our `cm-ui` executable, we also need to repeat the process for our `cm-lib` library. As you can imagine, this gets tedious very quickly.

Fortunately, the `macdeployqt` Qt Mac Deployment Tool is just what we need here. It scans an executable file for Qt dependencies and copies them across to our app package for us as well as for handling the reconfiguration work. The tool is located in the `bin` folder of the installed kit you have built the application with, for example, `/Qt/5.9.1/5.9.1/clang_64/bin`.

In a command terminal, execute `macdeployqt` as follows (assuming that you are in the `cm/installer/osx` directory):

```
$ <Path to bin>/macdeployqt cm-ui.app -qmldir=<Qt Projects>/cm/cm-ui -
libpath=<Qt Projects>/cm/binaries/osx/clang/x64/release
```

Remember to replace the parameters in angle brackets with the full paths on your system (or add the executable paths to your system PATH variable).

The `qmldir` flag tells the tool where to scan for QML imports and is set to our UI project folder. The `libpath` flag is used to specify where our compiled `cm-lib` file lives.

The output of this operation will be as follows:

```
File exists, skip copy: "cm-
ui.app/Contents/PlugIns/quick/libqtquick2plugin.dylib"
File exists, skip copy: "cm-
ui.app/Contents/PlugIns/quick/libqtquickcontrols2plugin.dylib"
File exists, skip copy: "cm-
ui.app/Contents/PlugIns/quick/libqtquickcontrols2materialstyleplugin.dylib"
File exists, skip copy: "cm-
ui.app/Contents/PlugIns/quick/libqtquickcontrols2universalstyleplugin.dylib
"
File exists, skip copy: "cm-
ui.app/Contents/PlugIns/quick/libwindowplugin.dylib"
File exists, skip copy: "cm-
ui.app/Contents/PlugIns/quick/libqtquicktemplates2plugin.dylib"
File exists, skip copy: "cm-
ui.app/Contents/PlugIns/quick/libqtquickcontrols2materialstyleplugin.dylib"
File exists, skip copy: "cm-
ui.app/Contents/PlugIns/quick/libqtquickcontrols2materialstyleplugin.dylib"
File exists, skip copy: "cm-
ui.app/Contents/PlugIns/quick/libqtquickcontrols2universalstyleplugin.dylib
"
File exists, skip copy: "cm-
ui.app/Contents/PlugIns/quick/libqtquickcontrols2universalstyleplugin.dylib
"
WARNING: Plugin "libqsqlodbc.dylib" uses private API and is not Mac App
store compliant.
WARNING: Plugin "libqsqlpsql.dylib" uses private API and is not Mac App
store compliant.
ERROR: no file at "/opt/local/lib/mysql55/mysql/libmysqlclient.18.dylib"
ERROR: no file at "/usr/local/lib/libpq.5.dylib"
```

Qt is a bit quirky with the SQL module, whereby if you use one SQL driver, it will try and package them all; however, we know that we are only using SQLite and don't need MySQL or PostgreSQL, so we can safely ignore those errors.

Once executed, you should be able to **Show Package Contents** again in Finder and see all the dependencies ready and waiting for deployment, as illustrated:

What a huge timesaver! It has created the appropriate file structure and copied all the Qt modules and plugins for us, along with our `cm-lib` shared library. Try and execute the `cm-ui.app` file now, and it should successfully launch the application.

Linux

Linux packaging and deployment is broadly similar to OS X, and we won't cover it in the same level of detail, so at least skim the OS X section first if you haven't already. As with all platforms, the first thing to do is build the solution using the kit of your choice in the **Release** mode in order to generate the binaries.

When building in Release mode for the first time, I received the "cannot find -lGL" error. This was because the dev libraries for OpenGL were not installed on my system. One way of obtaining these libraries is to install FreeGlut:

```
$ sudo apt-get update
$ sudo apt-get install build-essential
$ sudo apt-get install freeglut3-dev
```

Once compiled, copy the cm-ui binary to a new cm/installer/linux directory.

Next, we can take a look at what dependencies our application has. In a command terminal, change to the cm/installer/linux folder and run ldd:

```
$ ldd <Qt Projects>/cm/binaries/linux/gcc/x64/release/cm-ui
```

You will see an output similar to the following:

```
linux-vdso.so.1 => (0x00007ffdeb1c2000)
libcm-lib.so.1 => /usr/lib/libcm-lib.so.1 (0x00007f624243d000)
libQt5Gui.so.5 => /home/nick/Qt/5.9.1/gcc_64/lib/libQt5Gui.so.5
(0x00007f6241c8f000)
libQt5Qml.so.5 => /home/nick/Qt/5.9.1/gcc_64/lib/libQt5Qml.so.5
(0x00007f6241698000)
libQt5Xml.so.5 => /home/nick/Qt/5.9.1/gcc_64/lib/libQt5Xml.so.5
(0x00007f624145e000)
libQt5Core.so.5 => /home/nick/Qt/5.9.1/gcc_64/lib/libQt5Core.so.5
(0x00007f6240d24000)
libstdc++.so.6 => /usr/lib/x86_64-linux-gnu/libstdc++.so.6
(0x00007f62409a1000)
libgcc_s.so.1 => /lib/x86_64-linux-gnu/libgcc_s.so.1 (0x00007f624078b000)
libc.so.6 => /lib/x86_64-linux-gnu/libc.so.6 (0x00007f62403c1000)
libQt5Sql.so.5 => /home/nick/Qt/5.9.1/gcc_64/lib/libQt5Sql.so.5
(0x00007f6240179000)
libQt5Network.so.5 => /home/nick/Qt/5.9.1/gcc_64/lib/libQt5Network.so.5
(0x00007f623fde8000)
libpthread.so.0 => /lib/x86_64-linux-gnu/libpthread.so.0
(0x00007f623fbcb000)
libGL.so.1 => /usr/lib/x86_64-linux-gnu/mesa/libGL.so.1
(0x00007f623f958000)
libz.so.1 => /lib/x86_64-linux-gnu/libz.so.1 (0x00007f623f73e000)
libm.so.6 => /lib/x86_64-linux-gnu/libm.so.6 (0x00007f623f435000)
librt.so.1 => /lib/x86_64-linux-gnu/librt.so.1 (0x00007f623f22c000)
libicui18n.so.56 => /home/nick/Qt/5.9.1/gcc_64/lib/libicui18n.so.56
(0x00007f623ed93000)
libicuuc.so.56 => /home/nick/Qt/5.9.1/gcc_64/lib/libicuuc.so.56
(0x00007f623e9db000)
```

```
libicudata.so.56 => /home/nick/Qt/5.9.1/gcc_64/lib/libicudata.so.56
(0x00007f623cff7000)
libdl.so.2 => /lib/x86_64-linux-gnu/libdl.so.2 (0x00007f623cdf3000)
libgthread-2.0.so.0 => /usr/lib/x86_64-linux-gnu/libgthread-2.0.so.0
(0x00007f623cbf1000)
libglib-2.0.so.0 => /lib/x86_64-linux-gnu/libglib-2.0.so.0
(0x00007f623c8df000)
/lib64/ld-linux-x86-64.so.2 (0x0000562f21a5c000)
libexpat.so.1 => /lib/x86_64-linux-gnu/libexpat.so.1 (0x00007f623c6b6000)
libxcb-dri3.so.0 => /usr/lib/x86_64-linux-gnu/libxcb-dri3.so.0
(0x00007f623c4b2000)
libxcb-present.so.0 => /usr/lib/x86_64-linux-gnu/libxcb-present.so.0
(0x00007f623c2af000)
libxcb-sync.so.1 => /usr/lib/x86_64-linux-gnu/libxcb-sync.so.1
(0x00007f623c0a8000)
libxshmfence.so.1 => /usr/lib/x86_64-linux-gnu/libxshmfence.so.1
(0x00007f623bea4000)
libglapi.so.0 => /usr/lib/x86_64-linux-gnu/libglapi.so.0
(0x00007f623bc75000)
libXext.so.6 => /usr/lib/x86_64-linux-gnu/libXext.so.6 (0x00007f623ba63000)
libXdamage.so.1 => /usr/lib/x86_64-linux-gnu/libXdamage.so.1
(0x00007f623b85f000)
libXfixes.so.3 => /usr/lib/x86_64-linux-gnu/libXfixes.so.3
(0x00007f623b659000)
libX11-xcb.so.1 => /usr/lib/x86_64-linux-gnu/libX11-xcb.so.1
(0x00007f623b457000)
libX11.so.6 => /usr/lib/x86_64-linux-gnu/libX11.so.6 (0x00007f623b11c000)
libxcb-glx.so.0 => /usr/lib/x86_64-linux-gnu/libxcb-glx.so.0
(0x00007f623af03000)
libxcb-dri2.so.0 => /usr/lib/x86_64-linux-gnu/libxcb-dri2.so.0
(0x00007f623acfe000)
libxcb.so.1 => /usr/lib/x86_64-linux-gnu/libxcb.so.1 (0x00007f623aadb000)
libXxf86vm.so.1 => /usr/lib/x86_64-linux-gnu/libXxf86vm.so.1
(0x00007f623a8d5000)
libdrm.so.2 => /usr/lib/x86_64-linux-gnu/libdrm.so.2 (0x00007f623a6c4000)
libpcre.so.3 => /lib/x86_64-linux-gnu/libpcre.so.3 (0x00007f623a453000)
libXau.so.6 => /usr/lib/x86_64-linux-gnu/libXau.so.6 (0x00007f623a24e000)
libXdmcp.so.6 => /usr/lib/x86_64-linux-gnu/libXdmcp.so.6
(0x00007f623a048000)
```

That's some list of dependencies! Crucially, note the dependency on our cm-lib library:

```
libcm-lib.so.1 => /usr/lib/libcm-lib.so.1
```

This shows that the executable will look for our library in the `/usr/lib` folder, so let's ensure that it's available there before we move on by copying `libcm-lib.so.1` to `/usr/lib`:

```
$ sudo cp <Qt Projects>/cm/binaries/linux/gcc/x64/release/libcm-lib.so.1
/usr/lib
```

We can already guess what a nightmare managing all these dependencies manually will be, having discussed the OS X process and seen how many dependencies there are, so there must be a tool in our Kit's `bin` folder that does it all for us, right? Well, yes and no. There is no official Qt tool we get out of the box to do this for us like there is for OS X and Windows. Fortunately, a fantastic member of the Qt community `probonopd` has come to the rescue and plugged the gap with `linuxdeployqt`.

You can get a `linuxdeployqt` app image from the releases page of the GitHub project at `https://github.com/probonopd/linuxdeployqt`. Download the file (`linuxdeployqt-continuous-x86_64.AppImage`) and then make it executable:

```
$ chmod a+x <Path to downloaded file>/linuxdeployqt-continuous-
x86_64.AppImage
```

We can then execute it and have it work its dependency-based magic for us. Change the directory to `cm/installer/linux` first:

```
$ <Path to downloaded file>/linuxdeployqt-continuous-x86_64.AppImage cm-ui
-qmldir=<Qt Projects>/cm/cm-ui -appimage
```

The `qmldir` flag tells the tool where to scan for QML imports and is set to our UI project folder. The `appimage` flag is used to get the tool to create an application image file for us, which is a single file with everything bundled inside.

Things may not work perfectly the first time. Your output may look as follows:

```
ERROR: Desktop file missing, creating a default one (you will probably want
to edit it)
ERROR: Icon file missing, creating a default one (you will probably want to
edit it)
ERROR: "/usr/bin/qmake -query" exited with 1 : "qmake: could not exec
'/usr/lib/x86_64-linux-gnu/qt4/bin/qmake': No such file or directory\n"
ERROR: Qt path could not be determined from qmake on the $PATH
ERROR: Make sure you have the correct Qt on your $PATH
ERROR: You can check this with qmake -v
```

The first two errors are just because we haven't provided a desktop file or icon and defaults have been generated for us; we can ignore those. The rest are because `linuxdeployqt` doesn't know where `qmake` is. We can either provide the path as an extra parameter (-qmake=<PATH>), or to save us having to do it every time, we can add it to our PATH environment variable:

```
$ export PATH=<Qt Path>/5.9.1/gcc_64/bin/:$PATH
```

We can then check whether qmake can be found by trying to retrieve the version information:

```
$ qmake -v
```

If it is happy, you will see the version information:

```
QMake version 3.1
Using Qt version 5.9.1 in /home/nick/Qt/5.9.1/gcc_64/lib
```

With that fixed, we can now try running the `linuxdeployqt` command again. However, we've fixed one problem, but now experience another:

```
ERROR: Desktop file missing, creating a default one (you will probably want
to edit it)
ERROR: Icon file missing, creating a default one (you will probably want to
edit it)
ERROR: ldd outputLine: "libmysqlclient.so.18 => not found"
ERROR: for binary:
"/home/nick/Qt/5.9.1/gcc_64/plugins/sqldrivers/libqsqlmysql.so"
ERROR: Please ensure that all libraries can be found by ldd. Aborting.
```

Ignore the first two errors again. Now it can't find MySQL drivers, which is annoying, because we aren't even MySQL and it is the same Qt SQL quirk we saw on OS X. As a workaround, let's effectively "hide" the SQL drivers we don't want from the tool by temporarily renaming them:

```
$ cd <Qt Path>/5.9.1/gcc_64/plugins/sqldrivers
$ mv libqsqlmysql.so libqsqlmysql.so_ignore
$ mv libqsqlpsql.so libqsqlpsql.so_ignore
```

Run the `linuxdeployqt` command again. You will get lots of output this time, culminating in a success message, including the following:

```
App name for filename: Application
dest_path: Application-x86_64.AppImage
```

This is telling us that our app image has been named as `Application-x86_64.AppImage`, which it saves to the `Downloads` folder.

Take a look in file manager, and you will see that it has added various files and directories alongside our executable:

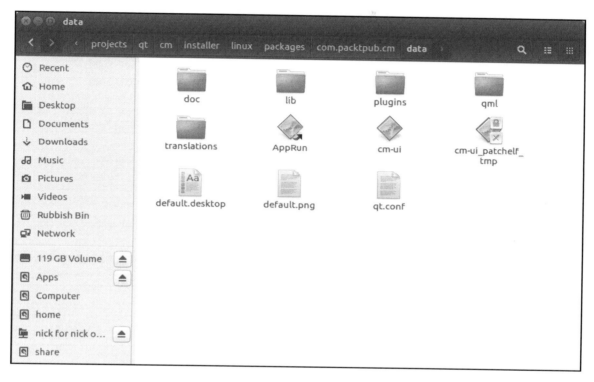

It has also deposited the `Application-x86_64.AppImage` file in the `Downloads` folder that is a single self-contained executable package with all dependencies. However, if you head over to `Downloads` and try and launch the `AppImage`, you may get an error (execute it via a Terminal command to see the error message):

```
QXcbIntegration: Cannot create platform OpenGL context, neither GLX nor EGL
are enabled
```

This appears to be an issue with `linuxdeployqt` missing some dependencies, but for some reason, running the tool a second time magically picks them up. Execute the `linuxdeployqt` command again, and hey presto, the `AppImage` now works correctly.

Windows

First, build the solution using the kit of your choice in the **Release** mode. Once complete, copy the `cm-ui.exe` and `cm-lib.dll` application binaries to a new `cm/installer/windows/packages/com.packtpub.cm/data` directory. This strange directory structure will be explained in the next section—Qt Installer Framework—and we are simply saving ourselves some additional copying later.

Next, let's remind ourselves of the dependencies we need to consider:

- Item 1: Custom libraries we've written or added to our solution manually (`cm-lib`)
- Item 2: The parts of the Qt framework that our application links to
- Item 3: Any internal dependencies of the Qt framework itself
- Item 4: Any libraries required by the C++ compiler we have built the application with

The good news is that item 1 is already done! Windows will look for the dependencies of an executable in the same folder that the executable is in. This is really helpful and by simply copying the DLL to the same folder as the executable, we've already taken care of that dependency. The Qt Installer framework takes all the files from a given folder and deploys them to the target machine in the same place relative to each other, so we know this will be preserved after deployment too.

The bad news is that the remaining steps are a bit of a nightmare to manage manually. We can have a decent first stab at what parts of Qt we need by reviewing the modules we've explicitly added to our `*.pro` files. This will be `qml`, `quick`, and `xml` from `cm-ui` and `sql`, and network and `xml` from `cm-lib` core is also included by default. In File Explorer, navigate to `<Qt Installation Folder>/5.9.1/<Kit>/bin`. In there, you can find all the binaries relating to these modules, for example, `Qt5Qml.dll` for the `qml` module.

We can use the approach that we did for `cm-lib.dll` and simply manually copy each of the Qt DLL files across to the data folder too. This will fulfil item 2 and while deeply tedious, it's fairly straightforward. However, item 3 is a painful exercise that we really don't want to do ourselves.

Fortunately, the `windeployqt` Qt Windows Deployment Tool is just what we need here. It scans an `.exe` file for Qt dependencies and copies them across to our installer folder for us. The tool is located in the `bin` folder of the installed kit you have built the application with, for example, `/Qt/5.9.1/mingw32/bin`.

In a command terminal, execute `windeployqt` as follows:

```
$ <Path to bin>/windeployqt.exe --qmldir <Qt Projects>/cm/cm-ui <Qt
Projects>/cm/installer/windows/packages/com.packtpub.cm/data/cm-ui.exe --
compiler-runtime
```

Remember to replace the parameters in angle brackets with the full paths on your system (or add the executable paths to your system PATH variable).

The `qmldir` flag tells the tool where to scan for QML imports and is set to our UI project folder. After we tell the tool which `.exe` to scan for dependencies, the `compiler-runtime` flag denotes that we want the compiler runtime files too, so it even takes care of item 4 for us as a bonus!

 By default, found dependencies will subsequently be copied to the same folder as the executable being scanned. This is a good reason to copy the compiled binaries to a dedicated installer folder first so that development project output and content for deployment remain separate.

Once executed, you should see a large block of output. Although it's tempting to think "oh, that's done stuff so everything must be ok", it's a good idea to scan through the output, even if you're not sure what it's doing as you can sometimes pick up obvious issues that you can can take action to resolve.

For example, when first deploying a MinGW kit build, I encountered the given line:

```
Warning: Cannot find GCC installation directory. g++.exe must be in the
path.
```

Although the command had executed successfully, and I can see a whole bunch of Qt dependencies in the installer folder, I was actually missing the GCC dependencies. It was a simple fix to follow the instructions and add `<Qt Installation path>/Tools/mingw530_32/bin` to the PATH variable in my system environment variables. After restarting the command terminal and running the `windeployqt` command again, it subsequently completed successfully without the warning, and the GCC files were present as expected in data alongside all the Qt binaries. Without picking up on this quiet little warning, I would have proceeded with some potentially critical missing files.

As you can see, `windeployqt` is a huge time saver, but unfortunately, it isn't a silver bullet and sometimes misses the required files. Tools like Dependency Walker exist, which can help analyze the dependency tree in detail, but a good starting point is to just manually launch the `cm-ui` executable from the data folder and see what happens. In our case, it is this:

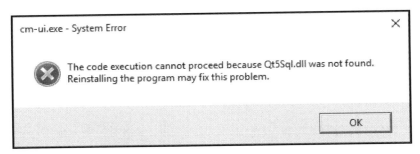

The bad news is that it doesn't work, but the good news is that at least it clearly tells us why it doesn't work—it is missing the `Qt5Sql.dll` dependency. We know that we do indeed have a dependency there, because we had to add the `sql` module to our `.pro` files when we started doing database work. However, wait, we've just executed a command that should pull in all the Qt dependencies for us, right? Right, I don't know why the tool misses out some dependencies that it really should know about, but it does. I don't know if it's a bug, an oversight, or a licensing restriction related to the underlying third-party SQLite implementation, but in any case, the simple solution is that we just need to copy it ourselves.

Head over to `<Qt Installation>/5.9.1/<kit>/bin` and copy `Qt5Sql.dll` over to our data folder. Launch the `cm-ui.exe` again and hurrah, it opens successfully!

One other thing to look out for apart from missing `.dll` files from the bin directory is missing files/folders from the plugins directory. You will see in our case that several folders have been copied successfully (bearer, iconengines, and such), but sometimes they don't, and can be very difficult to figure out as you don't get a helpful error message like we did with the missing DLL. I can only recommend three things in that situation: trial, error, and the internet.

So, we now have a folder containing our lovely application binaries and a whole bunch of similarly lovely other files and folders. What now? Well, we can simply copy the folder wholesale onto our users' machines and get them to launch the executable as we did. However, a neater and more professional solution is to bundle up everything into a pretty installation package, and that is where the Qt Installer Framework tool comes in.

Qt Installer framework

Let's edit our Qt installation and grab the Qt Installer framework.

Launch the **MaintenanceTool** application from your Qt installation directory, and you will be presented with a wizard virtually identical to the one we saw when we first installed Qt. To add Qt Installer Framework to your existing installation, follow these steps:

1. Either log in to your Qt Account or **Skip**
2. Select **Add or remove components** and click on **Next**
3. On the **Select Components** dialog, check **Tools > Qt Installer Framework 3.0** and click on **Next**
4. Begin the installation by clicking on **Update**

Once complete, you can find the installed tools in `Qt/Tools/QtInstallerFramework/3.0`.

> You can add further modules, kits, and such in exactly the same way. Any components you already have installed will be unaffected unless you actively deselect them.

The Qt Installer Framework requires two specific directories to be present: config and packages. Config is a singular piece of configuration that describes the installer as a whole, whereas you can bundle multiple packages (or components) together in the same installation package. Each component has its own subdirectory within the packages folder, with a data folder containing all the items to be installed for that component and a meta folder where configuration data for the package is held.

In our case, although we have two projects (`cm-lib` and `cm-ui`), it makes no sense to distribute one without the other, so we will aggregate the files together into one package. A common naming convention for packages is `com.<publisher>.<component>`, so we'll name ours `com.packtpub.cm`. We already created the required data folder in the previous section (yay for forward planning!) and `windeployqt` stuffed it full of files for us.

There is no required naming convention here, so feel free to name the package something else if you wish. If we wanted to bundle an additional, optional component with our application, we would do so by simply creating an additional package folder (for example, `com.packtpub.amazingcomponent`) containing the relevant data and meta files, including a separate `package.xml` to configure that component.

Create any missing folders so that you end up with the following folder structure inside `cm/installer/windows`:

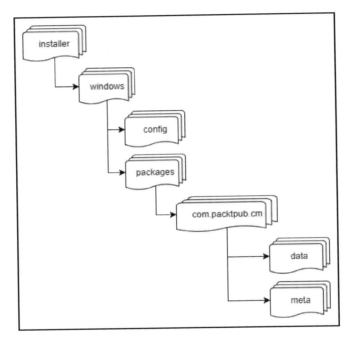

To compliment these folders, we also need to provide two XML configuration files.

Create `config.xml` in the config subfolder:

```
<?xml version="1.0" encoding="UTF-8"?>
<Installer>
    <Name>Client Management</Name>
    <Version>1.0.0</Version>
    <Title>Client Management Application Installer</Title>
    <Publisher>Packt Software Publishing</Publisher>
    <StartMenuDir>Client Management</StartMenuDir>
    <TargetDir>@HomeDir@/ClientManagement</TargetDir>
</Installer>
```

This configuration file customizes the behavior of the installer. The properties we have specified here are as follows:

Property	Purpose
Name	The application name
Version	The application version
Title	The installer name displayed in the title bar
Publisher	The publisher of the software
StartMenuDir	The default program group in the Windows Start menu
TargetDir	The default target directory for the application installation

 You will note strange @ symbols in the TargetDir property, and they define a predefined variable HomeDir that allows us to dynamically obtain a path to the end user's home directory. You can also access the values of other properties in the same way, for example, @ProductName@ will return "Client Management". Further information is available at http://doc.qt.io/qtinstallerframework/scripting.html#predefined-variables.

Next, create package.xml in the packages/com.packtpub.cm/meta subfolder:

```xml
<?xml version="1.0" encoding="UTF-8"?>
<Package>
    <DisplayName>Client Management application</DisplayName>
    <Description>Install the Client Management application.</Description>
    <Version>1.0.0</Version>
    <ReleaseDate>2017-10-30</ReleaseDate>
    <Licenses>
        <License name="Fictional Training License Agreement"
file="license.txt" />
    </Licenses>
    <Default>true</Default>
</Package>
```

This file configures the `com.packtpub.cm` package (our Client Management application) with the following properties:

Property	Purpose
`DisplayName`	The name of the component.
`Description`	The text displayed when the component is selected.
`Version`	The version of the component (used to promote component updates).
`ReleaseDate`	The date the component was released.
`Licenses`	A collection of licenses that must be agreed to in order to install the package. The text for the license agreement is obtained from the specified file that must be alongside the configuration file in the meta folder.
`Default`	Boolean flag denoting whether the component is selected by default.

You will also need to create `license.txt` in the meta folder; the content doesn't matter in this case as it's just for demonstration, so write any old nonsense in there.

With all the binaries, dependencies, and configuration in place, we can now run the Qt Framework Installer in a command terminal to generate our installation package. First, change directory to the `cm/installer/windows` folder and then execute `binarycreator`:

```
$ <Qt Installation Path> \Tools \QtInstallerFramework \3.0\ bin\
binarycreator.exe -c config\config.xml -p packages
ClientManagementInstaller.exe
```

The `-c` flag tells the tool where the `config.xml` file resides and `-p` where all the packages are. The final parameter is the name you want to give the resulting installer.

With our application neatly packaged up into a single installer file, `ClientManagementInstaller.exe`, we can now easily distribute it to our end users for installation.

Installation

Upon launching the installer, you will be presented with a welcome dialog, the content of which is derived from our `config.xml` file:

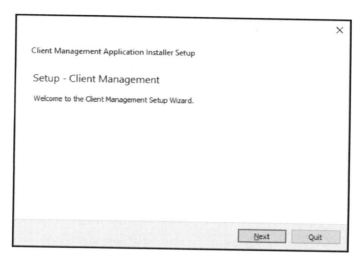

We are then prompted to specify the target directory for the installation and what we expect is that after installation, this folder will contain all the files and folders we pulled together in the data folder:

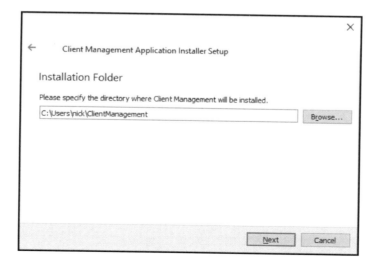

We are then presented with a list of all the components we defined via the packages directory, which in this case is simply the application and dependencies in the `com.packtpub.cm` folder:

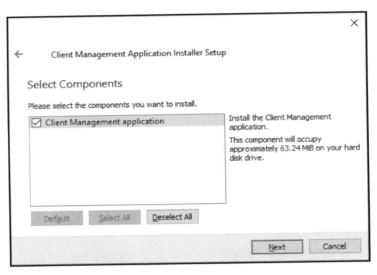

Next, we are presented with any licenses we defined in `packages.xml`, including the license information provided in the text files:

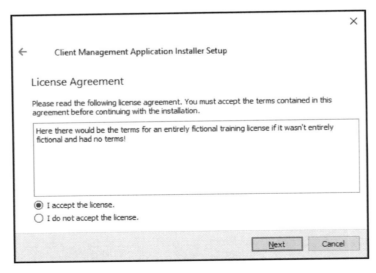

We are then prompted for the **Start Menu shortcuts**, with the default provided by
`config.xml`:

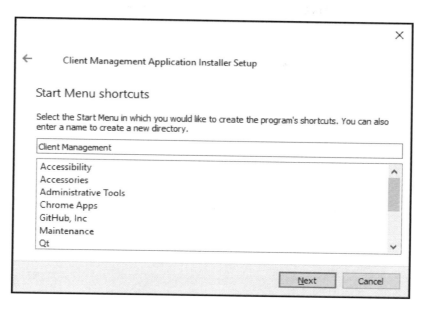

We're ready to install now and are provided with disk usage stats before we confirm:

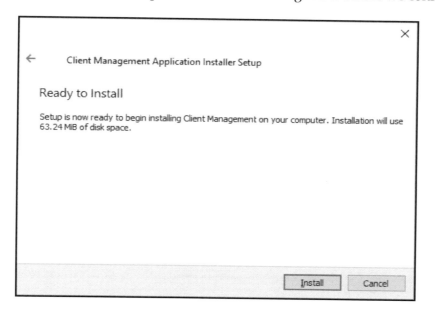

After a brief wait while the installation completes, we are presented with a final confirmation dialog:

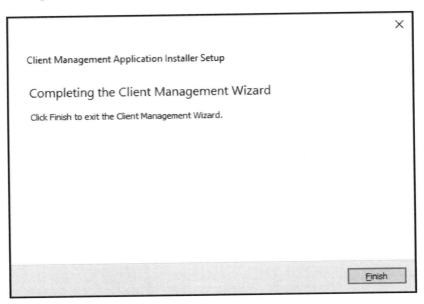

You should see a new `ClientManagement` folder in the target directory containing our installed application!

Summary

In this chapter, we made our application even more testable by introducing our first object factory. They are a really useful layer of abstraction that make unit testing so much easier, and on larger projects, it's common to end up with several factories. We then made our UI even more dynamic by having Style properties that can scale along with the Window. `EnumeratorDecorators` got some love and an editor component of their own, fully finger-friendly to boot. We then put that editor to use and implemented Contact management, showing how collections of objects can easily be viewed and edited.

With our application more fleshed out, we then took a look at how to get our shiny new work of genius into the hands of our end users. Different operating systems each have their own take on things, and you will undoubtedly discover quirks and encounter challenges in your own particular environment, but hopefully, you now have the tools you need to be able to work through them.

That sentiment goes not just for deployment, but for the whole project life cycle. The goal of this book was not to discuss theoretical problems that while interesting, will never come up in your day-to-day role as a developer. The goal was to present solutions to real-world problems. We have developed a functional Line of Business application from start to finish, working through common tasks that you will encounter on a daily basis, whether working on an initiative at work or on a personal project at home.

I hope that some of the approaches detailed in this book prove useful to you and that you go on to enjoy working with Qt as much as I do.

Other Books You May Enjoy

If you enjoyed this book, you may be interested in these other books by Packt:

Mastering Qt 5
Guillaume Lazar, Robin Penea

ISBN: 978-1-78646-712-6

- Create stunning UIs with Qt Widget and Qt Quick
- Develop powerful, cross-platform applications with the Qt framework
- Design GUIs with the Qt Designer and build a library in it for UI preview
- Handle user interaction with the Qt signal/slot mechanism in C++
- Prepare a cross-platform project to host a third-party library
- Build a Qt application using the OpenCV API
- Use the Qt Animation framework to display stunning effects
- Deploy mobile apps with Qt and embedded platforms

Computer Vision with OpenCV 3 and Qt5
Amin Ahmadi Tazehkandi

ISBN: 978-1-78847-239-5

- Get an introduction to Qt IDE and SDK
- Be introduced to OpenCV and see how to communicate between OpenCV and Qt
- Understand how to create UI using Qt Widgets
- Know to develop cross-platform applications using OpenCV 3 and Qt 5
- Explore the multithreaded application development features of Qt5
- Improve OpenCV 3 application development using Qt5
- Build, test, and deploy Qt and OpenCV apps, either dynamically or statically
- See Computer Vision technologies such as filtering and transformation of images, detecting and matching objects, template matching, object tracking, video and motion analysis, and much more
- Be introduced to QML and Qt Quick for iOS and Android application development

Leave a review - let other readers know what you think

Please share your thoughts on this book with others by leaving a review on the site that you bought it from. If you purchased the book from Amazon, please leave us an honest review on this book's Amazon page. This is vital so that other potential readers can see and use your unbiased opinion to make purchasing decisions, we can understand what our customers think about our products, and our authors can see your feedback on the title that they have worked with Packt to create. It will only take a few minutes of your time, but is valuable to other potential customers, our authors, and Packt. Thank you!

Index

Printed in Poland
by Amazon Fulfillment
Poland Sp. z o.o., Wrocław